COPYRIGHT LAW

Cases and Materials

COPYRIGHT LAW

Cases and Materials

DR. SHASHI NATH MANDAL

REGAL PUBLICATIONS

New Delhi - 110 027

COPYRIGHT LAW: CASES AND MATERIALS

ISBN 978-81-8484-266-1

Typeset by
THE LASER PRINTERS
8/15, 3rd Floor, Subhash Nagar, New Delhi-110027

Printed in India at
MAYUR ENTERPRISES,
WZ Plot No. 3, Gujjar Market, Tihar Village, New Delhi-110018

Published by
REGAL PUBLICATIONS
F-159, Rajouri Garden, New Delhi-110027
Phones: 45546396, 25435369
E-mail: regalbookspub@yahoo.com, regaldeepbooks@yahoo.com

The work is dedicated to my beloved mother

LATE M. DEVI MANDAL

CONTENTS

PREFACE

The book containing cases and materials on Copyright Law is of immense importance and relevance in the present age's requirement. This book generally aims at finding the essentials of Intellectual Property Rights in this modern age where idea is omnipotent and more particularly this project aims to search out the areas of copyright violation/infringement in our country which is not only affecting the individual property of an individual rather losing the revenues of the government to the tune of billions of rupees every year, and to find out the preventive measures. India is one of the biggest market of the world where the intellectual properties are being marketed more particularly. India is the biggest market of copyright-related properties but in reality, the practical market is being grasped by ingenuine product instead of original one which result in loss of revenues of government as well as the creator's or owner's property.

Intellectual property rights have never been more economically and politically important or controversial than they are today. Patents, copyrights, trademarks, utility models, industrial designs, integrated circuits and geographical indications are frequently mentioned in discussions and debates on such diverse topics as public health, food security, education, trade, industrial policy, traditional knowledge, biodiversity, biotechnology, the Internet, the entertainment and media industries. In a knowledge-based economy, there is no doubt that a better understanding of IPRs is indispensable to informed policy-making in all areas of human development. Technological progress and economic growth have been indisputably linked in the history of development. Technological progress requires both a system of encouraging innovation and a regulatory framework where innovative ideas and concepts can reasonably be fostered. The intellectual property system has long served this end, and it is likely to continue to do so for the foreseeable future. However, whether the future of copyright will produce the same bounty of creative expression, evident from its past, is debatable in the absence of positive means to encourage the use and dissemination of creative works. The international copyright system now occupies a central role in shaping the course of domestic legislation and in preserving a system that is capable of fulfilling the public good associated with a free press, freedom of information and access to basic educational tools. Thus, it is of no doubt that the concept Intellectual Property Rights is obviously a positive concept which always promotes the creativity, scientific development, tradition, cultural, geographical and feature-based industry in India. On the other hand, one of the important nomenclatures of IPR, i.e. Copyright is purely negative concept which recognises monopoly and does not permit any other to use the goods etc. of another without his consent.

This book has really given the author an opportunity to study and go through the detailed pros and cons of copyright-related matter and its effect on the socio-economic culture of the country like ours. This book also enabled the researcher to sharpen his intelligence in the interest of his own effectiveness and career progress. This book is his whole-hearted effort for the vast and a sensitive subject like "Intellectual Property Rights: A Case Study with Special Reference to the Infringement of Copyright in India", which has a great social, cultural and economic relevance so far as present digital and computer world is concerned.

In the book the author has made sincere efforts in comparing relevant provisions of the copyright laws of different countries. Each countries' law gave the researcher different ideas but one thing that the researcher has got that all laws rests on a distinct pedestal incorporating the ideals of the copyright policy which promotes the progress of art and creativity by giving for a limited time monopoly rights to the authors/owners of creative works so that these works pass on to the public domain after the expiry of the stipulated period. Copyright is considered to be the very engine of free expression.

Burdwan, West Bengal SHASHI NATH MANDAL

ACKNOWLEDGEMENT

In doing a project in law like the present a student is obviously reliant upon the guidance of those who have spent most of their lives of occupation or exertion in the field of Law either in the educational Institution or in practical field, i.e. in dealing corporate problems or involved in legal profession. During the present book the author has awfully taken the help of many known and unknown persons. The name of such personalities who provided their precious time and information to the researcher is not very small in this case. Among them the author would like to keep the contribution of his guide and supervisor Prof. (Dr.) Shiv Sahai Singh, Sr. Professor, Department of Law, University of Burdwan, above all because without his energetic co-operation, attachment and guidance the present book would not be possible in its present form and shape. In spite of his demanding schedule he has supervised the entire work and after a thorough eye he suggested a number of important insinuations which were booming for the researcher for the meaningful completion of the work. His unremitting inspirations and guidelines towards the completion of this work is the supreme source of the effort of the author to complete this work.

The author conveys sincere gratitude to Prof. Manick Chakraborty, Head of the Department of Law, Prof. Sarit Kumar Sadhu, Professor of Law, Prof. Mohammad Momin, Professor of Law, Dr. Dipak Das, Reader of Law, Dr. Sanjeev Kumar Tewari, Reader of Law and Dr. Jayanta Kumar Saha, Lecturer in Law, of the Department of Law, University of Burdwan, Burdwan, for lending their thoughts and providing their heartiest co-operation and approbation in process of the work.

The author is grateful to Dr. S.K. Mukhopadhayay, WB.E.S., Principal, Hooghly Mohsin College, for his constant encouragement and support.

The author sincerely puts across profound sense of gratefulness to Dr. Prem Kumar Agarwal, W.B.E.S., Head of the Department, Law Section, Hooghly Mohsin College, Chinsurah, Hooghly, whose everlasting and encouraging support round the clock in the work always inspired the researcher to proceed with the work. Sincere thanks also go to Dr. Subir Kumar Roy, Assistant Professor and Dr. Sadhna Gupta, Assistant Professor, Hooghly Mohsin College for their constant support and motivation towards the completion of the work.

The author sincerely convey thankfulness to Prof. V. Vijaykumar, Registrar and Professor of Law, National Law School of India University, Bangalore, who have taken the trouble to send lots of resources and guidelines electronically for the present work, Prof. Shivkumar, Research Associate, Indian Law Institute, who have continuously catered the requirements whenever requested and supplied lots of material and information electronically.

The author is thankful to Mr. A. Thakur, Deputy Controller, and Dr. G.C. Mondal, Librarian, Patent Office, Kolkata, who have supplied plenty of information, resources and materials for the work.

Sincere appreciation goes to Ms. Tutu Mukherjee, Librarian, NUJS, Kolkata for her cooperation by allowing the researcher to use their enriched library and provided lots of resources for the work.

The author expresses deep sense of gratitude to his father Shri Ram Deo Mandal for giving constant source of inspiration and mental support towards the completion of the present work. The author also expresses gratefulness to his late mother M. Devi Mandal whose sweet memory immensely inspired the author to finish the present work successfully and effectively. The everlasting help and inspiration from Punita Mandal, Sunita Mandal and Anita Mandal, sisters of the author encouraged the author to keep going successfully with the present venture. Heartfelt thankfulness goes to Mrs. Mamoni Mandal, wife of the researcher for her unending and steady inspiration, co-operation and support towards the successful completion of the work. Constant love of little baby Shirsha always make the author enthusiastic and energetic towards the momentous completion of present work.

Sincere appreciation goes to the friends of the author Mrs. Mousumi Mukherjee, Mrs. Himika Das, and Mr. P.P. Mitra who have immensely inspired and supported the author to proceed with the present work for successful completion. No words shall be sufficient to mention the inspiring words of Mr. Sukumar Khamrai, Ex-Librarian of LCD to carry on the present work eloquently. Instant support and help of Mr. Kishore Bhoumick, Mr. Arindam Chatterjee, Mr. Madhusudan Goswamy and Mr. Ashok Gorai for the present work shall be everlasting.

Sincere and deferential thanks also goes to Mr. Kankan Choudhury, Librarian, Hooghly Mohsin College, for his constant co-operation and support which enables the author to carry on the work and Mr. Amal Bhattacharjee and Mr. Provash Ghosh, Library associates for their hearties assistance. The author express thanks to Mr. Amal Bhattacharya, Mr. Partha Bhattacharya and Mr. Shyama Prosad Mukherjee and Mr. Durga Korel, office associates of Law Section, Hooghly Mohsin College, for their kind co-operation during my present work.

My sincere thanks also go to Mr. Birendra Das, Computer expert, Birendra Computer, Burdwan for his sincere technical and printing support.

Some of well wishers of the author who have immensely helped him in this work may be disappointed to find no mention of their imperative contributions in this acknowledgement, but the author can assure them that their labour have been most useful and precious to the author. They have made an indispensable contribution for meaningful accomplishment of the present work which shall be everlasting.

Last but not the least the author convey his deep sense of appreciation to those long listed students of Law College Durgapur, Hooghly Mohsin College and other Academic institutions, who have always enriched him by providing the sources of imperative informations and inspired him to study more and more for the successful completion of his work.

Burdwan, West Bengal SHASHI NATH MANDAL

ABBREVIATIONS

A.I.R.	:	All India Reporter
AHRA	:	Audio Home Recording Rights Act
ART	:	Article
Berne Convention	:	Berne Convention for the Protection of Literary and Artistic Works
CBD	:	Convention on Biological Diversity
EC	:	European Community
EEA	:	European Economic Area
EU	:	European Union
FTA	:	Free-Trade Agreement
FTAA	:	Free Trade Area of the Americas
ICTSD	:	International Centre for Trade and Sustainable Development
IP	:	Intellectual Property
IPR	:	Intellectual Property Right
ISP	:	Internet Service Provider
NSP	:	Network Service Provider
PMA	:	Post Mortem Auctoris
PIL	:	Public Interest Litigation
PPL	:	Phonographic Performance Limited
RAM	:	Random Access Memory
SC	:	Supreme Court
SCC	:	Supreme Court Cases

Sec	:	Section
SI	:	Statutory Instruction
TPI	:	Third Party Information
MPAA	:	Motion Picture Association of America
TPM	:	Technological Protection Mechanism
TRIPs Agreement	:	Agreement on Trade-Related Aspects of Intellectual Property Rights
TRIPs	:	Trade Related Intellectual Properties
UCC	:	Universal Copyright Convention
WCT	:	Wipo Copyright Treaty
WHO	:	World Health Organization
WIPO	:	World Intellectual Property Organization
WPPT	:	Wipo Performance and Phonograms Treaty
WTO	:	World Trade Organization

TABLE OF CASES

1

INTRODUCTION

> "If you have an apple and I have an apple and we exchange apples, then you and I will still each have one apple. But if you have an idea and I have one idea and we exchange these ideas, then each of us will have two ideas."
>
> —*George Bernard Shaw*[1]

The scientific and technological development has brought all the nations very close to each other and world have become very small one. The territorial boundaries no more remain the barriers for the expansion and dissemination of any concept. The concept of Intellectual Property Rights is not an exception. Hindu philosophy has a Vedic origin. Form the Vedic era the concept of **'Vasudhaib Kutumbkam'** i.e., the whole world is a big family also preachès us the tenets of co-existence, brotherhood and devotion for the universal peace, unity and integrity. In consonance with the Vedic spirit at present it seems that emergence of international organizations, international conventions and international treaties are in progress. The basic objects of the United Nations, 1945 are in conformity with the Vedic principles. The prime object of the pivotal and global organization is to maintain world peace and security with the additional functions of developing friendly relations among the

1. Mackay L. Mackay, *A Dictionary of Scientific Quotations* (Paperback, Jan., 1991), p. 113.

nations, of achieving international co-operation in economic, social cultural and humanitarian matters, of developing respect for human rights and fundamental freedom[2]. The acceptance of the concept of Intellectual Property Rights is effectual to one of the objects of the United Nations i.e., to achieve international co-operation in economic matters.

Intellectual Property Right (IPR) is the bunch of rights which are enjoyed by the person who have earned their intellectual property by application of their intellect. In the modern age the term intellectual property is indispensable one because no one can survive without intellectual property. The term 'Intellectual Property' has been justified at the conceptual level by many great philosophers like George Hegel, John Locke, etc. The theories of George Hegel and John Locke regarding the manner in which property is created raise a fundamental question: Can information be considered property in the same sense that a house or a car is considered property? The fundamental character of information is that it is non-rival goods, which means that the assumptions of depletion, scarcities, etc. that are used while analysing classical theories of property do not quite fit. Many explanations for the propertisation of intellectual creations are based on the Lockean theory of the creation of property. Locke's theory relies on three basic principles: firstly, that every person has property in himself/herself; secondly, everything that is in a state of nature i.e., not as yet propertised and still held in the commons was given by God to be propertised; and thirdly, that labour converts things in a state of nature into a state of property and adds value to things so laboured upon.

Locke was, therefore, of the opinion that if A mixes his/her labour into a thing that is in a state of nature, that thing becomes the property of A.[3] In terms of copyright, authors can be said to take ideas that are 'out there' in the commons, add their labour to it, and thereby create the 'work'. The question that Locke fails to answer is why, if authors add labour to ideas, the result becomes the property of the author? His theory simply rests on the assumption that property is the reward for labour.[4]

---

2. Article 1 of United Nations Charter.
3. John Locke, Two Treatises of Government.
4. Tom G. Palmer, Are Patents and Copyrights Morally Justified?, The Philosophy of Property Rights and Ideal Objects, *Harvard Journal of Law and Public Policy*, p. 817.

The next question that may come in this context is whether and how a person actually has property in himself or herself. This property in oneself cannot be a product of one's labour and, therefore, it must be premised upon something else. The core of Locke's theory lays the notion of personal freedom, with state power severely constrained and limited to the protection of liberty. It is in this context that he, again, presumes the ownership of oneself. Unlike Locke, however, Hegel does not see humans as naturally free and as having natural ownership rights in themselves. According to him, it is solely through the historical process of objectification and hence self-confrontation that one comes to be free:

> "It is only through the development of his own body and mind, essentially through his self-consciousness and apprehension of itself as free, that he takes possession of himself and becomes his own property and no one else's."[5]

In both theories, ownership of ours enables the ownership of natural objects as they become assimilated to our bodies. Such a proposition meets several objections. Philosopher *Robert Nozick* poses an interesting question: if I were to pour a bowl of radioactive soup (so that it could be traced), of which I was the owner, into the ocean, and this radioactive soup mixed throughout all the oceans and seas, could it be said that I am now the owner of all this?[6]

Locke locates the desire for propertisation of the commons in the need for the preservation of resources. According to him, if resources are left in the commons their utility will gradually diminish because of over-use or neglect. Land, for example, may be overgrazed or may by neglect become unmanable, and in both cases the utility that this land provides is diminished. Locke assumes that once a resource is taken from the commons and transformed into private property the owner of that property will use it in a manner that preserves its value in use.

Bernard Shaw's quotation concerning the 'sharing of ideas' is a simple, yet effective, demonstration of the nature of ideas and information goods. Information just does not possess the same characteristics as classical 'real property'. The dissemination of

---

5. *Supra* note 3.
6. Robert, Nozick, 'State Anarchy and Utopia', p. 57.

ideas, for instance, does not reduce their use value. Information is considered a 'non-rival' good, in the sense that usage of a particular piece of information cannot impair the utility of that information to another user. It has also been characterised as 'non-excludable' in the sense that use of a certain piece of information does not exclude other users from utilising the same information.[7] The best example of this is software. The only way a person can prevent the copying of software is by preventing third persons from accessing it. Once access is granted, it can be copied for almost no cost. This copying, moreover, does not affect the utility of the software itself, nor does it prevent the usage of that software by the original owner. The sharing of information goods, especially in the digital context, does not diminish in any manner the quality of the good that is shared. There is clearly a movement away from the idea of property as we have always understood it. However, the concept of copyright represents a stubborn drive towards taming this new monster of accessibility created by developments in information technology.

On the same traction it shall not be just that one person endowing his intellect to develop an idea, spending money to develop a concept, giving labour to develop useful skills, giving thought to create any information, providing consideration to construct any plan or investing brain to develop any goods, etc. and another will use the same without any hindrance and penny. If this will happen then the value less market shall be created which shall be against the human progress. Thus, to encourage the development in every fields of creation creative act had been welcomed by way of legal recognition and protection resulting in the monopoly of 'know-how'. Today's market is the product-based market and when anyone using his skill to make his creation marketable than that should be encouraged by governmental policy so that more and more creative works shall be possible. Until and unless the legal recognition and protection to the intellectual property is provided the encouragement is not possible. The realization of this prolonged problem has already been made and global initiatives have already been taken to boom the creative culture. India has also attempted a lot to

7. Hal, R. Varian, Microeconomic Analysis, ISBN 0-393-95735-7; Mas-Colell, Whinston & Green, Microeconomic Theory, ISBN 0-19-507340-1

protect the intellectual properties through various legislations but the available laws providing the security to the Intellectual property by some non-technological manner and protection is available to the established modes of violation or infringement only. The technological advancement throughout the world made the infringement an ordinary and common practice because of non-established/traditional or electronic or online mode of infringement. Indian law is still suffering from policy sickness in this area because different amendments of Copyright Act, 1957 are also unable to meet the challenge of the electronic advancement.

POSITION OF INTELLECTUAL PROPERTY RIGHT

To begin with the term Intellectual Property Right (IPR), it can be said that the term IPR is a heterogeneous term having mixture of many ideas. The term is not related to any one basic norm but rather it is a dynamic idea depending upon the application and market of the place. The term IPR can be analysed in the following way:

IPR is a bundle of exclusive rights given to persons over creations of the mind, both artistic and commercial. They usually give the creator an exclusive right over the use of his/her creation for a certain period of time. The former is covered by copyright laws, which protect creative works, such as books, movies, music, paintings, photographs, and software, and gives the copyright holder exclusive right to control reproduction or adaptation of such works for a certain period of time.

In this era of globalization, especially after the establishment of WTO, intellectual property law has assumed much importance, quite disproportionate to what they actually deserve. The reason might be the feeling that advanced industrial societies are undergoing a fundamental transformation from capital and labour-based economies into knowledge economies and aftermath of the recent information technology revolution.[8] Two interesting features of a knowledge-based economy are the astonishing speed and intensity of innovation and emergence of new technologies enabling dissemination of knowledge/ information in an unprecedented manner. These technological

8. Christopher May, A Global Political Economy of Intellectual Property Rights: The New Enclosures? The Routledge, 2000, p. 4.

development paved way for upsurge in the demand for the strengthening of protection of IPR. The proponents of expanded IPR protection try to justify their demand arguing that social progress in the technological age is inextricably connected with the creation and protection of intellectual property.[9]

The proponents of the arguments that stronger IPR is inevitable for industrial and economic development of a nation rely upon the commonly accepted belief that adequate protection of IPR is essential for promoting confidence among investors in research and development.[10] Their claim is that IPR acts as incentive to innovate to disclose the technology so as to facilitate further growth in science and technology. The progress of science and technology in the developed countries and the emergence of multinational corporation relating to the economic and industrial development are cited as example in this regard. They also try to propagate the view that the developing countries could reap the benefits of increased IPR as it attract more foreign direct investment and accelerates transfer of technology between countries, ensuring that all countries enjoy the benefit.[11]

There are many economists and jurists who share the feeling that knowledge is not like any other kind of goods as it is 'non-rival in use' and a proliferation of IPR inhibits access to information in areas of basic research, creating artificial scarcities in fields where abundance naturally prevails. Economists like Paul A. David[12] are of the opinion that the present system of intellectual property rights are economically imperfect in that the monopolistic nature of such rights may lead to waste of resources referred to by economic welfare. This is because of the tendency of the monopolists to raise the price of every product much above the cost of production thereby excluding many potential users form enjoying it.

---

9. Roberto Mazzoleni and Richard R. Nelson, The Benefits and Costs of Strong Patent Protection: A Contribution to the Current Debate, Research Policy, 27 (1998), pp. 273-84.
10. *Ibid.*
11. William M. Aandes and Richard A. Posner, 'The Political Economy of Intellectual Property Law' available at http://www.aei.org/docLib/20040608_Landes.pdf.
12. Edward Elgar, New Frontiers is the Economies of Innovation and New Technology: Essays in Honour of Paul A. David, ed. Cristiano Antonelli, Dominique Forany, Bronwyn H. Hall, W. Edward Stainmuller, p. 379, Cheltenham, UK, 2006.

However, internationally the current trend supports the former view. The TRIPs Agreement is the culmination of the efforts of the proponents of expanded IPR protection to set international standards base on their view.

Unlike the TRIPs Agreement, the initial International Conventions like Berne (1886) and Paris (1883) created only minimum principles of substantive law with adequate flexibilities so as to enable the member states to adopt the international norms without affecting their domestic requirements. This in fact enabled many countries to take advantage of the system to promote economic and technological development. TRIPs, on the other hand, attempted standardization of substantive law by listing out the scope, subject matter, duration etc., of different forms of IPR with very limited flexibilities in its implementation.

IDEA OF COPYRIGHT

It is important to remember the purpose of copyright which is public welfare, Enlightenment 'the encouragement of learning'.[13] **Justice Hugh Laddie** observed, **'The whole human development is derivative. We stand on the shoulders of the scientists, artists and craftsmen who preceded us. We borrow and develop what they have done, not necessarily as parasites but simply as the next generation. It is at the heart of what simply we know as progress.'**[14] The provisions for infringement and piracy may concentrate the copyright materials with the powerful corporation, particularly the Hollywood studios and this may not only lock way various copyrighted materials from public domain whose access would be unaffordable for the population of a country whose 70% still live in rural areas but may also seriously erode the common cultural products through a systematic homogenization thereby also affecting the most prolific, colourful and culturally diverse industry, Bollywood[15].

The issue of copyrights has until recently been in the foray for both its use and abuse since the dawn of the renaissance period, a time in history when the world marveled at the birth of new inventions, philosophies in science, arts and industry;

13. Layman, Ray Patterson, Copyright in Historical Perspective (1968), p. 147.
14. Hugh, Laddie, Copyright: Over-strength, Over-regulated, Over-rated? 5 E.I.P.R. 253 (1996).
15. India, Economic Survey, 2006.

inventions that redefined the limits of our capabilities at achieving hitherto what had been considered unachievable. The most remarkable feature worthy of appreciation would be the analysis of the development and evolution of copyright law in parlance with the development of legal theory. A systematic compilation of thought aimed at bringing about reforms, regulations, restrictions and punishments to certain identified behaviour considered detestable by a collective group of people called society. Although there are competing claims in defining the eternal question, what is law? Yet it is undeniable that Natural law theory affords a qualified understanding to copyright law, inherently an aspiration to secure individuality in realization of our right to liberty and property. Legal concepts of 'property' and 'right' in their extended applications brought a concrete materialization of determining the basis of Intellectual Property.

INFRINGEMENT OF COPYRIGHT

Copyright law confers upon the owner of the copyrighted work a bundle of exclusive rights in respect of the reproduction of the work and other acts. The owner of the copyright alone has a sole right in relation to such work without his permission[16]. If anybody else does any of the acts without the authority of the owner of the copyright, the owner of the copyright can maintain an action for infringement of his copyright against the wrongdoer.

The copyright in a work could be said to be infringed when someone without the permission of the owner of copyright does anything, the exclusive right being conferred upon the owner by the Copyright Act. In order to prove infringement, it has to be proved that the work alleged to be infringed has copyright and the infringing work is a copy of it. For proving the latter part, one has to have a clear understanding as to what amount to copying. How much of the original work need to be copied for constitution of infringement? Copying of the un-copyrightable material from the original work is not infringement. In order to constitute infringement not only that copyrighted material is copied but also such protected material is 'substantial'. In other words, there should be substantial copying between the original

16. H.M. Jhawala, Intellectually Property and Competition Law in India, p. 139.

work and the work alleged to be an infringing copy. However, the determination of the extent of copying that constitutes a substantial copying is one of the most difficult questions in the copyright law.[17] Substantial copying does not necessarily mean copying of substantial portion of the work. Even if the similar material is quantitatively small, it is enough to constitute substantial copying if it is qualitatively small important.[18] Copying need not be literal or verbatim. It is enough if the fundamental essence or structure of one work is duplicated. The mere fact that the defendant paraphrased rather than literally copied will not preclude a finding of substantial copying. Otherwise, a plagiarist would escape by immaterial variations.[19] However, both in literal and non-literal copying one of the most important considerations while deciding an infringement has the adverse effect on the market caused by the infringing work.

The question of infringement of copyright comes into picture when the people intend to take under advantage and cause economic loss to the people who by virtue of their intellect, expense and hard labour have earned those rights. What is apparent is that the technological change has made reproduction of copyright material easy and cheap, and also at the same time it has made piracy of copyright work simple and difficult to control. They have made copyright intringement international in character. When a work is transmitted from one point to another or made available for the public to access, numerous parties are involved in the transmission. These include entities that provide internet access or online services. When such service providers participate in transmitting or making available material provided by another, which infringe copyright or alter rights, they are liable.[20] Such liability could arise in one of the ways, if the service provider itself is found to have engaged in unauthorised acts of reproduction or communication to the public or if it is held responsible or contributing to a making possible the act of infringement by another. It is the potential liability of the online service and access providers for infringement taking place through their services. The important question that is raised is:

---

17. Nimmer, Melville; David Nimmer (1997): Nimmer on Copyright. Matthew Bender. ISBN 0-8205-1465-9, pp. 13-27
18. *Ibid.*
19. *Nichols Vs. Universal Pictures Co.*, 45 F 2d 119 (2d Cr 1930), at p. 121.
20. Rodeny, D. Ryder, Intellectual Property and the Internet, 1st edn., p. 66.

are service providers exercising the exclusive rights of copyright owners themselves, as they engage in acts that cause the material to be copied and transmitted?

Regardless, where the services make the transmission possible, the service providers are legally responsible for the unauthorised exercise of those rights. There is one reference to this issue in an Agreed Statement if the WCT, which says, 'It is understood that the mere provision of physical facilities for enabling or making a communication dies not in itself amount to communication within the meaning of this Treaty or the Berne Convention'.[21] Statement clarifies that simply providing the wires used to communicate, for example, does not constitute an act of communication. But the statement is limited in its application. It does not cover a number of activities that service provides may engage in, and it does not deal with concepts of liability for contributing to the infringement of another. The US Digital Millennium, Copyright Act, 1998 shields qualifying Internet Service Providers form much of the potential liability. It insulates service providers form vicarious liability (but not direct) for copyright infringement, both for acting as a conduit for infringing material (conduct activity) as well as infringing activities of their users and the content of those user's web pages (user activity) on the Internet Service Providers.[22] The Information Technology Act, 2000 provides that a network service provider is not subject to criminal or civil liability for third party material for which or to which the provider merely provides access.

Home taping by video-audio recording has posed further challenges to the rights of copyright owner of cinematographic films and sound recordings.[23] By using audio and video recording devices any number of copies of the films or sound recording can be made available at a very low cost which may result into a substantial loss to the copyright owners.[24] Further home taping reproduction of a broadcast may also be made by recording of the air from the satellite broadcast, thereby

21. Agreed statement concerning Article 8 of WCT.
22. Section 512(a) and (c) of US Digital Millenium Copyright Act, 1998.
23. Section 78 of Information Technology Act, 2000.
24. A.K. Kaul and V.K. Ahuja, Law of Copyright: From Gutenberg's invention to Internet, 1st ed., p. 22, Delhi, 2001.

infringing the rights of broadcasting organisations and performers.

Perhaps the most difficult task for intellectual property owners is detecting infringements and identifying the infringers. The worldwide reach of Internet, the millions of websites on the World Wide Web, the ease of access to the source of information/creation and copying others intellectual property and the framed anonymity of this new medium detection become cumbersome. The sufferings of a creator can best be seen by looking at *R.G. Anand Vs. Delux Films,*[25] where the Courts clearly held that if the mediums are different, proving violation becomes all the more difficult.

The next difficulty involved in answering the question of infringement is the idea/expression dichotomy in copyright. Since ideas are not protected under the copyright, similarly in ideas the question of infringement does not arise. It is not easy to identify when an imitator has gone beyond the idea and has borrowed its expression. According to Professor Zechariah Chafee, the protection covers the 'pattern' of the work; the sequence of the events and the development of the interplay of characters.[26]

EMERGENCE OF THE WORK

Due to rapid technological growth the copyright law becomes the weakest piece of legislation in terms of protection because the technological and other development makes this area most accessible and people can easily take the advantage of technology in the process of violation of the copyright resulting in two-fold economic crisis. Firstly, the crisis is available to the author or copyright owner and secondly the loss to the government's revenue. There are many other ways by which now-a-days the copyright can be violated. The most common use of statistics in the copyright tale concerns the losses caused by piracy. Thus, for instance, in case of computer software one would encounter the following narrative:

- The extent of software piracy and losses due to piracy cannot be given in exact quantitative terms though it is

25. AIR 1978 SC 1613.
26. Chafee, 'Reflections on the Law of Copyright', 45 Colum L Rev 503, at pp. 513-14 (1945).

believed that piracy in this sector is widespread. In India software piracy is costing the IT industry quite clear. According to a survey conducted jointly by Business Software Alliance (BSA) and NASSCOM in May 2006, total losses due to software piracy in India stood at a staggering figure of about Rs. 500 crores (US$ 151.3 million) showing about 60 per cent piracy rate in India.[27] In Europe alone the software industries lose an estimated $ 6 billion a year. In fact, Europe holds the dubious distinction of accounting for about 50 per cent of worldwide losses from software piracy, more than any other region including the number two, Asia. According to a study, losses due to piracy of personal computer business application software nearly equalled revenues earned by the global software industry. In 2006, piracy cost the software industry US $ 11.2 billion, a 16 percent decrease over the estimated losses of US $ 13.3 billion in 2005[28].

- In India a study by the Business Software Alliance (BSA), the international association of the world's commercial software industry found that, 73% of the software installed on PCs in India in 2004 was pirated representing a loss of Rs. 23,355 crore. It has been estimated that a 10% reduction in the infringement of copyright i.e. piracy in the next four years in India, would enable the IT sector to boom from Rs. 33,300 crore to Rs. 87,750 crore.[29]
- The failure to enforce Copyrights (IPR) laws has taken a heavy toll on government revenues and reduced employment opportunities, with the government forgoing tax revenue of over Rs. 10,000 crore annually due to the proliferation of counterfeit consumer products alone.[30]

---

27. MHRD Report on Copyright Piracy, 2006.
28. Study Conducted by Software Publishers' Association, a US-based body, published in 2006.
29. *The Times of India*, Jan. 10, 2006.
30. Chief Justice of the Delhi High Court, S.B. Sinha, in the inauguration of a seminar on new IPR laws organised by the Associated Chambers of Commerce and Industry of India (ASSOCHAM), *The Hindu*, September 22, 2002.

- The 2007 report of the International Intellectual Property Alliance (IIPA) on the Indian documented that India suffered trade losses worth 496.3 million US dollars due to copyright infringement.[31]

It is often lamented that there is a difference between enacting a law and ensuring that it is properly enforced. The copyright laws in India offer a very good illustration of this enigma. Despite the protection provided by the India Copyright Act, 1957, India has acquired notoriety by being on the priority watch list year after year mainly because of abominable high piracy rates and dearth of appropriate measures of encouragement.[32] It is critical to adjust the legal system to respond rapidly to the new technological environment in an effective and appropriate way, because technologies and markets evolve increasingly and rapidly. This will ensure the continuous furtherance of the fundamental guiding principles of copyright and related rights, which remain constant whatever may be the technology of the day. It would involve giving incentives to creators to produce and disseminate new creative materials; recognising the importance of their contributions providing appropriate balance for the public interest, particularly education, research and access to information and thereby ultimately benefiting society by promoting the development of culture, science and the economy."[33]

Apart from the above mentioned facts the present research work is undertaken to cope with the following supplementary objects:

The excerpts from news reports quoted above provide just a glimpse of the discourse that has become a regular staple of the media's coverage of copyright-related issues. Yet there is a stubborn logic that refuses to accede so easily to the threats, blackmail and pleas of copyright protectionists. The spectral

31. International Intellectual Property Alliance, 2007, Special 301 Report India, 12 February 2007, pp. 49, 51, 53-54, 117 at www.iipa.com/rbc/2007/2007/SPEC301INDIA.pdf (21 September 2008).
32. Desai, Rachna, Copyright Infringement in Indian Film Industry, *Vanderbilt Journal of Entertainment, Law & Practice* (Spring 2005), pp. 259-78.
33. Minister of State for Coal, Mines, Law and Justice, Ravi Shankar Prasad, in his keynote address in the inauguration of a seminar on new IPR laws organised by the Associated Chambers of Commerce and Industry of India (ASSOCHAM), *The Hindu*, September 22, 2002.

figure of copyright looms large over, but fails to entirely haunt our imagination. As with any other conflict, the 'battle for souls' is perhaps as important as the transformations taking place in the material world of practices. And it is within these spaces of the human imagination that we insert our current intervention. The promoters of copyright have a rather straight forward justification for it. We shall begin with what may be considered a rather typical account of the necessity of copyright law. In recent years copyright law has been amended to include protection for performers' rights. The key assumption that sustains copyright law is that authors have a natural right over their works of intellectual labour, and copyright protection is required to provide an incentive to create intellectual works. Copyright, therefore, grants an exclusive right to the author over his or her works; this includes a basket of related rights such as the right to authorise reproduction, adaptation, performance, and distribution, etc. of the work. In the absence of a system like copyright, it is argued, there would be no incentive for authors to produce and hence there would be a general decline in the world of creativity and the arts. However, copyright inherently includes a balance between the protection of authors, on the one hand, and the interests of the public, on the other. Since it is recognized that excessive protection may result in curbing the ability of the public to use works, copyright protects only unique expressions and not ideas *per se*. Some balance is also sought to be achieved by providing a limited term of protection (i.e., the lifetime of the author plus 60 years). Within these limits, any person who uses the works of another person's intellectual labour without permission is, according to copyright law, guilty of indulging in an act of stealing the other person's ideas. The rationale is that such theft will result in unacceptable losses of the author for the work. As with any other totalising story, the tale of copyright appears to have some intrinsic appeal, relying as it does on a progress account (copyright promotes creativity) and the despotic world that it prevents (there will be no creativity without copyright).[34] There are a number of contradictions in the attempt to equate information goods with classical property which are becoming ever more glaring. Some of these are internal

34. Santa Clara Computer and High Technology Law Journal, Vol. 24, p. 31, 2007.

contradictions within the larger machinery of production and consumption. Thus, on the one hand, we have hardware manufacturers creating better CD writers at a cheaper price and advertising their products with the magical words, BURN, RIP, COPY, DUPLICATE, STORE, etc. On the other hand, we have the content industry screaming itself hoarse at these new technologies that are making it easier for people to steal information unethically. Copyright has acquired all-pervasive status in recent years, entering the realms of the everyday in various forms. It appears in the public sphere most commonly as a newspaper story about the losses caused by piracy or the latest 'threatno-innovative' attempt to fight piracy. Post-September 11, 2001, the war against terrorism and the war against piracy have become close allies. Sometimes the battle acquires a certain glamorous appeal when one celebrity sues another for copyright infringement, as in the recent case of ***Bappi Lahiri against Dr. Dre***[35] for using his song, ***Kaliyon Ka Chaman***, or ***Rajnikant***, Famous Hindi and Tamil film actor, claiming rights over a sign that he uses in his film, ***Baba***.[36] The recognition of the legal tender shall certainly helpful in achieving the target of prevention of copyright infringement in India.

Copyright infringement (or copyright violation) is the unauthorized use of material that is covered by copyright law, in a manner that violates one of the copyright owner's exclusive rights, such as the right to reproduce or perform the copyrighted work, or to make derivative works. It is the authorized use of copyrighted material in a manner that violates one of the copyright owner's exclusive rights, such as the right to reproduce or perform the copyrighted work, or to make derivative works that build upon it. There are different ways through which copyright owners may find their copyright has been infringed. For example, in this world of technology apart from illegal copying, Bootlegging Piracy, Counterfeiting, Plagiarism, etc. which may be related to writing, software, film and music industry, etc. are other forms of infringement. Anyone who violates the exclusive rights of the owner of copyrighted work by using or copying it for its commercial exploitation or its communication to the public, without the author's consent or

35. *The Telegraph*, Calcutta, India, Friday, November 01, 2002.
36. *The Hindu*, Saturday, September 28, 2002.

authority, is infringing the copyright. Under the Indian Copyright Act for electronic and audio-visual media, unauthorized reproduction and distribution is occasionally referred to as piracy.[37] The legal basis for this usage dates from the same era, and has been consistently applied until the present time. Critics of the use of the term 'piracy' to describe such practices contend that it is pejorative, unfairly equates copyright infringement with more sinister activity,[38] though courts often hold that under law the two terms are interchangeable.[39]

We are constantly delighted with stories of how copyright as a system acts as the basic protection for poor, struggling authors who would otherwise have no means of protecting themselves against pirates who reproduce their goods or others who steal their ideas. Let us, at the very outset, clarify that we certainly not enemies of creative workers and we would, of course, like to see all creative labour recognised and rewarded. But the question that begs an answer is: does copyright really achieve that and, if not, why does this image of the poor, struggling author keep coming to mind? What the metaphor of the poor, struggling author does is render invisible the critical difference between the authorship of a work of intellectual labour and the ownership of the same.

Copyright scholar *Peter Jaszi* states that:

> "while there is a tendency in copyright law to invoke liberal individualism to justify economic structures that frustrate the aspirations of real-life individuals, it is somewhat surprising to encounter the individualistic romantic conception of 'authorship' deployed to support a regime that disassociates creative workers from a legal interest in their creations: the 'work-for-hire' doctrine of American copyright law, where this doctrine applies, the firm or individual who paid to have a work created,

---

37. http://www.med.govt.nz/templates/ContentTopicSummary_34357. aspx.
38. Geiger, Andrea (2008-04-30), A View From Europe: The high price of counterfeiting, and getting real about enforcement, at http://thehill.com/business--lobby/a-view-from-europe-the-high-price-of-counterfeiting-and-getting-real-about-enforcement-2008-04-30.html.
39. Pilieci, Vito (2008-05-26). "Copyright deal could toughen rules governing info on iPods, computers", available at http://www.canada.com/vancouversun/story.html? id=ae997868-220b-4dae-bf4f-47f6fc96ce5e&p=1

> rather than the person who created it, is regarded as the 'author' for purposes of copyright ownership."[40]

When a work is deemed to have been made 'for hire', the alienation of labour is formally and legally complete: the 'author' of the 'work' is the person on whose behalf the 'work' was made, not the individual who created it. In this legal configuration, the employer's rights do not derive from the employee by an implied grant or assignment. Rather, those rights are the direct result of the employer's status. Ironically, the employer's claims are rationalised in terms of the Romantic conception of 'authorship' with its concomitant values of 'originality' and 'inspiration'. Recently, J.K. Rowling, author of the Harry Potter series, has been in the news for enforcing her copyright against cheap pirated copies. In more ways than one she stands as a role model for copyright enforcers, and her status as a struggling single mother is often used as the analogy for the way copyright protects the rights of poor authors. While we are all happy for Ms Rowling, what is not convincing is how the example applies even after the publication of the fifth or sixth Harry Potter book, by which time the writer had become one of the highest paid authors in the world, with many millions of pounds in excess. Clearly pirates respond only to a market demand, and not every book is pirated. There is a particular popularity or price limit that has to be achieved before it enters into the piracy circuit. Presumably, if a book has achieved a certain status that leads to it being pirated, its author is no longer poor and struggling. Encouraging creation of authors by protecting their interest shall undoubtedly be helpful to minimise the rampant practice of infringement of copyright through different modes.

The unauthorized downloading of copyrighted material and sharing of recorded music over the internet in the form of MP3 files and other audio files is more prominent now than since before the advent of the internet or the invention of MP3, even after the demise of Napster and a series of infringement suits brought by the American recording industry. Promotional screener DVDs distributed by movie studios (often for consideration for awards) are a common source of unauthorized

40. Woodmansee, M., The Construction of Authorship: Textual Appropriation in Law and Literature, Duke University Press, 1994 (also published as a law journal issue, 10, *Cardozo Arts and Entertainment Law Journal*, 274, 1992).

copying when movies are still in theatrical release, and the MPAA has attempted to restrict their use. Movies are also still copied by someone sneaking a camcorder into a movie theater and secretly taping the projection (also known as 'camming'), although such copies are often of lesser quality than copied versions of the officially released film. Some copyright owners have responded to infringement by displaying warning notices on commercially sold DVDs; these warnings do not always give a fair picture of the purchaser's legal rights, which in the US generally include the rights to sell, exchange, rent or lend a purchased DVD. Sharing copied music is legal in many countries, such as Canada, and parts of Europe, provided that the songs are not sold but under Indian copyright law it is gross infringement since it is not permitted. A blanket ban on reproduction of a work of science, literature and arts, either in full or part may, in certain circumstances, become inimical to the public purpose that a copyright is intended to serve. For example, such a total ban may, instead of promoting and stimulating study and research in science, humanities and arts, lead to thwart it and become counter-productive. Promotion of music and cinematographic industry not only protect the copyrights of the creator or investor but also encourage the scope of employment in this industry.

To understand how to protect and promote the markets in creativity, it is important to first define creativity. Creativity is the production of something novel that offers value in a particular situation. What is valuable differs according to the situation. The value may stem from the usefulness, merit, importance, uniqueness, or desirability of that product, service, process, or idea. The copyright industries savour their role as critical intermediaries in the copyright supply chain. To this end they are continually seeking to strengthen their legal entitlements by arguing that stronger copyright incentives fuel future creative action. But the reality of creativity is different from the linear economic reward/action relationship that these industries promote. This reality has been brought into sharp focus by the seemingly limitless creativity that the internet has unleashed. Much of this creativity occurs without reference to the incentive structure provided by copyright law and demonstrates the potential redundancy of several existing industry functions. The result has been a seemingly intractable tension between established industries and emergent modes of production and dissemination. The clearest examples of this tension are the current debates over the utility of peer-to-peer technology and the competition between proprietary and open source software development models.[41] This tension, and the realities of creativity that underpin it, are the challenges for the researcher. Many of us think of the arts and sciences as being the sole domains of creative expression, but creativity is manifested in many different ways and in many different fields. The people and organizations produce novelty and value by way of Expressions, Potential, Experiences and Capabilities. The last category of creativity that emerges from individual and organizational capabilities is what is at stake in the question about the future of copyright.

Historically software has been considered to be a subject matter that may be protected by copyright. It is obvious that any item protected by copyrights automatically comes under the ambit of the Berne Convention, and all statutory provisions under the copyright law become applicable to the software protected by copyright. One has to be very clear about the concepts of authorship and ownership of computer programs. The programmer or programmers are to be considered as joint authors of a work. If the work is created in the course of one's employment, then the first ownership goes to the employer in the absence of any contrary contractual agreement. If someone is specifically hired to do develop the program then it is implied that the ownership is assigned to the one who commissioned the work. However, one has to exercise considerable care as issues of prior knowledge, proprietary object codes from one's library may be used for the development of the program and the associated applications and hence the issue of authorship and ownership can get fairly murky under such circumstances. Different data of the days shows that the software industry shall have the potential to contribute to the state fund remarkably if nurtured properly. The protection of the software industry from the curse of infringement and promotion of this industry to its proper shape and size are amongst the duties of the researcher.

Apart from the statutory provisions as laid down under

41. Ganley, Paul, The Internet, Creativity and Copyright Incentives, *Journal of Intellectual Property Rights*, Vol. 10, p. 188, 2005.

Indian Copyright Act the infringement of copyright cases can also be dealt with by High courts and Supreme Court of India under different lawful provisions of constitution of India. Even though certain important fundamental rights including right to carry on any trade or business are guaranteed only to citizens, all persons including non-citizens can claim equality before the law and equal protection of the laws under the constitution. Therefore, any arbitrary discrimination against a person, who is a non-citizen *qua* his claim to be treated equally as others before the law, can be challenged before the Courts. Recourse to Court by law is a well recognized concept world over and firmly entrenched in the Constitutional and other laws of India. Therefore, any person can claim a statutorily or customarily recognized right to property. In case of infringement of a legally recognized right recourse to law cannot be denied and the rule of law enshrined under the Constitution will enable any person including a non-citizen to move to the appropriate forum of the country for redressal of his grievances. In India the Code of Civil Procedure allows alien friends also to sue in any Court otherwise competent to try the suit, as if they were citizens of India. Ordinarily, violation of Copyrights has a private dimension in as much as it affects the proprietary rights of individuals and may cause financial loss and loss of credit to the owner. Therefore, the questions of national or public interest would rarely arise when redressal is sought by a non-citizen for violation of such proprietary rights by the infringer. The judiciary is bound to implement the laws and redress grievances of all persons including aliens to uphold their common law or statutorily recognized rights. The Indian Judiciary has many things to achieve in present time to establish a society with minimum of infringement of copyright or any Intellectual Property. Some cases may be summarized to mobilize the concept of judicial response in real sense. Infringement of Copyright is century old problem but the infringement of copyright in ancient age was not as harmful as in today's situation. In ancient time the creator were not so worried because the dimension of this right did not receive the present economic values. In present time copyright has not only the creative values but rather it has becomes economic right of the owner. At the same time the challenge to protect copyright is also very difficult which was not to centuries back. Today, due to the development of technology, electronic and digital mechanism the scope of infringement is higher and value of copyright is also increasing day-by-day. Results from past studies indicated that apart from protecting their economic, cultural, moral etc. rights rather contributing to the state exchequer that now a day copyright is not only benefiting the owner/creator of the copyright by contributing in state exchequer, in some of these nations (e.g. USA, Germany, Sweden, Australia, and U.K.) the contribution from copyright-based industries to their respective Gross Domestic Product (GDP) is significantly high. Unfortunately in the Indian context no systematic effort is undertaken to arrive at fair indicators of the sector's contribution to GDP whereas India is one of the largest creator of the copyrighted works whose benefit cannot enjoyed due to rampant infringement of copyright and related rights.

The copyright is one of the highly demanded mode of intellectual property which has immense role to play so far as the advancement of the country and the contribution to the revenue of the government is concerned but due to the excessive available modes of infringement of copyright it has remained only a dream for a country like India which is one of the largest market of copyright-related IP. Whereas in developed countries having lesser market in comparison to Indian market, the copyright-based industries comprise mainly the print and publishing industry, audio cassettes/CDs industry, film and video industry and computer software, etc. which contribute handsomely to the state exchequers. Worldwide it is recognized that copyright piracy is a serious crime which not only adversely affects the creative potential of the society by denying the creators their legitimate dues, it also causes economic losses, to all who had invested their money in bringing out copyrighted materials in various forms for use by end-users. Globalization forced the copyright issues to the forefront because a large number of copyrighted products area are traded internationally. Protection of copyright, therefore, is a priority matter in the national agenda of many countries especially in the developing world. Surely, it has also emerged as an important factor governing international relations. India is losing its revenues to the tune of crores every minute due to infringement activities but due to unknown modes or cases of the infringement it is not able to protect the same. Moreover, sometime due to unavailable legal measures, known infringement activities area is also not prevented resulting is loss to the owner/author of the creation. Another problem for which the work has been taken is that maximum population in India even, today do not know what copyright infringement is and how it is caused at all? The protective acts could not be expected from a person who has no basic idea about the Copyright and its infringement. This is caused because of lack of awareness and consciousness about consequences of infringements. The present available laws in India are insufficient and are not able to protect every aspect of the copyright infringement in India. Another object is to analyse the current position of law and to find out the proper measure for the protection of the copyright and related rights. Judiciary always plays an important role in the development of any civilised countries. Basically in federal countries the judicial pronouncements are playing the role of path finder both for the legislature as well as other branches of judiciary. In India, Article 141 of the Constitution made Supreme Court as the highest Court having supremacy in judicial decision with binding effect on the subordinate judiciary and after administrative and quasi-judicial bodies of the country. The proposed work shall analyse the different judicial decision and try to find out the areas of infringement, mode of infringement and the available modes of protection of the copyright from infringement.

Thus, the abovementioned data and situations clearly speak regarding the emergence of the present research in the field of copyright and its protection from infringement. The research propose to find out the modes by which the copyrights have been infringing and on the same track the ways by which reasonable protection can be given to copyright-based creation as well as industries so that less loses to the creator/owner or investor shall be caused and at the same time more revenues shall be contributed to the government revenues. The research work seeks to identify and interrogate some of the assumptions that underlie most media stories about copyright. The greatest success of the concept of copyright has been its successful elevation to the status of myth through the constant rendering of certain familiar figures (the poor struggling author), arguments (people deserve to own the fruit of their labour) and rhetorical data (billions of dollars lost due to piracy). By specifically labelling these assumptions myths, the researcher seek to question their truth premise. This is, however, a task that has just begun and more collective works are required to strive towards making arguments that go beyond merely providing counter-facts if we are to effectively counter the totalising rhetoric of copyright. The importance of the work can easily be measured from the facts and informations discussed in the foregoing paragraphs. It also shows that the Copyright protection in India is still not strong and effective enough to take care of the copyright of individual and copyright based industry and business so far as the protection of copyrighted works are concerned. Though sometimes it is claimed that our law is enough for the protection of copyright works but it is a utopian thought because Indian laws on copyright is capable to protect the copyright from the established or manual methods of infringement only not otherwise. The technological and technical advancement is adding to the process of the infringement of copyright throughout the globe now-a-days. The protection extends only to the Copyright as understood in the traditional sense but not in its modern aspect. Thus, on-line copyright issues are also not adequately protected. Neither the country has developed a sound strong legal base for the protection of copyrights nor is the judiciary playing a proactive role in the protection of these rights. Hence, the situation is very alarming as it is growing and the existing legal system cannot effectively take care of all problems associated with copyright infringement. In this thesis the researcher has tried to find out the non-obvious or electronic/digital/technological modes of infringement of copyright and possible methods of its protection so that the monopoly of the know-how based property exists and more and more endeavour is made in the process of creativity and development which consequently contributes more and more to the government revenues from the Intellectual Property market particularly from the Copyright based market.

In order to explore the possibilities of better use of copyright without its infringement the author has classified the entire work project into six heads:

The First Chapter introduces introduction, The Second Chapter highlights on the historical background of copyright. The Third Chapter of the work discusses the International position of copyright. The Fourth Chapter explains the Indian position of copyright especially during post-constitutional period. The Fifth Chapter of the book studies on cases and its analysis in the context of copyright. The Sixth Chapter finally concludes the whole work project.

2

COPYRIGHT AND ITS HISTORICAL BACKGROUND

Anticipation and effort of human civilisation to pin down the certainty that life may offer is an irony to the inherently uncertain character of life. Amidst this engulfing uncertainty is but one real attribute of humankind and any other life form, to mimic itself in varying environments whereby he brings to fore a plethora of responses, those which we, as an evolved species have come to classify as knowledge, tradition, custom, culture, etc. The issue of copying and its ethics has always been of much concern to the academia. The present era of rapid extension of human capabilities in frontiers hitherto unmapped and unrealized has come to alter the very sense of perception that man has lived with. It has been rightly termed as the age of information, an age where information decides the triumphant; it has correspondingly brought along with it a deep insecurity and fear within men, to protect all that is precious to him, learning apparently has fallen prey to this ardent zeal of man and his society to seek his own self-preservation.

Copyright has its root in the privileges, laws and regulations associated with the advent of printing in the fifteenth century; these mainly protect the printer rather than author.[1] The issue of copyrights has until recently been in the foray for both its use

1. M.C. Dock, Etude sur le droit d'auteur (L.G.D.G., Paris, 1963; Ricketon/ Ginsburg, Ch. 1.

and abuse since the dawn of the renaissance period, a time in history when the world marveled at the birth of new inventions, philosophies in science, arts and industry; inventions that redefined the limits of our capabilities at achieving hitherto what had been considered unachievable. The most remarkable feature worthy of appreciation would be the analysis of the development and evolution of copyright law in parlance with the development of legal theory. A systematic compilation of thought aimed at bringing about reforms, regulations, restrictions and punishments to certain identified behaviour considered detestable by a collective group of people called society. Although there are competing claims in defining the eternal question, what is law? Yet it is undeniable that Natural law theory affords a qualified understanding to copyright law, inherently an aspiration to secure individuality in realisation of our right to liberty and property. In this context it can be said that Gutenberg and Caxton changed the possibilities of copying a work with the introduction of mechanical printing, and the subsequent viability of commercial publishing. Half a millennium later, the Internet has further revolutionised matters, because it permits virtually unlimited duplication of documents at a single key-stroke.

DEVELOPMENT OF LAW OF COPYRIGHT

One of the earliest copyright disputes reputedly took place in 557 A.D. between Abbot Finnian of Moville and St. Columba over St. Columba's copying of a Psalter belonging to an Abbot. The dispute over ownership of the copy led to the Battle of Cúl Dreimhne (also known as Battle of Cooldrumman), in which 3,000 men were killed.[2]

The Copyright law was first introduced in the United Kingdom in response to the need to protect the new printing trade against the unauthorized copying of books (piracy). Ever since, it has developed to keep pace with the introduction of new technologies. As copyright law developed in the eighteenth and nineteenth centuries it was mainly concerned with the field of literature and the arts but, following the advancement in technology of the twentieth century, the protection given by

2. Gantz, John and Rochester, Jack B. (2005), Pirates of the Digital Millennium, Upper Saddle River: *Financial Times*, Prentice Hall, pp. 30-33; ISBN 0-13-

copyright law has been considerably expanded over the years, both with respect to the subject-matter of protection and also to the classes of acts which constitute infringement. Thus, today protection is not only given to literary, dramatic, musical and artistic works, but also to sound recordings, films, broadcasts, and the typographical arrangements of published editions. Infringement of copyright was originally limited to copying but the acts restricted by copyright now cover the issue of copies to the public, the rental or lending of works to the public, the performance, showing or playing the work in public, communicating the work to the public and making adaptation of the work or doing of the above in relation to an adaptation.

It is helpful to an understanding of the modern law of copyright to study its history i.e. to see how it has developed from its origins to the present day position.

Copyright is a comparatively modern concept, born in the late fifteenth century, following the invention of printing, which for the first time made it possible to produce multiple copies of books quickly and comparatively cheaply. The classical world did not recognize as such; there is no mention of much concept in Justinian era although there is plenty of evidence that Greek and Roman authors were greatly concerned to be identified as the author of their works and that their authorship should be recognized.[3] The word plagiarism, the practice of copying the work of another and passing it off as the copier's own, derives from the Latin *plagiarius,* an abductor or kidnaper, and has been condemned as an immoral and contemptible practice from the earliest historical times, but in those days there was no law against it. In today's terms, classical authors were concerned that their moral rights be respected, but they enjoyed no economic rights. The earliest copyright case of which there is any record is an Irish sixth century case involving *St. Columbia,* who while on a visit to the monastery of his former teacher, Abbot Finnian, copied the latter's Psalter; Finnian demanded the return of the copy and getting no satisfaction referred the dispute to the King,

3. A. Birell, the Law and History of Copyright in Books (Cassell and Co., London, etc. 1899), p. 411; S.M. Strwart, International Copyright and Neighbouring Rights (2nd ed. Butterworths, London, 1989), p. 13; G.H. Putnam, The question of Copyright (2nd, ed., The Knicker Bocker Press, New York, 1896).

who ruled in his favour; "to every cow her calf and consequently to every book its copy".[4]

Before the invention of printing, there was little practical need for legal protection of authors against the copying of their works. To start with, the bulk of the population was illiterate and had no use for books. Moreover, the copying of manuscripts was a meticulous and time consuming occupation mainly done by monks and limited to the copying of religious works for religious orders and the royal courts of Europe. The possibility of printing multiple copies of books cheaply resulted in a new market for books for a public which has not previously has access to the manuscripts which, in the past, had been available only to the most privileged members of society.

Gutenburg Invention of Printing Press and Early Control of Printing

Prior to Johannes Gutenberg's invention of the printing press in 1440, copying manuscripts was a painstaking task requiring weeks, sometimes months of labour. As such, the task was traditionally left to monks, and few people considered it worth their time to copy manuscripts for mass distribution. However, with the development of Gutenberg's revolutionary machine, copying became much less time-intensive, and making multiple copies of a work was no harder than making one.

Throughout its history copyright law has been closely linked to development in technology. It was only after the introduction of printing that any serious question as to the copyright in literary works could be expected to arise. An early statute of Richard III in 1483 encouraged the printing of books, and permitted their importation, but this statute was repealed 50 years later on protectionist grounds, it being alleged, in the preamble of the repealing statute in 1533, that such a marvelous number of printed book were imported into the realm to the prejudice of the King's natural subjects who have given themselves so diligently to learn and exercise the said craft of printing that at this day there be within this realm a great number cunning and expert in the said science or craft of printing as able to exercise the said craft in all points as any stranger in any other realm or country. A similar plea was urged

4. R.R. Bowker, Copyright, its history and its law, Houghton Mifflin, 1912, p. 3.

on behalf of the bookbinders who having no other faculty wherewith to get their living, be destitute of work and likely to be undone, except some reformation herein he had.

As the member of printers increased in England, the King assumed a prerogative of granting printing privileges, and the earliest copyright protection took the form of printers' licenses granted by the sovereign to regulate the book trade and to protect printers against piracy.[5] These privileges became a source of considerable profit to the Crown and used as an instrument of censorship by the authorities.

Censorship and Privileges

Within a few years after the introduction of printing, European states began to adopt legal measures to deal with consequences of this development. The simplest way to control the distribution of printed material, and protest local printing industries against piracy and foreign impost, was to introduce control of the printing presses, so that the state authority would know what was being printed and by whom.

The state authority took unto itself the sole right of printing, and the authority to grant permissions to print. The control was exercised through general regulations providing that nothing could be printed without state's (or academic or ecclesiastical) authority, and by issuing decrees or ordinances authority particular persons to print and sell books of certain classes, or copies of particular works. These instruments are generally described as "privileges", in the sense of legislative instrument referring to a particular person as distinct from the community at large. The turning point in the history of copyright was reached when authors in general, as opposed to particular individuals named in privileges, were granted rights to reproduce their works. The first printing privileges were apparently the Decrees issued by the State Councillors of Venice in the fifteenth century, The first Venetian privileges in this area was granted to a printer (Johannes of Speyer, by Decree of September 18, 1469), conferring an exclusive right to carry on the art of printing. The second of these privileges was granted to an author (Marc Antony Sabellico, by Decree of September 1, 1486), conferring the

5. An Act of Henry-VIII (*Cum privilegio regali as imprimendum solum*) set-up the system of privileges for the printing of books in England in 1529.

exclusive right of author in printing of one of the author's named works. The 1486 Decree is the first recorded instance of the formal grant of an author's right to an author. The distinction between the first two recorded privileges is of much importance, the beneficiary of the 1469 privilege was a printer, given a monopoly to exercise a certain production method and may be likened to a patent. The beneficiary of the 1486 privilege was the author himself.

In the main, the Venetian privileges of the fifteenth and sixteenth century were related to particular works, or to works in a particular language (e.g. Greek, Arabic), or to particular typefaces, or methods of reproducing drawings (such as the *chiaroscuro process).* Of particular note in this respect are the privileges granted to Ariosto for his poetry and Aldus for his typeface. The privileges were often for a term of years, but were sometimes for life, or for an indefinite period. Like modern copyrights, they were territorial in nature, having effect solely in the jurisdiction of the issuing authority. Other Italian States also adopted the privilege system, as did those in northern Europe.

Generally the privileges systems were of two classes:

(1) Those issued by the sovereign, as part of the royal prerogative, and
(2) Those issued by legislative and official bodies under the general powers of the state.[6]

Decrees of the Star Chamber

In the year 1556, by a decree of the Star Chamber, it was forbidden, amongst other things, to print contrary to any ordinance, prohibition or commandant in any of the statutes or laws of the realm, or any injunction, letters patent, or ordinance set forth, or to be set forth by queen's grant, commission or authority. By a later decree, this time in the reign of Mary's Protestant sister, Elizabeth I, dated June 23, 1585, every book was required to be licensed and all persons were prohibited from printing any book, work, or copy against the form or meaning of any injunction made by Her Majesty or her Privy Council or against the true intent and meaning of any letters patent commissions or prohibitions under the great seal or contrary to

6. J.A.L. Sterling, World Copyright Law, 3rd edn., London, Sweet and Maxwell, p. 8.

any allowed ordinance set down for the good government of the Stationers' Company.[7]

In 1623, a proclamation was issued to enforce this decree reciting that it had been evaded amongst other ways by printing beyond the sea such allowed books, works or writings, as have been imprinted within the realm by such person to whom the sole printing authority thereof by letters patent or lawful ordinance or authority doth appertain.

In 1637, the Star Chamber codified its law on book licensing and printing and again decreed that

> "no person is to print or import (if printed abroad) a book or copy which the Company of Stationers, or any person, hath or shall, by any letters patent, order or entrance in their register book, or otherwise, have the right, privilege, authority, or allowance, solely to print."[8]

Stationers' Copyright

From 1557 to 1641, the English Crown exercised authority over printing and the Stationers' Company through the Star Chamber. After the abolition of the Star Chamber in 1641, the English Parliament continued to extend the Stationers' Company's censorship/monopoly arrangement through a series of ordinances and Licensing Acts between 1643 and 1692. During its time, the Stationers' Company developed a private system for handling disputes between its members. Under this system, specific Guild members held monopoly rights in a particular work that were treated as being perpetual. Although Guild members could purchase a manuscript from an author, authors could not become members of the Guild and were not entitled to any royalties or additional payments after purchase. Members were allowed to buy and sell rights over particular works to each other. As a method to keep track of which members claimed rights in what works, the Guild required that copyrights be recorded in a registration book at the Guild's Hall. The Licensing Act of 1662 also required printers to deposit a copy of each work with the Guild to prevent changes to the work after it was reviewed by censors. Many aspects of the Stationers' system were later incorporated into modern copyright laws.

---

7. Latter decree of Elisabeth dated 23.06.1585.
8. 4 Burr, 2312.

Copyright and Public Performance

There was another area which concerned the state in the literary field, namely the public presentation of plays and other dramatic works. Throughout Europe theaters were subject to rigorous control by the state authorities, but the dramatist's remuneration was generally earned under contract with the theatre managers rather than by exercise of any right of performance of published work.[9]

Original Charter of the Stationers' Company

In 1556, the original charter of Stationers' Company was granted by the Catholic Queen Mary and her consort, Philip II of Spain.[10] It was the declared object of the Crown at that time to prevent the propagation of the reformed religion, and it seems to have been thought that this could be brought about most effectively by imposing several restrictions on the publishing trade and press to prevent the publishing of seditious and heretical books and pamphlets. Until 1640, the Crown, using the Star Chamber as its instrument, rigorously enforced several decrees and ordinance of that Chamber regulating the manner of printing, the number of presses permitted to operate throughout the Kingdom, and prohibiting all printing against the force and meaning of any of the statutes or laws of the realm. This restrictive jurisdiction was enforced by the use of summary powers of search, confiscation and imprisonment, free of any obstruction from parliament.

Emergence of Author's Right

In the seventeenth century, there had been discussions and learned writing in England, France, Germany and other countries on the principle that authors of works were entitled to the rights of controlling, the copying and public performance of their works, but with no positive results in the fork of legislation.[11]

---

9. J.A.L. Sterling, World Copyright Law, 3rd edn., London, Sweet and Maxwell, 2008, p. 10.
10. Confirmed by Queen Elizabeth-I in 1559.
11. B. Shermen, A. Strowel, Of Authors and Origins, Oxford, Clarendon, 1994, J.A.L. Sterling, World Copyright Law, 3rd edn., London, Sweet and Maxwell, p. 10.

First Licensing Act

In 1640, however, the Star Chamber was abolished with the Cromwellian revolution, the King's authority was set at naught; all the regulations of the press and restraints previously imposed upon unlicensed printers by proclamations, decrees of the Star Chamber and charter powers given to the Stationers' Company were deemed and certainly were illegal. The scandalous nature of some libelous publications induced Parliament to pass an ordinance in 1643 which prohibited printing unless the book was first lawfully licensed and entered in the register of the Stationers' Company. The ordinance prohibited printing of any such licensed book without the consent of the owner, or importing it (if printed abroad), upon pain of forfeiting the same to the owner or owners of the copies of the said books and such further punishment as shall be thought fit. The provision necessarily presupposed the property to exist; it would have been of no effect if there had been no admitted owner. An owner could not at that time have existed otherwise than by common law. In 1647, 1649 and 1652 further ordinances were passed in similar terms. Finally in 1662, the Licensing Act was passed which likewise prohibited the printing of any book unless first licensed and entered in the register of the Stationers' Company. It ordered that no person should presume to print any heretical, seditious, schismatical, or offensive books or pamphlets, wherein any doctrine or opinion shall be asserted or maintained which contrary to the Christian faith, or the doctrine or discipline of the church of England or which shall or may tend to be the scandal of religion or the church or the government or governors of the church, state or commonwealth or of any corporation or particular person or persons whatever. It further prohibited the publications of unlicensed books, prescribed regulations as to printing and empowered the Kings' messengers and the master and wardens of the Stationers' Company to seize books suspected of containing matters hostile to the Church or Government. It was necessary to print at the beginning of every licensed book the certificate of the licenser to the effect that the books contained nothing contrary to the Christian faith, or the doctrine or discipline of the Church of England, or against the state and government of this realm or contrary to good life or good manners, or otherwise, as the nature and subject of the work shall require. To prevent fraudulent changes in a book after it had been licensed a copy was required to be submitted with the licenser when application was made for a licence.

The Act further prohibited any person from printing or importing, without the consent of the owner, any book which any person had the sole right to print by virtue of letters patent or by force or virtue of any entry or entries thereof duly made or to be made in the register book of the said Stationers' Company or in the register book of other universities. The penalty for piracy was **forfeiture of the books and six-shilling and eight pence for each copy of which half to go to the King and half to the owner.** The sole property of the owner is here acknowledged in express terms as a common law right and so the legislature which passed that Act must have recognized the concept that the productions of the brain could be the subject-matter of property. To support an action on this statute the ownership of the book had to be proved or the plaintiff could not have recovered because the action was to be brought by the owner who was to have a half share of the penalty. The various provisions of this Act in effect prevented piracy, without actions of law or Bills in equity. Cases of disputed property did, however, arise. Some of them were between different patentees of the Crown and in some the point was whether the property belonged to the author from his invention and labour or the King, from the subject-matter.

End of the Licensing Act

The Licensing Act, 1662 was continued by several Acts of Parliament for almost 19 years, but expired in May 1679. The system had fallen into disrepute because the power of members of the Stationers' Company to claim copyright in perpetuity had led to high prices and a lack of availability of books. Powerful arguments were also being heard in favour of freedom of the press. The control of the book trade exercised by the Stationers' Company was broken with the result that piracy flourished. Soon thereafter, a case was reported in Lilly's Entries of Hilary Term,[12] in which action was brought for printing 4000 copies of the Pilgrim's Progress, of which the plaintiff was the true proprietor, as a result of which he had lost the profit and benefit of his copy.

12. *Ponder Vs. Brady, Lilly's Entries*, 67, 31 Car. 2, B.R.

Ordinances of the Stationers' Company

In 1681, all legislative protection having ceased, the Stationers' Company adopted an ordinance or bylaw of its own which recited that several members of the company had great part of their estates in copies that by ancient usage of the company when any book or copy was duly entered in their register to any member, such person has always been reputed and taken to be the proprietor of such book or copy and ought to have the sole printing thereof. The ordinance further recited that this privilege and interest had of late been often violated and abused and it then provided a penalty against such violation by any member or members of the company where the copy had been duly entered in their register. This ordinance was an attempt by the members of the Stationers' Company who on finding their property in copies of books (their estates in copies, which belonged to them by the common law) no longer under the protection of the Licensing Act to provide for the failure of legislation and to regulate the printing trade themselves although the ordinance was, of course, only applicable to their own members. The ordinance, however, shows what the common law right was then deemed to be. The situation was much the same as if an association of persons were to agree that any one of their number should pay a penalty for violating the acknowledged rights of property of any other person in the association, provided such rights were duly entered in their common records. It would not be an attempt to create the right but it would justly be regarded as acknowledgement of the existence of such a right.[13]

In another byelaw, passed in 1694, it was stated that copies were constantly bargained and sold amongst the members of the company as their property bequeathed to their children and others for legacies and to their widows for maintenance; and it was provided that if any member should, without the consent of the member by whom the entry was made, print or sell the same, he should pay a **fine of 12 pence for every copy.**

New Law Demanded

Parliament was regularly petitioned for a new Licensing Act. The booksellers argued that failure to continue exclusive rights of

13. Curtis on Copyright, Clark, New Jersey: The Lawbook Exchange, 2005, p. 38.

printing had resulted in disincentives to writers. Without some form of protection to encourage authors, the public interest would be harmed by the decreased flow of works.[14]

The submissions of the members of the Stationers' Company were added in 1690, the plea of the philosophers, John Locke who although opposed to licensing as leading to unreasonable monopolies injuries to learning, demanded a copyright for authors which he justified by the time and effort expended in the writing of the work which should be rewarded like any other work.[15] In one of the petitions presented to the House of Commons in support of applications to parliament in 1709 for a Bill to protect copyright, the last clause or paragraph was as follows:

> "The liberty now set on foot of breaking through this ancient and reasonable usage is no way to be effectually restrained by an Act of Parliament. For, by common law, a bookseller, can recover no more costs than he can prove damage, but it is impossible for him to prove the tenth, nay, perhaps, the hundredth part of the damage he suffers; because a thousand counterfeit copies may be dispersed into a many hands over the kingdom, and he not be able to prove the sale of them. Besides, the defendant is always a pauper, and so the plaintiff must lose his costs of suit. Therefore, the only remedy by the common law is to confine a beggar to the rules of the King's Bench of Fleet, and there he will continue the evil practice with impunity. We therefore pay that confiscation of counterfeit copies be one of the penalties to be inflicted on offenders".[16]

Statue of Anne, 1709

In 1709, the first copyright Act was passed and came into force on April 10, 1710.[17] The Statue of Anne was the first copyright law in the world and it is the foundation on which the

14. L. Patterson, Copyright in Historical Perspective, Vanderbult University Press, Nąshvillę, 1968, p. 142.
15. John Locke, Two Treatises of Government (1690), P. Laslett, ed. , Cambridge University Press, 1988, para. 27.
16. 4 Burr. 2318.
17. 8 Anne, c. 19.

modern concept of copyright was built.[18] Two of the principles established by the statue of Anne were revolutionary at that time: firstly, recognition of the author as the fountainhead of protection and secondly, adoption of the principle of a limited term of protection of published works.[19] It was not the first English statute to deal with copyright but the first to be adopted by Parliament as opposed to royal decree and the first to be unconnected with censorship. According to its Preamble, the Act responded to several objectives like the encouragement of learning, the prevention of the practice of piracy for the future and the encouragement of learned men to compose and write useful books. The Act gave authors of books already printed the sole right and liberty of printing them for a term of 21 years from the date of entry into force of the Act and of books not then printed, the sole right of printing for 14 years with a proviso that, after the expiration of the said term of 14 years, the sole right of printing or disposing of copies should return to the authors thereof, if they were then living, for another term of 14 years. Thus, the statutory copyright was not to be limited to the members of the Guild and it was not to exist in perpetuity. The title to the copy of a book had to be registered before publication with the Stationers' Company and nine copies had to be delivered to certain libraries. Penalties for infringement were severe, i.e. **infringing books were subject to forfeiture and a fine of a penny for every sheet copied**. This resulted in a steep fine when many copies of a substantial book were pirated. The fine was divided equally between the Crown and the complainant. It is of interest to note that the Act also expressly provided that the importation and sale of books in Greek and other foreign languages printed beyond the seats should remain unaffected by its provisions. The idea that foreign authors also merited protection was not ripe.

18. A. Birrell, The law and history of copyright in books, Cassell and Co., London, 1899, p. 68; G. Davies, copyright and the public interest 2nd ed., Sweet & Maxwell, 2002, p. 11.
19. Lord Hailsham of St. Marylebone in Halsbury Law's of England, 4thed., Butterworths. London, 1974, Vol. 9.

DEVELOPMENT OF CONCEPT OF COPYRIGHT

Resonance understanding of the problem of Copyright as it relates to modern concepts of the rights of authors requires an understanding of the origin of the right and what the right was designed to protect. Before entering to the main discourse on the history of the copyright the researcher wish to clarify the meaning of the word 'copyright'. The common assumption is that it means 'right to copy'. The unfortunate historical incident that gave rise to this understanding has done much to the muddy modern thinking on the subject. The actual meaning of the term 'Copyright' is much closer to the term 'Copyhold'. Under the common law a number of rights could be derived from inscription (copying) on a register. Thus, one might obtain the right to farm a particular piece of land by virtue of having his name inscribed on a register of tenants; this is a copyhold interest in land. In the case of publishing, the publisher inscribed his name and the title of the work that he would be publishing on a register of Stationers' Company, giving him a copy of the work. The rights attendant to the copy constitutes the 'copyright'. Copyright begins with Censorship or more properly, the relationship between the desire of the Crown to censor and the technology available to circumvent the Crown's wishes. Before the development of the printing press it was relatively easy for the Crown to maintain control over the publication of ideas within the realm. Since publications had to be hand copied the books were few and expensive.

In a political move, England enacted its first official 'copyright' in 1556. In an effort to control printing of heretical or seditious material which might undermine the authority of the crown, Mary-I awarded the Stationers' Company (a printer's guild), the exclusive right to print manuscripts. In return for the economic success she guaranteed the Stationers' Company, she also exercised substantial control over what was and was not allowed to be printed. Until the law's expiration in 1694, the Stationers' Company held complete control over both the publishing and sale of printed works, establishing a publishing monopoly of sorts. The most significant thing to note about this 'copyright law' is that it bears little resemblance to most copyright law today. Mary-I granted exclusive rights to printers not to the creators of the works printed. The Charter continues to give the individuals the exclusive right to own a printing press and the implementation of printing and also the exclusive right to practice the art of printing. It also gives the Stationers' Company the right to enforce its monopoly by burning the books and presses of its competition and imprisoning any one owning a press or found engaged in printing without the consent of the authority. The grant allows the Stationers to conduct search and destroy missions on their own outside of other legal processes. It appears that frequently such proceedings were instituted in conjunction with the Star Chamber and the Privy Council under whose order at least one publisher of illegal material was publicly disemboweled.

Statute of Anne and Copyright

Following the English Civil War, which was partly fought over the Crown's abuse of monopolies the Stationers' power was threatened when the last Licensing Act expired in 1694. Without their monopolies London's booksellers faced an unregulated influx of cheap texts printed outside Britain and in Scotland that began flooding the English market. After years of lobbying by authors and members of the Conger the world's first modern Copyright Statute was enacted by the British Parliament.[20]

The Statute of Anne was introduced by English Parliament in 1710. In a shift away from the former publishing monopoly of the past, the Statute of Anne granted authors fourteen years of exclusive rights to their work (accompanied by the option of another fourteen years under the renewal policy.) To obtain these rights, authors were required to complete a series of registrations, notices and deposits. A publisher could purchase the right to a work, edit the text, typeset and promote a work. He would, of course, have set a price that would allow him to make back what he laid out plus a profit for himself plus a reserve for those works that did not sell well enough to pay for themselves. Now let us suppose this work was successful. Without the copyright protection, another publisher could take the work, retype it and sell it at a lower price because he doesn't have to pay the author nor the editor. He doesn't have to pay for promotion and he doesn't have to worry that the book won't sell. Since, anyone foolish enough to print a new work would, if the

20. Statute of Anne, 8 Anne, Ch. 19 (1710).

work were successful, be immediately undercut on the market. Suddenly no publisher was willing to print new works and there was no market for new ideas.

The Statute of Anne was the first real copyright Act and gave the author rights for a fixed period after which the copyright expired. Unlike previous laws that gave broad monopoly power to the Stationers' Company who would then administer a private system of copyright between Guild members, the Statute of Anne directly outlined a public copyright system that applied to the public in general. Secondly, the Statute recognized a copyright as originating in the author rather than a Guild member. Lastly, it placed a time limitation on the monopoly enjoyed by holders of a copyright. Specifically, the Act provided that an owner of the copyright in any book already printed should have the exclusive right of publishing it for twenty-one years. For works not yet published, the act provided an exclusive right to publish for fourteen years from the time of first publication with the stipulation that the right could be extended by an author for another 14 years. However, printers argued that the texts were property owned by the authors and therefore, could be sold as such to the printers who would then own the rights.

An act for the encouragement of learning by vesting the copies of printed books in the authors' or purchasers of such copies during the times therein mentioned (1710, but commonly referred to as the Copyright Act of 1709, 8 Ann. c. 19) carries many similarities to the Anti-monopoly Act of 1624. It is the world's first true Copyright Act (as opposed to Censorship Act) and is the model for most of the succeeding legislation on the subject. This Act recited the problems associated with the intervening years.

Whereas printers, booksellers and other persons have of late frequently taken the liberty of printing, reprinting, and publishing or causing to be printed, reprinted and published, books and other writings without the consent of the authors or proprietors of such books and writings to their very great detriment and too often to the ruin of them and their families. For preventing, therefore, such practices for the future and for the encouragement of learned men to compose and write useful books, new law was passed.

Licensing Act of 1662 and Copyright

Historically, in the period of beginning of second half of seventeenth century the governments issued monopoly rights to the publishers for sale of printed works. Copyright was not invented until after the advent of the printing press and with wider public literacy. As a legal concept its origins in Britain were from a reaction to printers' monopolies at the beginning of the eighteenth century. In Britain the King was concerned by the unfair copying of books and used the royal prerogative to pass the Licensing Act, 1662 which established a register of licensed books and required a copy to be deposited with the Stationers' Company essentially continuing the licensing of material that had long been in effect. These provisions were strengthened under Queen Elizabeth in 1586. The Printers who were designated as members of this monopoly, of course, were not stupid. Very quickly, they determined the best means of maximizing their own profits was to agree not to compete with each other as the agreements in restraint of trade were quite legal at this time.

It is no longer the purpose of the law to provide the Crown with a method for regulating the press but rather, it is intended to provide regulation under which the printing industry could grow and prosper. Further, the rational for wanting the printing industry to grow and prosper was not because the crown, legislature and people had pity on the plight of the publisher but they suffered the monopoly because it was a necessary evil to promote the free exchange of ideas. Again, we need to note that the protection was specifically designed for the printing industry as the technology existed in the early 1700's. The nature of the printing and publishing industry requires that publishers speculate a certain amount of money on the success of a particular work. When a publisher purchases the rights to a work from the author, he puts out money. While it is unclear when editors came into the picture, the cost of editorial revisions became an expense. The cost of putting a work in type must be advanced by the publisher. The cost of promoting the work to the booksellers and public is a significant cost. All of these costs come before a publisher really knows whether the work will sell well enough for him to recoup his investment. Regardless how good the publisher is some of the things that he chooses will be poor sellers. Consider the situation immediately before the Copyright Act of 1710.

The basic provisions of the Act involved the fine and imprisonment of authors, publishers, sellers, and buyers of scandalous or libelous materials or inaccurate accounts of Parliamentary sessions. All printed materials needed to be licensed by Parliament and published by a member of the Stationer's Company. All presses outside of London, Oxford and Cambridge were banned. Every item printing needed to have a title page giving the author, publisher and place of publication. Most significantly for this discussion the Act specifically affirmed the rights of individual publishers to their copies and forbade other publishers to counterfeit the works belonging to other publishers. This last provision was necessary because Parliament had done away with the Star Chamber under whose provision the copyright system had developed. The restoration naturally did little to change the *status quo*. A law for preventing the frequent abuses in printing seditious treasonable and unlicensed Books and Pamphlets and for regulating of Printing and Printing Presses[21] was quickly adopted in keeping with the prior laws and was renewed regularly under Charles-II, James-II and the early years of William & Mary. The Golden Age of the Stationer's Company ends with the expiration of the censorship laws in 1694 and, with it, copyright. There passed a period of sixteen impoverishing years for the Stationers wherein it was discovered the extent to which the industry had become dependent upon the monopoly. There were a number of attempts to restore the old system during the late 1690's and early 1700's but it was not until 1710 that a watered down version of the old system was enacted.

Copyright and Development of Period of its Protection

The Act provided that books already in publication would be protected from unauthorized republication for 21 years and future works would be protected for 14 years. At the end of 14 years the right reverted to the author (if living) to sell publication rights for an additional 14 years. The penalty for violation of this right was turning all unauthorized copies of the work in the possession of the violator into 'waste paper' and a fine of one penny per sheet in civil court. It further provided for registration

21. 14 Car. 2. c. 33 (1662).

of works with the Stationer's Company to prevent accidental publication of protected works however, anyone could make such a registration not just the members of the Company (The act set fines in the event the clerk refused or 'neglected' to register such works and allowed publishers to utilize other means of notice in the event they were refused by the clerk). To prevent publishers from price scoring as a result of the monopoly they had been given a number of public officials including the Archbishop of Canterbury, the Lord Chancellor and the Chief Baron of Exchequer who were also given the authority to fix the price of sale.

Copyright in Mainstream

The Copyright Act served to create a market, but it was not designed to protect the publishers or authors but rather society's interest in new ideas. While the Copyright Act of 1709 restored profitability to the printers it did not restore their previous status. Specifically, anyone could print not just the members of the company. More importantly, the copyright did not exist in perpetuity. The Act provided for a renewable 14 year term for the copyright. Of course, during the period of statutory copyright the publishers were quite willing to bring enforcement under its provisions. However, once the copyrights started to expire the publishers began to conspire as to how they might regain their lost right to hold copies in perpetuity.

A number of cases were brought during the 1750's to enforce a common law copyright independent of the statutory copyright but most were uncontested. In 1761, the case of *Tonson Vs. Collins*[22] brought the matter to a heard. Plaintiffs argued that an author is entitled to enjoy the work of his labour. Property right may be acquired either by physical labour or by mental labour. It would be wrong not to secure the value of an author's work to another but rather to allow others to profit from his industry without compensation. A publisher is merely an assignee of the rights of the author by which the author might obtain his value. Therefore, since the author's rights exist in perpetuity independent of statute so also does the publishers. It appears that the publishers might have won with this argument but for the

22. 1 Wm. Blackstone 301, 96 Eng. Rep. 169 [1761]; 1 Wm. Blackstone 322, 96 Eng. Rep. 180 [1762].

fact that it was suspected that the defendant was in collusion with the plaintiff to throw the case in order to create a precedent. The judges did not render a decision on the matter. The issue came up again in *Miller Vs. Taylor*[23] in 1769 wherein one of the most extensive treatments of the history of English printing was found. This case was found in favor of the publishers on the same arguments. However, five years later it was overturned by the House of Lords in *Donaldson Vs. Becket*[24] in 1774. This case in 1774 brought disagreements on the length of copyright to an end. The outcome of the case resulted in the decision that Parliament could and had put a limit on copyright length. This decision reflected a shift in English ideas of copyright. The English Lords who made the decision in 1774 decided that it was not in the public's best interest to have London publishers control books in perpetuity, particularly as English publishers commonly kept prices high. There were some notions that this was a cultural or class issue. Works in perpetual copyright were seen to have limited access by some citizens to the cultural history of their own land.

Concepts of the roles of the author and publisher of copyright law and of general Enlightenment notions interacted in this period. Authors had been previously seen to be divinely inspired. Patronage was a legitimate way to support authors in part. Authors who were paid rather than entering into patron-relationships were often regarded as hacks and looked down upon. However, the notion of individual genius was becoming more common during the 1770s (the generation after *Donaldson Vs. Beckett*[25]) and being a paid author, therefore, became more accepted.

Development of Copyright Law in Colonies

In Great Britain's North American colonies, reprinting British copyright works without permission had long happened episodically but only became a major feature of colonial life after 1760. It became more commonplace to reprint British works in the colonies (mostly in the 13 American colonies). The impetus for this shift came from Irish and Scottish master printers and

23. 4 Burrow 2303, 98 Eng. Rep. 201 [K.B., 1769].
24. 7 Parl. Hist. Eng. 953 [H.L., 1774].
25. 7 Parl. Hist. Eng. 953 [H.L., 1774].

booksellers who had moved to the North American colonies in the mid-18th century. They were already familiar with the practice of reprinting and selling British copyrighted works and continued American printing and publishing trade. Robert Bell was an example. He was originally Scottish and had spent almost a decade in Dublin before he moved to British North America in 1768. His operations and those of many other colonial printers and booksellers ensured that the practice of reprinting was well-established by the time of the American Declaration of Independence in 1776. Weakened American ties to Britain coincided with the increase of reprinting outside British Copyright controls.

The Irish also made a flourishing business of shipping reprints to North America in the 18th century. Ireland's ability to reprint freely ended in 1801 when Ireland's Parliament merged with Great Britain and the Irish became subject to British Copyright laws.

The printing of uncopyrighted English works for the English-language market also occurred in other European countries. The British government responded to this problem in two ways: (1) it amended its own copyright statutes in 1842 explicitly forbidding import of any foreign reprint of British copyrighted work into the UK or its colonies; and (2) it began the process of reciprocal agreements with other countries. The first reciprocal agreement was with Prussia in 1846. The US remained outside this arrangement for some decades. Such authors as Charles Dickens and Mark Twain objected to this.[26]

The development of copyright gradually became the subject matter of the whole world because a common medium of protection for the creative work throughout the globe was highly needed for protecting the know-how globally. The copyright law has its root in Britain started developing in international field. Apart from the Statue of Anne of England in the year 1710 many international laws contributed the protective movement of the copyright throughout the globe.

---

26. S.M. Stewart, International Copyright and Neighbouring Rights, 2nd ed., London, Butterworths, 1989, Ch. 1, 2.

Denmark's Ordinance of 1741

The Danish Ordinance of January 7, 1741 forbade the unauthorised printing of published books, the title which had lawfully been acquired, without the permission of the author or first publisher. The Danish Ordinance thus has some claim to be the second legislative provision recognising a general statutory right for authors, albeit with the publisher's right also recognised.[27]

France (Laws of 1791 and 1793)

Before the French Revolution, authors had no specific statutory rights in France permitting them to control the printing or performance of their works. As in other countries, uses of authors' works were controlled by the State through the system of privileges. These had, since the sixteenth century, been claims for an author's right but printing rights were generally granted to the publishers and performance rights to the theatre directors, the authors had to obtain their remuneration by contract with these right holders.

Here as in so many other fields, the French Revolution brought fundamental changes. Privileges were abolished on August 4, 1789; the Declaration of the Rights of Man and the Citizen was adopted on August 26, 1789. These measures effectively destroyed the previous systems of privileges and licensing for the printing and performance of authors' works. Two laws of the Constituent Assembly laid down the foundation of the French laws on author's right—that of January 13/19, 1791 (completed by a Decree of July 19/August 6, 1791) on the right of performance and that the July 19/24, 1793 on the right of what would be called reproduction or copying. Briefly summarized, the law of 1791 dealt with theatres and performance rights and provided, among other things, that:

(a) Works of living authors could only be publicly performed with the written consent of the author; and
(b) The term of the right was for the life of the author and five years after his death.

27. J.A.L. Sterling, World Copyright Law, 3rd ed., London, Sweet and Maxwell, 2008, p. 16.

The Law of 1793 provided that:

(a) Authors, composers, painters and engravers enjoyed the exclusive right to sell and distribute their works in France; and

(b) The term of the right was for the author's life and 10 years after his death.

During the nineteenth century, two categories of rights of authors were developed in French jurisprudence: economic rights that is, rights to control commercial or other exploitation of works and moral rights which is rights associated with the author's personality and enabling him to ensure, among other things, recognition of his authorship and maintenance of the integrity of his work.

The economic rights were derived from the Laws of 1791 and 1793. The right developed respectively was: (a) the right of representation (performance), and (b) the right of reproduction (copying). The moral rights developed from case laws and the writings of learned authors during the nineteenth century. The French law of author's right is still based on these two fundamental economic rights, together with the moral rights.

Germany

The German States adopted legislation for the regulation of the printing trade in the eighteenth and early nineteenth centuries, but it was the Prussian Law of June 11, 1837 which presented the form of what would today be recognised as a comprehensive text.

The Prussian Law of 1837 influence the basis of the Law of June 11, 1870, adopted throughout the German Empire from the beginning of 1871. During the nineteenth century other European States also adopted statutes giving statements and Statutes giving specific rights to authors to control the printing and performance of their works.

China

Copyright law made its first appearance in the wake of the invention of the printing in China necessitating official copyright protection as early as 1068 when the emperor of the north song dynasty issued an order forbidding the reproduction without authorisation of the "Nine Books" published by the official publisher, *Guo Zi Jian*, in 932.[28] The first official copyright legislation in China came about in 1991, with the approval of the State Council. The State Administration issued the Implementing Regulations for the Copyright Law of the Peoples' Republic of China, also in 1991. China has also a mechanism set out for the Regulation of Computer Software. It became a party to the Berne Convention and the Universal Copyright Convention in 1962. In pursuance of its international commitment to protect works from infringement, China came to promulgate measures on computer software copyright registration. In 1994 the Decision of the Standing Committee of the National People's Congress concerning punishment of the crime of copyright infringement was incorporated. Copyright protection in China is constitutionally accorded in its Article 47.[29]

Japan

Copyright law in Japan owes its origin to the Meiji Revolution[30] which proved responsible in giving the country its rudimentary copyright law, the Publishing Ordinance of 1869. The Ordinance soon paved the way to the passing of Copyright Act, 1887. Japan acceded to the Berne Convention in 1899 and in compliance with the provisions of the convention the Copyright Ordinance came to be overhauled in the Act of 1899 which can be truly referred to reflect the modern copyright law of Japan. The Act witnessed its expansion to include architectural works in 1910. In 1920, musical works too came under the expanding umbrella of protected works. In the following decades Japan along with the rest of the international community has come to

28. Evolution of the Copyright system on http://www.china-laws-online.com/intellectual-property-rights/evolution-copyright-system.htm
29. It elicits the freedom of the people to engage in scientific research literary and artistic creation and other cultural pursuits. The corresponding provisions that aid in constructing a constitutional safeguard, and guarantee for the protection of copyright are to be found also in Articles 19-24. Article 94 of The General Principles of Civil Law of China acknowledge ownership of the author in his work and also provide for a transmission of such right to another. The enforcement mechanism is to be found in Article 118 of the General principles.
30. The Revolution marks an important phase in the transition of Japanese society from isolation to open up to global development in the fields of industry, trade and commerce. The revolution can be said to be the reformation period in Japanese history.

expand the scope of copyright and neighbouring rights protection to include moral rights of authors, the right to broadcasting, the protection of cinematographic works and the right of publication. In 1939, Japan enacted the law on Intermediary Business Concerning Copyright which provided for regulations on collective administration of musical, literary and dramatic works for the benefit of copyright owners and users aiming at a fair exploitation of works. The present governing law is the Copyright Act, 1971.

Development of Modern Copyright

Modern copyright has been influenced by an array of older legal rights that have been recognized throughout history, including the moral rights of the author who have created a work, the economic rights of a benefactor who paid to have a copy made, the property rights of the individual owner of a copy and a sovereign's right to censor and to regulate the printing industry. Prior to the invention of movable type in the west in the mid-fifteenth century texts were copied by hand and the small number of texts generated few occasions for these rights to be tested. Even during a period of a prospering book trade during the Roman Empire when no copyright or similar regulations existed[31] copying by those other than professional booksellers was rare. This is because books were typically copied by literate slaves who were expensive to buy and maintain. Thus, any copier would have had to pay much the same expense as a professional publisher. Roman booksellers would sometimes pay a well regarded author for first access to a text for copying but they had no exclusive rights to a work and authors were not normally paid anything for their work.

During the centuries following the destruction of the Roman Empire, European literary undertakings were confined almost entirely to the monasteries. The Roman usage under which authors could dispose of their works to booksellers and the latter could be secure of some commercial control of the property purchased was entirely forgotten. (In Ken Follet's novel *The Pillars of the Earth,* a character is astonished to meet a woman who actually owns books, which were normally owned only by churches and monasteries.)

31. Martial, The Epigrams, Penguin, 1978, James Mitchie.

United Kingdom

In United Kingdom Copyright started as a licence granted to publishers as an exercise of the Royal Prerogative. Initially Copyright existed as a property right that existed only at the level of common law and it lasted in perpetuity. Statutory Copyright was introduced for published works by the Copyright Act, 1709 and unpublished works received Copyright protection by virtue of common law. For the next two centuries Copyright law advanced by means of piecemeal legislation which gradually increased the types of works protected as the need arose. The Copyright Act, 1911 attempted to unify all the divergent branches of the existing laws into one coherent system and along with this objective the existence of common law Copyright was also abolished. In 1956, a further Act was passed in order to bring the United Kingdom in line with further developments both on an international scale and from the point of view of technology. The most recent Act was passed in 1988, and encompassed the area of patents and registered designs as well as the traditional view of Copyright. The initial idea of Copyright as a property law consisted of it being a 'chose in action' that is an intangible property.

The 1709 Act (commonly referred to as the 'Statute of Anne') stated that the author of a new book had the sole printing right on that book for 14 years, when this period had expired, the book could be freely printed. If the author was still alive at the end of this period, a further extension of 14 years was granted. Authors whose books were already in publication had a 21 year sole publication right granted to them from April 10, 1710. It was also a requirement that all books were registered with the Stationers' Company. A House of Lords decision in the *Donaldson Vs. Beckett*[32] case had the effect of destroying common law copyright in unpublished works but common law remained in position until 1911 and could now only exist in statute.

Copyright Act, 1814 by Sec. 4 provided sole right to author to print a work for 28 years from the first day of publication and again if the author was still alive at the end of this period his sole right of publication was increased to last the rest of his natural life. The duration of Copyright was increased yet again by the

32. 1 E.R. 837 (1774); 2 Brown's Parl. Cases 129, 1 Eng. Rep. 837; (1774) 4 Burr 2408.

time the 1842 Act was passed and was placed this time at the life of the author plus 7 years or 42 years from the first date of publication whichever was longer. If the work was published posthumously, the period it was covered by Copyright was for 42 years. Another change was also that the requirement of registering at Stationers Hall was no longer remain compulsory, it was however, still a precondition before any action of infringement could be taken. The decision of *Donaldson Vs. Beckett*[33] had a fundamental influence in determining the development of Copyright law in succeeding centuries, because it blatantly highlighted the conflict between common law and statutory law.

The Copyright Act, 1842 provided similar protection for the performance of musical works and the period granted was extended to bring it into line with the protection offered to literary works. The range of works protected was greatly increased. However, many different statutes were passed with no consideration to creating a unified system. A Royal Commission was formed in 1875 to solve the problems of the disjointed laws, the report of which was published in 1878.

In 1886 the first international treaty on Copyright law was introduced. The Berne Convention which was a multinational agreement that enabled reciprocal Copyright protection to be secured in all member-states so long as the author is connected with a member-state or the work was first published in a member-state. The United Kingdom was a signatory to this convention and the international Copyright Act was passed in Great Britain in 1886 in order to fulfil obligations to foreign authors that arose upon the UK ratifying the Berne Convention on September 8, 1887. To cope with the revision of the Berne Convention in 1908 (in Berne again) the existing Act was revised in 1911 and an Act was passed that repealed all previous copyright legislation that had been in force in the UK. The 1911 Copyright Act came into force on July 1, 1912, the most significant measure it introduced was the abolition of common law copyright and the protection could now only be conferred by statute. Copyright also existed in both published and unpublished works as the Act stated that copyright arose in the

33. 2 Brown's Parl. Cases 129, 1 Eng. Rep. 837; 4 Burr. 2408, 98 Eng. Rep. 257 (1774).

act of creation not the act of publishing.[34] Literary, dramatic and musical works could be infringed by the making of a film or other mechanical performance incorporating the above vessels of creation (section 1(2)(d)).

Another international agreement called the Universal Copyright Convention (UCC) and was signed in Geneva in 1952. The United Kingdom was also a founding signatory of the UCC and so another parliamentary committee was appointed to consider whether or not any changes were needed in the existing domestic legislation to comply with increasing international obligations. The committee also considered the effect of new technology on Copyright works, it was known as the Gregory Committee after its chairman, and reported to Parliament. The report was published in 1952 and as a result the 1956 Copyright Act was passed. This Act came into force on June 1, 1957 which repealed the few remaining Acts of copyright that remained despite the 1911 Act.

The principle change in the Copyright Act, 1956 was brought about by the Design Act, 1968, this was intended to deal with the position of Copyright in design drawings for is mass produced items. Protection was offered by the Dramatic and Musical Performers' Protection Act, 1925 which offered some limited sanctions to these creative groups further strengthened by the Dramatic and Musical Performers' Protection Act, 1958, Performers' Protection Act, 1963 and Performers' Protection Act, 1972. The recording industry complained that none of these provided sufficient protection and this was indeed one of the major commercial pressures that led to the repeal of the Copyright Act, 1956. Other issues that needed consideration were computers and the software and databases that accompany them along with major advances in audio and visual reproduction and transmission. 1973 saw another committee appointment which also considered recent international developments. The Committee submitted its report in 1977 and is known as the Whitford Report after the Judge who presided over its preparation. There were two important papers presented to Parliament before the full report was presented: (i) The Reform of Law Relating to Copyright, Designs and Performers' Protection, 1981, and (ii) Intellectual Property Innovation, 1986.

34. *Gramophone Co. Ltd Vs. Stephen Cawardine* [1934] 1 Ch. 450.

As a result of both the papers and the 'Whitford Report', the 1988 Copyright, Designs and Patents Act was passed. This forms the current framework for today's legislation and repealed the 1956 Copyright Act, the Copyright Computer Software Act, 1985 and the Performers' Protection Act, 1988. The new provisions provided by this Act came into force on August 1, 1989. The 1988 Act introduced a number of new rights, such as rental rights in respect of sound recordings, films and computer programmes [section 18(3)]. The issue of Industrial Designs which had troubled both the courts and parliament for many years resulted in the creation of a new property right called the Design right. Although this is now the principal legislation covering Copyright, it is not the sole source to be consulted, and certain areas have been amended by the Broadcasting Act, 1990. Intellectual Property issues continue to arise within the European Union and the International market, the United Kingdom for example, officially revised the Berne Convention (Paris, 1971) with effect from January 2nd 1990.

The European Union is continually struggling to cope with the wishes of its member states, as well as remaining in line with international thinking and the new technological state society is finding itself and it is widely accepted that Copyright as a law will never be fully complete and can only ever exist as a continually evolving law adapting to the new challenges faced by it and the governments that create the legislation. The Copyright Directive has been accepted by the EU and is due to become UK law at the end of this year.

United States of America

Copyright law has been modified many times since to encompass new technologies such as music recording to extend the duration of protection and to make other changes. U.S. courts have interpreted this clause of the Constitution to say that the ultimate purpose of copyrights is to encourage the production of creative works for the public benefit and that therefore the interests of the public are primary over the interests of the author when the two conflict. These rulings have since been formalized into fair use laws and decisions. Certain attempts by copyright owners to restrict uses beyond the rights provided for by copyright law may also subject them to the copyright misuse doctrine preventing enforcement against infringers.

The U.S. Congress first exercised its power to enact copyright legislation with the Copyright Act of 1790. The Act secured an author the exclusive right to publish and vend maps, charts and books for a term of 14 years with the right of renewal for one additional 14 year term if the author was still alive. The act did not regulate other kinds of writings such as musical compositions or newspapers and specifically noted that it did not prohibit copying the works of foreign authors. The Copyright Act of 1831 extended the term to 28 years with 14 year renewal. The Copyright Act of 1909 extended term to 28 years with 28 year renewal and Universal Copyright Convention ratified by the U.S. in 1954 and again in 1971, this treaty was developed by UNESCO as an alternative to the Berne Convention. The Copyright Act of 1976 extended term to either 75 years or life of author plus 50 years, extended federal copyright to unpublished works, preempted state copyright laws, codified much copyright doctrine that had originated in case law. The Berne Convention Implementation Act of 1988 established copyrights of U.S. works in Berne Convention countries. The Uruguay Round Agreements Act (URAA) of 1994 restored U.S. copyright for certain foreign works then the Sonny Bono Copyright Term Extension Act of 1998 extended terms to 95-120 years or life plus 70 years. The Digital Millennium Copyright Act of 1998 which criminalized some cases of copyright infringement was landmark to deal with the electronic challenges to the field of copyright. The Family Entertainment and Copyright Act of 2005 criminalized more cases of copyright infringement and permitted technology to 'sanitize' works. The statutory provisions relating to copyright currently in effect are codified in Title 17 of the United States Code.[35] Key international agreements affecting U.S. copyright law includes Berne Convention for the Protection of Literary and Artistic Works, The Universal Copyright Convention and Agreement on Trade-Related Aspects of Intellectual Property Rights.

The United States became a Berne Convention signatory in 1988 and the treaty entered into force with respect to the U.S. on

35. A History of Copyright in the US, at http://eon.law.harvard.edu/property99/history.html

March 1, 1989. The U.S. is also a party to TRIPS which itself requires compliance with Berne provisions and is enforceable under the WTO dispute resolution process. To meet the treaty requirements protections were extended to architecture (where previously only building plans were protected from copying not buildings though currently the law makes exception for reproduction of buildings in photographs or paintings if they are ordinarily visible from a public place) and certain moral rights of visual artists.[36]

India

History and the development of Copyright Law in India closely parallels the history of British Copyright Laws as Administration in British occupied India was streamlined on English principles of justice, liberty and good conscience.[37] As a result, British legal framework has been available in India since beginning of copyright concept. Copyright Law began in England when the Crown passed the Statute of Anne in 1710. The Statute of Anne conclusively laid down Copyright as a creature of statute and not a natural law right in perpetuity, thereby curtailing the term of copyright and preventing an absolute monopoly on the part of booksellers. Since, the Statute of Anne, copyright law has been revised to broaden the scope of what is covered by a copyright, to change the term of a copyright and to incorporate new technologies.

Emergence of Indian Copyright was nothing but the idea of Copyright protection which only began to emerge with the invention of printing which made it possible for literary works to be duplicated by mechanical processes instead of being copied by hand. This led to the appearance of a new trade that of printers and booksellers in England called 'Stationers'. These entrepreneurs invested considerable sum in the purchase of paper in buying or building press and in the employment of labour involving an outlay which could be recouped with a reasonable return over a period of time.

---

36. http://www/patent.gov.uk
37. M.P Jain, Outlines of Indian Legal History, 5th ed., Wahdwa & Co., Reprint 2001.

The development of copyright law in India was gradual and based on British system. The development of law relating to copyright in India can be studied in the following way:

Copyright Development in India[38]

The ever first copyright law applied to Indian Copyright was English Copyright Act, 1842. Tracing the historical graph, it has been discovered that the English Copyright Act, 1842, was held to be applicable to India by the High Court of Bombay in *Macmillan Vs. Khan Bahadur Shamsul Ulama Zaka,*[39] even when this Act was not expressly made applicable to India.[40] India had its first copyright law, Indian Copyright Law, 1847 enacted on 18th December 1847 which was based upon the British Copyright Act, 1942, much earlier than many other countries.[41] The historical growth of Indian Copyright can be discussed in the following phase for the better understanding of its development. Modern Copyright law developed in India gradually in what we may identify roughly as three distinct phases spanning more than 150 years. Here the researcher has attempted to briefly navigate through the major changes brought in by each successive wave of copyright amendment which have cumulatively resulted in the way Indian Copyright law stands today.

PHASE I—East India Company Statute
The Copyright Act, 1887

The law relating to copyright begins in India when East India Company extended the English Copyright Act of 1847 to the territories under its control.[42] It was the part of common law regarding the recognition and enforcement of copyright as a part of the common law or administration of justice. The law was developed on the basis of 'Justice, equality and good conscience'

---

38. History of Copyright in India, by Brian Rowe, October 1, 2008.
39. ILR (1895) 19 Bom. 557 as referred in Lal's Commentry on the Copyright Act, 1957(Act 14 of 1957) with the copyright rules, 1958 and neighbouring rights 4th edn., Delhi Law House at p. 5.
40. *Kumari Karnaka Vs. Sundarajan*, 1972 Ker LR 536. Followed in *R. Madhawan Vs. S.K. Nayer*, AIR 1988 Ker 39(45).
41. James, T.C., Copyright Law of India and the academic community, Volume IX, JIPR 207(212), May 2004.
42. Baxi, Upendra, Copyright Law and Justice in India, *Journal of Indian Law Institute* (1986), pp. 497-540.

as regards the application of British statutes to territories then administered by the East India Company. The term of copyright was for the lifetime of the author plus seven years *post mortem auctoris* (PMA). But in no case the total term of copyright was exceeded the period of forty-two years. The government was empowered to licence publication of the book if the owner of copyright upon the death of the author refused to allow its publication. Unauthorized printing of copyright work for (or as a part of attempt of) 'sale or hire or exportation', or 'for selling, publishing or exposing to sale or hire' constituted in fragment. Suit or action for infringement was to be instituted in the highest local court exercising original civil jurisdiction. The Act provided specifically that under a contract of service copyright in any encyclopedia, review, magazine, periodical work or work published in a series of books or parts shall vest in the proprietor, projector, publisher or conductor. Infringing copies were deemed to be copies of the proprietor of copyrighted work. Importantly, unlike today, copyright in a work was not automatic. Registration of copyright with the Home Office was mandatory for the enforcement of rights under the Act. However, the proviso to Sec. 14 of the Act also specifically reserved the subsistence of copyright in the author, and his right to sue for its infringement to the extent available in law other than the 1847 Act. As we shall see, this reservation of other 'copyright-type' laws was done away with in later legislations.

At the time of its introduction in India, copyright law had already been under development in Britain for over a century and the provisions of the 1847 enactment reflected the learnings from deliberations during this period. Thus, in its very first avatar, copyright had arrived in India as a modern law that was both abstract (encompassing 'all works' of literature and art) and forward looking in the way that it sought to accommodate both existing and new forms of subject matter. As a result, many of the philosophical debates over the nature of 'literary property' that had animated the initial years of copyright development in Britain were conspicuous by their absence in the sub-continent. On the precise manner that the 1847 enactment operated, very little is known. However, this enactment created the conceptual milieu that eased the passage of succeeding legislations. This statute was made applicable to India during the East India Companies regime and continued to operate till 1911.

An interesting features of British, this phase of copyright protection in the country is that while in Britain, the university of Cambridge and Oxford, the four Universities in Scotland,[43] and the several colleges of Eton, Westminster and Winchester as well Trinity college, Dubbling, had the right 'to hold in perpetuity their copyright in books given or bequeathed to them for the advancement of useful learning and other purposes of education', whereas, Universities in India such as Kolkata, Mumbai and Chennai did not have such a right.[44]

PHASE II—Indian Copyright Law
The Copyright Act, 1914

In 1914, the then Indian legislature enacted a new Copyright Act which merely extended most portions of the United Kingdom Copyright Act of 1911 to India. It is a replacement of British Copyright Act, 1911 in new form. It, however, make a few minor modifications. Upendra Baxi identifies two of the major changes. First, it introduced criminal sanctions for copyright infringement (sections 7 to 12). Second, it modified the scope of the term of copyright; under Sec. 4 the 'sole right' of the author to 'produce, reproduce, perform or publish a translation of the work shall subsist only for a period of ten years from the date of the first publication of the work'. The author, however, retained his 'sole rights' if within the period of ten years he published or authorised publication of his work or a translation in any language in respect of that language. So far as the first change is concerned it has been criticised that the property rights with criminal remedies can probably be understood as a part of general colonial legal and political policies which sought to protect, generally, right to property over rights to personal freedom. The modification of term of copyright for translation rights had adverse impact and disadvantageous to the authors and boon to publishers. This Act has been elaborated by judicial decision like *Macmillan Vs. R.C. Cooper.*[45] Vesting violations or

43. University of St. Andrews, Glassgow, Aberdeen and Edinberg.
44. T.C. James, Copyright Law of India and the Academic Community, Volume IX, JIPR 207 (212), May 2004.
45. AIR 1924 PC 75.

property rights with criminal sanctions can probably be understood as a part of general colonial legal and political policies which sought to protect the right to property over rights to personal freedom.

The modification of term of copyright for translation rights however cannot be explained by any reference to dominant characteristics of colonial policy. The language of the Act might suggest a laudable policy objective of promoting wider diffusion of Indian works in one language into other Indian languages, a consideration which might have appeared distinctive to India as compared with UK. There might also have been the desire to promote the growth of publication industry in numerous Indian languages. But whatever be the intention, the impact was disadvantageous to the authors and a boon to publishers. This can be seen from the following observations in a note of dissent when the continuation of the same provision was urged by the Joint Select Committee of the Indian Parliament in 1956 (a recommendation which did not ultimately prevail). Ram Dhari Singh 'Dinkar' (renowned Hindi poet designated as national poet for his contribution to national literature) argued that this provision has worked to the utter detriment of the authors. Referring to the plight of two distinguished Bengali authors he observed:

> "Most of the novels by Sarat Chandra Chatterjee were translated in Hindi, while the author was yet alive. The author's novels, in translation sold thousands of copies, but the author did not get a pie out of the sale proceeds something like this happened in the case of Gurudeva (Tagore). Publishers in Hindi and other languages were making good money out of the translations of his works, but the poet, revered by the nation, was in his extremely old age touring the country for money to support the Shanti-Niketan."[46]

The 1914 Act was continued with minor adaptations and modifications till the 1957 Act was brought into force on 24 January 1958 very shortly after the attainment of independence.

This phase of copyright law generated some important 'classical' decisions on the law of copyright. Simultaneously,

46. Report of the Joint Select Committee, The Gazette of India Extraordinary, pt. 2, s. 2, p. 907 (1956) cited in Baxi, U.

however, it also sowed the seeds of a trend that Upendra Baxi terms as 'a juristic dependencia'—the tendency of Indian judicial decisions as well as forensic styles relying excessively on United Kingdom (UK) precedents. On the impact of this trend, he notes:

> "The heavy hand of UK law still lies on Indian creative works despite the reformulation of the law in 1957. Judicial interpretation is perhaps most heavily influenced by UK precedents in the area of copyright law than in any other. The slavish imitation of foreign precedents has occasionally led intrepid Indian justices to remind the Bar and the Bench that the 1957 Act is made by 'a sovereign legislature of this land' and its interpretation 'must be based upon the object of the legislation and the language used' and that the 'historical roots' of the Indian law in the UK law of copyright should have no higher function than that of providing an 'aid to thinking.'"[47]

PHASE III—First Independent Law
The Copyright Act, 1957

Independent India accorded high priority to formulation of her own law on copyright. The Indian Copyright Act, 1957 ('the 1957 Act') repealed the Indian Copyright Act, 1914 ('the 1914 Act') which had virtually incorporated the most of the Imperial Copyright Act, 1911. The revision of the 1914 Act occurred within a mere seven years of Independence. In other words, this Act was the nothing but the modifications of the previous Act of 1914 which was affected from 24th January 1958. This Act was the outcome of Indian aspects only. It did not cover even the Brussels Act of 1948 and Universal Copyright Convention of 1952. It was the introduction of first Indian Copyright law of Independence India with advance method of communications covering modernisation of the required law. This Act meted up the social requirement of an independent and self-contained law which was highly sought for in terms of the past experience of the Copyright law of 1914. This Act also for the first time fulfilled the growing public consciousness about the rights, duties and

47. Baxi, Upendra, Copyright Law and Justice in India, *Journal of the Indian Law Institute*, 28.4: p. 501.

obligations of the author.[48] This Act for the first time specifically stated that there shall be no copyright in any work beyond the provisions of this Copyright Act.[49]

This Act was the first in Independence India but it was the replica of English legislative proposals. This Act was not at all able to protect all-round areas of copyright for example it does not protect the right of the performers properly. It was sensibly work for judges and lawyers though not always. The main fact was that the country had first independent law in the field of Copyright. It provided the guidelines and policy advancement to the legislature. Thus, it can be said that this Act was primarily discover the prime features of the law related to the administration of justice in case of copyright-related cases and offences since its inception. It is considered as the roadmap to the development of the copyright law in India.

The general discourse of this Act was to deal with the cases of Copyright and its ownership, its infringement and protection, national and international character of the copyrights, registration of copyright and the remedies for its infringement in the provided manner. This Act was originally divided into fifteen chapters and seventy-nine sections. A copyright rule was also framed under Sec. 78 of this Act under which government is empowered to make an order directing that any or all the provisions of this Act may apply to foreign copyright works or in international organisations. This Act also recognised certain administrative set-up of the implementation and protection of copyright in India. These are The Copyright Office and the Copyright Board. The Ministry of Education and Social Welfare is the administrative body regulating and controlling the Copyright Office. Copyright Board has been given the appellate status.

A number of factors, according to Upendra Baxi, impelled this early revision. First, it was clear that continued existence of the 1911 Act through the 1914 Act was unbecoming to 'the changed constitutional status of India.' Second, the 1914 Act did not accord with the 1948 Brussels Act of the Berne Convention and the 1952 Universal Copyright Convention—chiefly in the much longer terms that the Berne Convention mandated. Third, 'new and advanced method of communications' rendered

48. The Gazette of India, Extraordinary, pt.-2, Section-2, p. 907 (1956).
49. Section 16 of the Copyright Act, 1957.

modernisation of the law necessary. Fourth, the need for an 'independent self-contained law' was also felt in the light of the experience of the 'working' of the 1911 Act, and more important, 'the growing public consciousness of the rights and obligations of the authors.' To aid them in this task of indigenisation, the Indian legislators appointed a 'Select Committee' to propose a model Copyright Act. The Committee appears to have consulted the report of the English Copyright Committee, the models provided by the relevant international conventions; they received evidence from twelve organisations, including the International Confederation of Societies of Authors and Composers (Paris), the Performing Right Society (London), British Copyright Council and the Columbia Gramophone Company Ltd. The Report of the Select Committee, says Baxi 'appears to be among the briefest in the annals of the Indian Parliament but, in many senses, it made major innovations which were ultimately enacted.' One of the key legacies of the Committee's Report, for instance, was the abolition of registration as a pre-condition for infringement proceedings. Another significant area where the new Indian Copyright Act parted ways from the UK Act was in its omission of sections contained in the latter providing for 'gratuitous' supply of books to designated libraries.

In his evaluation of the new Copyright Act, Upendra Baxi notes:

> "it was as not in any sense a replication of the English legislative proposals. In this sense, the 1957 Act was the first truly Indian legislation after well over two centuries of the subjection to the 'imperial law'. The Act was not sufficiently far-sighted; it, for example, does not protect the right of the performers adequately. In many respects it is drafted in ways which make it meaningful only to judges and lawyers and sometimes not even to them. But the fact remains that the country had its own law of copyright for the first time in contemporary history; and, for weal or woe, it represented the law-policy choices made by its independent legislature."[50]

50. Baxi, Upendra, Copyright Law and Justice in India, *Journal of the Indian Law Institute*, 28.4: p. 503.

Three sets of ancillary amendments succeeded the 1957 Act. In 1983, several new sections were introduced into the Act. Sections 32A and 32B provided for 'compulsory licence' for publication of copyrighted foreign works in any Indian language for the purposes of systematic instructional activities at a 'low price' with the permission of the Copyright Board on certain conditions. The other crucial change was the insertion of section 19A, relating to the conferral of power in the Copyright Board, upon a due complaint to it, to order revocation of the assigned copyright where either the terms are 'harsh' or where the publication of the work is unduly delayed. In addition the 1983 Amendment provides for power in the Copyright Board to publish unpublished Indian works, and for the protection of 'oral works'. The amendment made it mandatory for the copyright office to publish details of all copyright registrations in the Gazette of India. Lastly, they disallowed the importation of an 'infringing copy' of a copyright work for 'private and domestic use' which had been permissible prior to the amendment.

Of all the certainty that one can see in life, is undeniably the human attribute of imitating. To imitate nature has been one of man's oldest triumphs, learning through copying is, considered by modern educationists, the best tool to dispense knowledge. However, inculcating the thought of respecting a creative contribution, be it to art, science or literature is the intrinsic quality of wisdom and needs to be imbibed by the human being in its pursuit of knowledge. Acknowledgement of the source of information is said to inculcate respect, not only to the author of the work, but more so to oneself, to establish ones credibility is much more important than to seek the greatest of all treasures, knowledge. Copyright, is one of the four cornerstones to the establishment of the new world economic order.[51] John Oswald had opined that, "if creativity is a field, copyright is the fence,"[52] the growth and development of copyright law world over reflects primarily the human endeavor in its colorful variations of

51. http://www.culturaleconomics.atfreeweb.com/cpr3.3htm
52. Oswald, John, Plunderphonics, or Audio Piracy as a Compositional Prerogative, this paper was initially presented by Oswald at the Wired Society Electro-Acoustic Conference in Toronto in 1985. It was published in Musicworks #34, as a booklet by Recommended Quarterly and subsequently revised for the Whole Earth Review #57 as 'Bettered by the borrower' in 1986.

creative ingenuity. The efforts to protect originality from plagiarism have traversed a journey of 500 years in human history. To receive the sanctity now made available to it by the international regime that has bonded the understanding to protect works, is but a debt, owed to our turbulent past and a guarantee to a promising future.

3

COPYRIGHT: HIGHLIGHT ON INTERNATIONAL LAW

The idea of Copyright began with a view to protect the creativity in terms of copyrights and related rights purely on municipal basis. The gradual addendum of value in the copyright-related work makes this a property of international community. The international economic philosophy behind the copyright is playing the vital role in this respect. Actually there is no such thing as an 'international copyright' that will automatically protect an author's creations throughout the world. Protection against unauthorized use in a particular country depends on the national laws of that country. However, most countries offer protection to foreign works under certain conditions that have been greatly simplified by international copyright treaties and conventions. Though the copyright laws now-a-days has become of international character but originally the notion of copyright began in England where it evolved following the introduction of the printing press at the end of the fifteenth century. As book publishing and selling (activities that were not readily distinguished from one another at the time) became profitable, the stationers (publishers) sought ways to protect their trade. The "stationer's copyright" gave a particular member of the Company of Stationers, the right to copy a particular work. It was awarded and enforced by the Company. Lyman Ray Patterson describes the purpose in his book on the history of copyright:

> "The stationer's copyright was literally a right to copy, that is, a right to reproduce a given work for sale. The basic purpose of this right was to provide order for the book trade by establishing a method to enable publishers to have the exclusive right to publish a work without competition as to that work. And the sanctions for copyright came from the company, for it was the company, not the author, which granted the copyright. From the stationers' viewpoint, copyright was protection against rival publishers, not against authors."[1]

Since, authors were not members of the Company, they could not hold the copyright. Copyright was perpetual. During the course of the seventeenth century copyright became entangled with politics and censorship. The Company of Stationers which received its legitimacy from a royal charter rode through the turmoil of the civil war and restitution of the crown but the previous arrangements to bring order to the trade slowly changed into arrangements to control the press. The Licensing Act that governed the book trade expired in 1692 and the House of Commons refused to renew it. There were many reasons but one of them was the belief that the Stationers had abused their monopoly and chaos ensued. The book trade went from a tightly regulated enterprise to a wide-open free-for-all. The stationers petitioned Parliament for relief and it finally came in 1709 with the Statute of Anne. The outcome wasn't exactly what the stationers wanted.

In the field of Copyright, the Statute of Anne was an attempt to restore order to the book trade and, at the same time, to address perceived abuses by the stationers. It provided two kinds of copyright. For past works, it extended the stationer's copyright for a period of 21 years. For future works it gave the author (or any assignee) the exclusive right to print the work for 14 years with the stipulation that the right could be extended by an author for another 14 years. There are two important points here: Firstly, the statute allowed people outside the Stationer's Company to hold the copyright (although it was the assignees rather than the authors who normally held it). Secondly, the statute attempted to

1. Patterson, Lyman Ray, The History of Copyright, 1968, p. 71.

break the monopoly of the stationers by limiting the term of copyright, a radical change for the stationers, who until then had enjoyed perpetual copyright. The booksellers were outraged. While the statute restored order to the trade, it also fundamentally changed the nature of their monopoly. A copyright that expired meant a decrease in its value, as well as an increase in risk. The booksellers fought back.

PHILOSOPHY OF INTERNATIONAL COPYRIGHT LAW

Copyright continued to change, often driven forward by the call for author's right. Nowhere were author's rights more embedded in the notion of copyright than in France. During the mid-eighteenth century, French copyright was both a tool for control of literature and a system of trade agreements just as it had been a century before in England. Copyright was perpetual and administered by powerful guilds but increasingly regulated by the Crown (much to the displeasure of the guilds). But while the stationers in England used legal challenges to the Statute of Anne, the French used philosophy. When the Paris Book Guild saw its literary privilege threatened by the royal Administration of the Book Trade, the guild hired the great encyclopedist, Denis Diderot, to write a treatise that defended the guild's right to literary property. According to *Diderot*, 'Ideas' were the highest form of property because they were so closely associated to the individual who created them:

> "What form of wealth could belong to a man, if not a work of the mind, if not his own thoughts, the most precious part of himself, that will never perish, that will immortalize him?"[2]

This was the strongest possible form of an 'author's copyright', grounded in epistemology rather than finance. It was based on high moral principles, glorifying the rights of individuals and their creative intellect. It was written at the request of a guild, the publishers of Paris. Of course, there were opposing philosophical arguments. For over 100 years, intellectuals had argued that the enlightenment was grounded on the free exchange of ideas that belonged to the world and not to the individuals who discovered them. This was a view eloquently expressed in 1776 by *the marquis de Condorcet.*

2. Diderot in Hesse, 1991, p. 101.

Individuals could not own ideas as they did property, he argued:

> "There can be no relationship between property in ideas and that in a field, which can serve only one man. Literary property is not a property derived from the natural order. It is not a true right, it is a privilege."[3]

As a consequence, copyright existed to protect the free exchange of ideas not the rights of authors.[4] This view, however, was soon overwhelmed in 1788-89 by the Revolution. In the Declaration of the Rights of Man, the National Assembly officially sanctioned freedom of the press. Without effective copyright, the freedom was wild and destructive. Naturally, anonymous and seditious pamphlets appeared; piracy of literary works was rampant; publishers faltered and became insolvent. Officials recognized the need to act but they debated endlessly ensnared by the politics of censorship in the midst of the Revolution's turmoil.[5] As early as 1790, Condorcet himself co-sponsored a proposal that provided copyright for the author's life plus ten years. The proposal violated the principles Condorcet had declared just 14 years earlier but he now had another goal in mind following the Revolution (to make authors accountable for what they wrote). His proposal did in fact place some limitations on literary property but not surprisingly; these were widely criticized by the Paris Book Guild and the royally privileged theatre directors. Once again they used author rights as their central argument[6]. The proposal never came to a vote.

Astonishingly, after the original sponsors departed almost exactly the same measure was passed into law in 1793 without discussion partially propelled by the revolutionary call to respect individual rights and property. French copyright law was a compromise. The law sanctioned the notion of literary property yet it limited such property and created the notion of public domain. It gave something to those with corporate interests in literary property but it also took something away. During the nineteenth century those corporate interests worked steadily to take back whatever they had lost.

---

3. Condorcet in Hesse, 1991, p. 103.
4. Condorcet went so far as to propose a publishing industry that sold ideas rather than works by authors. Such an industry would be based on the subscription model of periodicals rather than the sale of individual books.
5. Hesse, 1991, pp. 20-32.
6. Hesse, 1991, p. 110.

Some claim that French copyright law was delivered in the Revolution as *droit d'auteur* author rights. But French copyright continued to change for one-hundred years following the Revolution (Ginsburg, 1990). What was initially an uneasy compromise between the philosophies of Diderot and Condorcet slowly became dominated by the notion of authors and moral rights until copyright became synonymous with *droit d'auteur* in France.

The lacking of unified international law of copyright for the global recognition of author's creation round the globe laid the basic foundation for the establishment of international law in respect to Copyright which enabled the protection of creativity of authors particularly, and encourage creative works throughout the world generally.

REASON OF INTERNATIONAL COPYRIGHT PROTECTION

The brief history shows that copyright is far more complicated than *Peter Givler* suggests:

> "Copyright is not merely giving authors legal control over their own texts. Copyright is far more complex, more nuanced"[7].

But why should we care? Why bother with esoteric subtleties? Why worry about publishers who boast that their only goal is to protect authors? Because allowing such boasts to go unchallenged may lead us to seek the wrong solutions to the copyright problem. It's hard to solve a problem if you don't know its cause.[8] A good example is the recent attempt to fix copyright for scholarly journals by demanding that authors retain the copyright. Give authors control of their work, the argument goes and the publishers' monopoly will be thwarted. Give authors control and the real owners will once again be in charge. Give authors control because it's fair[9]. The argument

---

7. Peter Givler, 2003. "Copyright: It's for the Public Good," Chronicle of Higher Education, Volume 45, issue 35 (9 May), p. B20.
8. It should be noted that copyright experts who advocate reform do not make these mistakes. Lessig (2001) makes a number of suggestions for reform in Chapter 14, none of which merely shift copyright to authors.
9. S. Harnad, 2001, For Whom the Gate Tolls? How and Why to Free the Refereed Research Literature Online Through Author/Institution Self-

sounds convincing at first but in practice the case was not so. A single publisher produces journals with thousands of articles by thousands of authors each year. If all authors retain the copyright but give the publisher an exclusive license to publish for a period of time then who really benefits? After the exclusive period expires anyone who wants to make the journals available to the public (for example, in a new format online) will have to contact all those thousands of authors to obtain permission. Some authors will decline; some will be hard to find; some will be missing. Who then controls the journals? Surely not the public, the publishers retain control of the journals even if they do not control the individual articles themselves.

The problem of copyright is not author's rights but the problem is the balance between rights and unauthorise use. Copyright is control with a purpose. Copyright controls the dissemination of works in order to provide incentive to creators and to publish that's good for everyone, authors and the public alike. But perpetual (or nearly perpetual) control works against the public interest and that's true whether it's the publisher or the author who exercises the control. Encouraging every author to retain copyright simply replaces the deliberate tyranny of the few by the inadvertent tyranny of many.

BENEFIT OF INTERNATIONAL COPYRIGHT PROTECTION

The problem of copyright is balance. It is therefore ironic that *Peter Givler* ends his essay on copyright's benefit to authors with a quote from *Justice Ruth Ginsburg*:

"Indeed, copyright's purpose is to promote the creation and publication of free expression".[10]

Justice Sandra Day O'Conner in *Harper & Row Publishers, Inc. Vs. National Enters.*, observed:

> "It should not be forgotten that the Framer's intended copyright itself to be the engine of free expression. By establishing a marketable right to the use of one's

Archiving, at http://cogprints.soton.ac.uk/documents/disk0/00/00/16/39/index.html.

10. Peter Givler, 2003, Copyright: It's for the Public Good, Chronicle of Higher Education, Volume 45, issue 35 (9 May), p. B20.

> expression, copyright supplies the economic incentive to create and disseminate ideas."[11]

Justice Ginsburg was writing the majority opinion in a recent Supreme Court case[12] upholding the extension of copyright to 70 years beyond the life of the author (or 95 years for corporations). The decision was remarkable for its lack of balance. And surely no one can argue that extending copyright to 70 years after an author is dead (or 95 years for Walt Disney Inc.) benefits authors. Given the title of his essay, Givler might have quoted instead a portion of the dissenting opinion in that case from Justice *Steven Breyer*, who wrote:

> "It is easy to understand how the statute might benefit the private financial interests of corporations or heirs who won existing copyrights. But I cannot find any constitutionally legitimate, copyright-related way in which the statute will benefit the public."[13]

Justice Stevens was concerned about the public good. He was concerned about bringing balance to copyright[14]. Copyright has drifted out of balance over the years. What can we do to bring it back? Alas, there are no simple answers. Changing copyright laws is difficult. The U.S. Supreme Court ruling above shows why; so does the entire history of copyright. As authors, however, we may be able to restore balance to copyright without changing the law itself. There are many groups working to find appropriate ways for authors to dedicate their work to the public domain after a suitable length of time. That's a solution that addresses the real problem balance. For centuries, publishers have convinced authors that they are helpless victims in need of

---

11. 471 US 539 (1985).
12. *Eric Eldred, et al. Vs. John Ashcroft, Attorney General*, 537 U.S. 186; 683, 71 U.S.L.W. 4052, which challenged the Sonny Bono Copyright Term Extension Act.
13. Peter Givler, 2003, Copyright: It's for the Public Good, Chronicle of Higher Education, Volume 45, issue 35 (9 May), p. B20.
14. In *Feist Publications. Inc. Vs. Rural Telephone Service Co.*, 499 U.S. 340, 349 (1991), Justice Sandra Day O'Connor wrote: "The primary objective of copyright is not to reward the labor of authors, but [t]o promote the Progress of Science and useful Arts. 'To this end, copyright assures authors the right to their original expression, but encourages others to build freely upon the ideas and information conveyed by a work. This result is neither unfair nor unfortunate. It is the means by which copyright advances the progress of science and art."

protection. Copyright is for authors, copyright is fair and resistance is futile and foolish. But it's possible to resist that's why we should do so in spite of the difficulty.

Thus, International copyright at one hand provide international protection to the authors and at the another footing disseminate the knowledge and information throughout the word which shall certainly encourage creative works of the creators/authors/publishers. It also provided bigger market to the creator in terms of economic benefit of the creator. So, to provide a common mode of protection to all the creators throughout the globe and at the same time to provide source to the information and knowledge for everyone after a certain period of monopoly of creators/authors, a uniform international copyright law is highly sought for.

CURRENT POSITION OF INTERNATIONAL COPYRIGHT LAW

The international laws of Copyrights are the law which provides new guidelines to the entire community of the globe. The member-state shall follow the guidelines in the process of making their own domestic laws relating to copyright. The laws of copyright working in the international community are the product of the whole community and any contracting parties shall implement the international principles of copyright laws at the time of making their own municipal copyright laws. Since the inception of the copyright and related laws in the world many international Conventions, Treaties, Agreements and Covenants have been adopted by the international communities in order to protect the copyright of the authors/owners but still the result is not very encouraging and proper laws are still lacking in the national scenario because the member-countries are not under compulsion to adopt the international principles entirely. In course of time many international agreements, conventions, treaties, etc. have been adopted out of that some are highly remarkable like Berne Convention, UCC and TRIPs Agreement and having global admiration in the area of protective measures of copyright. These are as follows:

EVOLUTION THROUGH INTERNATIONAL INSTRUMENTS
The Berne Convention for the Protection of Literary and Artistic Works, 1886

The Berne Convention in 1886 first settled the recognition of copyrights between sovereign nations. It set out the scope of copyright protection and is still enforce to this day. Copyright's history has taken it from a legal concept regulating copying rights in the publishing of books and maps to one with a significant effect on nearly every modern industry covering such items as sound recordings, films, photographs, software, and architectural works.

The Berne Convention similar to the Paris Convention had its beginnings in the world meet that took place in the late 19th century. The making of numerous bilateral treaties for the protection of copyright had not served to protect the interests of the authors who were denied protection from rampant plagiarism in the foreign market. An International Literary Association came to be established under the guidance of renowned litterateurs like Victor Hugo. The association held regular meetings and at the Berne session in 1883 produced a draft text for an international agreement on copyright. Three inter-governmental meets came to be organized at Berne in 1884, 1885 and 1886 the Berne Convention for the Protection of Literary and Artistic Works was opened for signature, envisioning an international system for the protection of copyright and related rights. Formulated on parameters as laid out for the Paris Convention, the Berne Convention too, was based on the principle of minimum standards and national treatment.[15] The important feature of the international system ushered in by the Paris and Berne Conventions was the abandonment of the principle of reciprocity. The Berne Convention signed in 1886, underwent a series of changes in the succeeding decades and the authoritative text of this convention till this date is the Paris text of the Convention. This text was adopted in 1971 to incorporate changes suggested by the Revision Committee that met at Stockholm in 1967.[16] The objective of the Berne Convention as

15. Matt Elsmore, Intellectual Property Rights Within the International Community at http://wwwsolent.ac.uk/law/netsc.html
16. The Paris Act of July 24, 1971, was amended on September 28, 1979; the Treaty it stood on September 9, 1886, was completed at Paris on May 4, 1896,

agreed upon by the signatories provided as "equally animated by the desire to protect, in as effective and uniform manner as possible, the rights of authors in their literary and artistic works".[17]

Before the Berne Convention, national copyright law usually only applied for works created within each country. Consequently, a work published in United Kingdom (UK) by a British national would be covered by copyright there, but could be copied and sold by anyone in France. Likewise, a work published in France by a French national could be copyright there, but could be copied and sold by anyone in the UK. The Berne Convention followed in the footsteps of the Paris Convention for the Protection of Industrial Property of 1883, which in the same way had created a framework for international integration of the other types of intellectual property: patents, trademarks and industrial designs, etc.

Like the Paris Convention, the Berne Convention set-up a bureau to handle administrative tasks. In 1893, these two small bureaus merged and became the United International Bureau for the Protection of Intellectual Property (best known by its French acronym BIRPI) situated in Berne. In 1960, BIRPI moved to Geneva to be closer to the United Nations and other international organisations in that city. In 1967, it became the World Intellectual Property Organisation (WIPO) and in 1974 became an organisation within the United Nations. The Berne Convention was revised in Paris in 1896 and in Berlin in 1908, completed in Berne in 1914, revised in Rome in 1928, in Brussels in 1948, in Stockholm in 1967 and in Paris in 1971, and was amended in 1979. India signed it on April 1, 1928 and Bilateral in August 15, 1947 and by its subsequent legislation implemented some principles in national level. The UK signed in 1887 but did not implement large parts of it until 100 years later with the passage of the *Copyright, Designs and Patents Act of 1988*. Since, almost all nations are members of the World Trade Organisation, the Agreement on Trade-Related Aspects of Intellectual Property Rights requires non-members to accept almost all of the conditions of the Berne Convention. As of November 2009, there

reviewed at Berlin on November 13, 1908, completed at Berne on March 20, 1967, and at Paris on July 24, 1971 and amended on September 28, 1979.

17. Objective of the Berne Convention, 1886.

are 164 countries that are parties to the Berne Convention. The Berne Convention requires its signatories to recognize the copyright of works of authors from other signatory countries (known as members of the *Berne Union*) in the same way it recognises the copyright of its own nationals. For example, French copyright law applies to anything published or performed in France, regardless of where it was originally created. In addition to establishing a system of equal treatment that internationalised copyright amongst signatories, the agreement also required member-states to provide strong minimum standards for copyright law. Copyright under the Berne Convention must be automatic; it is prohibited to require formal registration (note however that when the United States joined the Convention in 1988, they continued to make statutory damages and attorney's fees only available for registered works).

The Berne Convention states that all works except photographic and cinematographic shall be copyrighted for at least 50 years after the author's death, but parties are free to provide longer terms, as the European Union did with the 1993 Directive on harmonising the term of copyright protection. For photography, the Berne Convention sets a minimum term of 25 years from the year the photograph was created and for cinematography the minimum is 50 years after first showing or 50 years after creation if it hasn't been shown within 50 years after the creation. Countries under the older revisions of the treaty may choose to provide their own protection terms and certain types of works (such as phonorecords and motion pictures) may be provided shorter terms. Although the Berne Convention states that the copyright law of the country where copyright is claimed shall be applied. Article 7.8 states that "unless the legislation of that country otherwise provides, the term shall not exceed the term fixed in the country of origin of the work", i.e. an author is normally not entitled a longer copyright abroad than at home even if the laws abroad give a longer term. This is commonly known as the rule of the shorter term. Not all countries have accepted this rule. The purpose of the Berne Convention is to protect the rights of authors in their literary and artistic works. This convention is based on two principles: National Treatment and Automatic Protection.

National Protection

The Berne Convention Provides that works originating in one of the member-states of the Berne Union must be given the same protection in each of the other member-states as the latter grants to the works of its win nationals.

Automatic Protection

The Berne Convention also based on the principles of automatic protection which provides that enjoyment and the exercise of rights under the national treatment principle shall not be subject to any formality and such enjoyment and such exercise shall be independent to the existence of protection in the country of origin of the work. This means that the protection is granted automatically and is not subject to any registration, deposit or to any formal notice in connection with the publication.

Apart from two basic principles, the Convention also contains a set of provisions of minimum standards of protection that each member-state undertakes to implement through its national legislation. Developing countries may depart from these minimum standards of protection with regard to the right of translation and the right of reproduction for certain works under certain circumstances.

The Universal Copyright Convention (and Protocols), 1952

The Convention brought into force on September 6, 1952 and subsequently revised in Paris in 1971. The reason for the adoption of UCC was that many states, including two most powerful states, the United States and the Soviet Union were not members of the Berne Convention. The countries were no willing to join Berne Convention due to the reason that its level of protection was high. The Copyright system of the United States and many Latin American countries also differed from that of the Berne Convention. Ultimately the UNESCO adopted UCC by removing several hurdles which came in its way.

The Convention was initiated as a result of an urge to ensure copyright protection of literary, scientific and artistic works in all countries. The members agreed to accord recognition to work produced in any member-country just as if the work had been composed within their own territory. Thus, universality came to be accorded to works of authors without discrimination of any kind. The agreed term of protection came to be not less than the life time of the author and to twenty-five years after his/her death. The Convention also came to provide separate provisions relating to the position of copyright for the developing nations.

All signatories came to acknowledge their obligation to provide, *inter alia,* for the 'adequate and effective' protection of the rights of authors as well as others to copyright proprietors in literary, scientific and artistic works. The UCC obligates contracting states to adhere to the principal of 'national treatment'. The symbol © together with the year of publication and the name of the copyright owner may be required by any contracting states under the UCC as satisfying all formalities which are otherwise required by the domestic laws in such contracting states.

The International Convention for the Protection of Performers, Producers of Phonograms and Broadcasting Organisations, 1961

International Convention for the Protection of Performers and Producers of Phonograms and Broadcasting Organisations commonly known as Rome convention was concluded on October 26, 1961 and brought into force on May 18, 1964. Its object is to protect neighbouring rights which has also been called related rights. It came to provide protection to performers, producers of phonograms and broadcasting organisations based on parameters of the performance/broadcast/phonograms either undertaken by its nationals, fixed first within their territory, first published within their territory or where the head office is located within the territory of such State. The signatory States agreed to accord 'national treatment' to performers, producers and broadcasting organisations only on the satisfaction of the conditions set out in the convention.

The Rome Convention contains the principle of reciprocity in respect of certain rights expressed by reservations which any contracting states can make at any time. Like the UCC, under the Rome Convention also, the symbol P in a circle together with the year date of first publication and the name of the owner of the rights of the produces may be required by any contracting states as satisfying all formalities which are otherwise required for the protection of the rights of producers of phonograms and the performers by the domestic law in such contracting states.

Convention Establishing the World Intellectual Property Organisation (Stockholm, 1967)

The Convention establishing the World Intellectual Property Organisation known as WIPO Convention came to be signed at Stockholm on July 14, 1967 and entered into force in 1970 and amended on September 28, 1979. Since 1974, WIPO has the status of a specialised agency of the United Nations. The Convention[18] elicits the scheme of the signatory states to contribute to a better understanding and co-operation among States for their mutual benefit on the basis of respect for their sovereignty and equality so as to encourage creative activity, promote the protection of intellectual property and the protection of throughout the world and modernize and render more efficient administration of the Union established in the fields of the protection of industrial property and the protection of literary works, while fully respecting the independence of each of the Unions.

The objectives of the Organisation are two-fold, firstly, to maintain and increase respect for intellectual property throughput the world, in order to favour industrial and cultural development by stimulating creative activities and facilitating the transfer of technology and the dissemination of literary and artistic works. Secondly, the promotion of the protection of intellectual property throughout the world through the co-operation among the states in collaboration with any other international organisation and ensuring administrative co-operation among Unions like Paris Union, Berne Union, etc.[19] The Organisation also undertakes to facilitate services relating to the protection of IPR's especially with regard to the co-ordination of

18. Initially there were two secretariats (one for industrial property, one for copyright) for the administration of the two conventions, but in 1893 the two secretariats united. The most recent name of the organisation, before it became WIPO, was BIRPI, the acronym of the French-language version of the name: United International Bureau for the Protection of Intellectual Property (in English). In 1960, BIRPI moved from Berne to Geneva.
19. The unions referred are Paris Convention, the Special Union and Agreements created in relation to it, as for instance the International Union for the protection of New Plant Varieties (UPOV), the Berne Convention and such other agreements which have been created for the purpose of protection of intellectual property, whose administration is assumed by the WIPO in accordance with the provisions of Article 4 (iii).

registration services and the publication information regarding registrations.[20]

The functions for which WIPO has been established are as follows:

- Normative activities, involving the setting of norms and standards for the protection and enforcement of intellectual property rights through the conclusion of international treaties;
- Programme activities, involving legal technical assistance to states in the field of intellectual property;
- International classification and standardisation activities, involving co-operation among industrial property offices concerning patents, trademarks and industrial design documentation; and
- Registration activities, involving services related to international applications for patents for inventions and the registration of international marks and industrial designs.

The Convention for the Protection of Producers of Phonograms against the Unauthorised Duplication of Their Phonograms (Geneva, 1971)

The Convention for the Protection of Producers of Phonograms Against Unauthorised Duplication of Their Phonograms, commonly known as the Phonograms Convention, was concluded at Geneva on October 29, 1971, and came into force on April 1973.[21]

The Geneva Convention of 1971 came to be signed by 72 members as on April 2003 to curb the widespread and increasing unauthorized duplication of phonograms and the damage to the interest of authors, performers and producers of phonograms. The signatories agreed upon the working of a nationality status being conferred upon nationals of the Union States. The protection accorded however, varied in accordance with the enforcement mechanism of the individual States.[22] It aimed at international protection against the piracy of sound recordings.

20. Article 3 WIPO Convention.
21. World Intellectual Property Organisation, Guide to the Rome Convention and to the Phonograms Convention 91-118 (1981).
22. http://www.wipo.int

The Contracting states, concerned at the widespread and increasing unauthorised duplication of phonograms and the damage, this is occasioning to the interests of authors, performers and producers of phonogrammes. They convinced that the protection of producers of phonograms against such acts will also benefit the performers whose performances, and the authors whose works, are recorded on the said phonograms. This convention was to recognise the value of the work undertaken in this field by the United Nations Educational, Scientific and Cultural Organisation and the World Intellectual Property Organisation. The members were also anxious not to impair in any way international agreements already in force and in particular in no way to prejudice wider acceptance of the Rome Convention of October 26, 1961, which affords protection to performers and to broadcasting organisations as well as to producers of phonograms.

Vienna Agreement for the Protection of Type Faces and their International Deposit, 1973

The Vienna Agreement for the protection of type faces and their international deposits, 1973 was concluded on June 12, 1973 at Vienna. This agreement for the protection of the type faces concluded within six chapters apart from introduction having 41 articles. This agreement was formulated in order to encourage the creation of type faces and provide an effective protection thereof. According to the provisions of this agreement the contracting states undertake to ensure the protection of the type faces, by establishing a special national deposit, or by adapting the deposit provided for in their national industrial design laws, or by their national copyright provisions.

The Convention Relating to the Distribution of Programme-Carrying Signals Transmitted by Satellite, 1974

The Convention Relating to the Distribution of Programme-Carrying Signals Transmitted by Satellite came to be concluded at Brussels on May 21, 1974. The Convention's main aspect is to curb the appropriation and distribution of programmes transmitted by communications a pace satellites. The Convention covers transmissions made through point-to-point satellites and through distribution satellites that transmit signals to earth stations for subsequent retransmissions, such as by cable distribution systems. The main consensus to provide for a global system to restrain the unintended distribution of program carrying signals transmitted by satellite by distributors as this had its impact felt on the use of the satellite communications. The Brussels Convention enjoyed a membership of 24 nation-states as on the 15th of April 2003.[23] The Brussels Convention was concluded because the member states were aware that the use of satellites for the distribution of programme-carrying signals is rapidly growing both in volume and geographical coverage and this convention was to convinced that an international system should be established under which measures would be provided to prevent distributors from distributing programmes carrying signals transmitted by satellite which were not intended for those distributors. This is popularly known as Satellite Convention.

Geneva Treaty of International Registration of Audio-Visual Works, 1989

The Treaty on the International Registration of Audiovisual Works is also known as film Register Treaty. It was concluded on April 20, 1989, came into force in 1992. It is concluded with a view to increase the legal security in transactions relating to audio-visual works and thereby to enhance the creation of audio-visual works and the international flow of such works and to contribute to the fight against piracy of audiovisual works. 'Audio-visual work' means any work that consists of a series of fixed related images, with or without accompanying sound, capable of being made visible and, where accompanied by sound, capable of being made audible. The International Register of Audio-visual Works is established for the purpose of the registration of statements concerning audio-visual works and rights in such works, including, in particular, rights relating to their exploitation.

Any natural person who is a national of, is domiciled in, has his habitual residence in, or has a real and effective industrial or commercial establishment in, a contracting state; and any legal entity which is organised under the laws of, or has a real and effective industrial or commercial establishment in, a contracting state is entitled to make an application for the registration of

23. http://www.wipo.org/treaties/documents/english/word/p-vie&sa.doc

statements concerning his/its audio-visual works. It is basically connected with registration of audio-visual works at international level. It is administered by WIPO's International Bureau. In the Register of the bureau, the information about particular works, their nature, rights as to reproduction, distribution and performance, place of enforceability of such rights, and limitation if any on such rights are to be kept and maintained.

Agreement on Trade Related Aspects of Intellectual Property Rights, Including Trade in Counterfeit Goods (Geneva, 1993)

This agreement was concluded at Geneva on December 15, 1993.[24] The agreement desired to reduce distortions and impediments to international trade, and taking into account the need to promote effective and adequate protection of intellectual property rights, and to ensure that measures and procedures to enforce intellectual property rights do not themselves become barriers to legitimate trade. This agreement was required due to new rules and disciplines concerning:

- The applicability of the basic principle of the GATT 1994 and of relevant international intellectual property agreements or conventions;
- The provision of adequate standards and principles concerning the availability, scope and use of trade-related intellectual property rights;
- The provisions of effective and appropriate means for the enforcement of trade-related intellectual property rights, taking into account differences in national legal systems;
- The provision of effective and expeditious procedures for the multilateral prevention and settlement of disputes between governments; and
- Transitional arrangements aiming at the fullest participation in the results of the negotiations.

This agreement contains VII parts, 73 articles and 5 sections covering different aspects of international relations and control of intellectual property rights internationally.

---

24. Concluded at Geneva on December 15, 1993, GATT document MTN/FA II-AIC.

The Agreement on Trade Related Aspects of Intellectual Property Rights (TRIPs), 1994

On September 20, 1986, a Special Session of the Contracting Parties to the General Agreement on Tariffs and Trade, held in Punta del Este, Uruguay, and attended by representatives from more than seventy countries, formally launched the Uruguay Round of GATT. A Ministerial Declaration identified the Round negotiating objective for intellectual property:

> "In order to reduce the distortions and impediments to international trade, and taking into account the need to promote effective and adequate protection of intellectual property rights, and to ensure that measures and procedures to enforce intellectual property rights do not themselves become barriers to legitimate trade, the negotiations shall aim to clarify GATT provisions and elaborate as appropriate new rules and disciplines."[25]

By the time the 'Draft Final Act Embodying the Results of the Uruguay Round of Multilateral Trade Negotiations' was presented on December 20, 1991, the parties had agreed that the Agreement on Trade Related Aspects of Intellectual Property Rights should incorporate the norms of the major intellectual property treaties, including the Berne and Rome Conventions augmented by specific minimum standards introduced by the Agreement. Yielding to vigorous objections from the United States, the negotiations expressly excluded the Berne Convention's moral rights obligations form the obligations enforceable under the TRIPs Agreement.[26] The Negotiations specified extensive remedies including measures for interdicting infringing goods at national borders and made concessions to developing and least developed country members in the form of an extra four years' and ten years' leeway, respectively, from the date of entry into force of the Agreement Establishing the WTO to bring their intellectual property laws into compliance with all but a prescribed handful of TRIPs standards.

The Trade Related Aspects of Intellectual Property Rights

25. Statement by the Chairman, GATT: Ministerial Declaration on the Uruguay Round of Multilateral Trade Negotiations (Sept. 20, 1986), 25, I.L.M. 1623, 1626.
26. Terence P. Stewart, the GATT Uruguay Round: A Negotiating History 2288-2289 (1986-1993).

Agreement is Annex-IC of the Marrakesh Agreement which established the World Trade Organisation. This agreement was signed on April 14th 1994 at Marrakesh, Morocco. An endeavor came to be made for the very first time in the history of international affairs to conjoin issues of trade and intellectual property rights.[27] This objective of the WTO came to be crystallized in the preamble to the TRIPs Agreement, which explicitly lays down that at the conclusion of the agreement the signatories had been desirous of flattening the curves acting as impediments to international trade, simultaneously ensuring the prevalence of efficient and adequate measures to combat infringement of intellectual property rights.

TRIPs agreement is divided into seven parts and consists of 73 articles. Part I deal with general provision and basic principles; part II deals with standard concerning the availability, scope and use of intellectual property rights; part III deals with the enforcement of intellectual property rights; part IV deals with acquisition and maintenance of intellectual property rights and related inter-parts procedures; part V deals with dispute prevention and settlement; part VI deals with transitional arrangements; and part VII deals with institutional arrangements and final provision.

Part I of the agreement sets out general provisions and basic principles, notably a national-treatment commitment under which the nationals of other parties must be given treatment no less favourable than that accorded to a party's own nationals with regard to the protection of intellectual property. It also contains a most-favoured-nation clause, a novelty in an international intellectual property agreement, under which, any advantage a party gives to the nationals of another country must be extended immediately and unconditionally to the nationals of all other parties.

Part II of the agreement sets the minimum substantive standards of protection for the intellectual property, i.e. copy-right and related rights; trademarks; geographical indications; industrial design; patents; layout-designs (topographies) of integrated circuits; undisclosed informations (trade secrets) and

27. United States of America was the first nation to identify the relevance of the conjugality and pursuant thereto it amended the Trade Act of 1974 to include Section 301 which effectively imposed trade sanctions on countries without an effective Intellectual Property Protection System.

control of anti-competitive practices in contractual licensed.

With respect to copyright, parties are required to comply with Articles 1 to 21 of the Berne Convention (Paris Act, 1971), except Art 6 *bis* and the appendix thereto. It ensures that computer programs will be protected as literary works under the Berne Convention and lays down on what basis databases should be protected by Copyright and Rental rights have also been added in the area of copyright and related rights.

Wipo Copyright Treaty (WCT), 1996

After adoption of the TRIPs Agreement, it was realised that all challenges posed by the new technologies have not been addressed by the agreement. Some of the issues raised by the spectacular growth of the use of digital technology particularly through the Internet were not addressed by the TRIPs Agreement. In order to fill this gap, the WIPO Diplomatic Conference on Certain Copyright and Neighbouring Right questions adopted the WIPO Copyright Treaty, 1996 at Geneva in between December 2 to 20, 1996.

WIPO Copyright Treaty (WCT) 1996 is a special agreement within the meaning of Article 20 of the Berne Convention, as regards contracting parties that are countries of the union established by that convention and obligate them to comply with Articles 1 to 21 and the appendix of the Berne Convention. It lays down provisions for contracting parties to protect two subject matters, firstly, Computer Programme, whatever may be the mode or form of their expression, and secondly, compilations of data or other material (database) in any form which by reason of the selection or arrangement of their contents constitute intellectual creations.[28] It obligates the contracting parties to provide legal remedies against the circumventions of technological measures, e.g. Encryption, used by authors in connection with the exercise of their rights and against the removal or altering of information, such as certain data that identify works or their authors, necessary for the management, e.g. Licensing, collecting and distribution of royalties of their rights (right management information).

28. The Instrument came to include material which constituted an intellectual creation even by virtue of its selection or arrangement.

The WIPO Copyright Treaty reflected the aspiration to develop and maintain the protection of rights of authors in their literary and artistic works in a manner as effective and uniform as possible on a universal scale. The Treaty having 25 articles had a membership of 51 countries as on the 19th of July of which 8 nations had ratified the same. Member-countries were provided the privilege of prescribing limitations or exceptions to the rights granted to the authors of literary and artistic works by way of their domestic legislation. Authors of computer programs, cinematographic works and works embodied in phonograms received the exclusive right to authorize for the commercial rental of their works either of originals or copies thereof, subject however to the rules prescribed by the domestic laws of such member-states.

The WIPO Performances and Phonograms Treaty (WPPT), 1996

The WIPO Performances and Phonograms Treaty, 1996 (WPPT) was also concluded at Geneva in between December 2 to 20, 1996. The WIPO Performances and Phonograms Treaty, 1996 having five Chapters and 33 Articles, came to usher in the modernity to the realm of copyright, a characteristic of the age of information technology. This treaty was concluded to develop and maintain the protection of the rights of performers and producers of phonograms in a manner as effective and uniform as possible in order to introduce new international rules to provide adequate solutions to the questions raised by economic, social, cultural and technological developments, protects performances of performers (actors, singers, musicians, etc.) and phonograms of the phonograms procedures. Unlike, WCT and WPPT do not have any connection with any other treaties.

The Protection under WPPT is to be accorded to the performers and producers of phonograms who are nationals of other contracting parties. The nationals of other contracting parties will have to meet the eligibility criteria as laid down in the Rome Convention. The contracting parties are required to adhere to the principle of national treatment with regard to the exclusive rights specifically granted in WPPT and to the right to equitable remuneration provided under Article 15 of the WPPT. However, this obligation does not apply to the extent that another contracting party makes use of the reservations permitted by Art. 15(3) of the WPPT. It is noteworthy that the provisions of WIPO Copyright Treaty and WIPO Performances and Phonograms Treaty are fully applicable in the digital environment. The compatibility came to correspondingly provide for authors, composers, writers, performers and artists using the internet,[29]in furtherance of expanding their target audience.[30] The WPPT established in 1996 came into force on May 20th 2002. As on 19th July 1999, 50 countries had signed the treaty of which six had ratified.

RATIFICATION OF INTERNATIONAL COPYRIGHT LAWS BY INDIA

Many international Conventions like Berne, Rome, Universal Copyright, Geneva, Paris, Stockholm, Vienna, Brussels, TRIPs, WCT, WPPT, etc. have been concluded and among them Berne Convention is the world's most important international copyright convention. Except for one section, all of the important sections of the Berne Convention have now also become part of the 1994 Agreement on Trade-Related Intellectual Property Rights, better known as the TRIPs Agreement. It would be possible to discuss the key concepts of international copyright with reference to the particular clauses of the TRIPs Agreement. It is easier, however, to explain these concepts within the Berne Convention context because this is their original source and because in various ways, the architecture of the TRIPs Agreement is based on the Berne Convention.[31] Some of the changes that TRIPs have made to international copyright are also duly noted. Though, India is not the contracting members of all of the above Conventions till date like WCT, WPPT, etc. India concluded Berne Convention in April 1, 1928, Bilateral in August 15, 1947, it

---

29. The Internet means a public network of computer networks known by that name which enables the transmission of information between users or between users and a place on the network. For further information see Internet Industry Code of Practice, Code for Industry and Self-regulation in Areas of internet content Pursuant to the Requirements of the Broadcasting Services Act, 1992 as amended May 2002, Version 7.2; http://www.iia.net.au.
30. http://www.usinfo.state.gov/topical/econ/ipr03012001.htm
31. Haochen Sun, Overcoming the Achilles Heel of Copyright Law, *Northwestern Journal of Technology and Intellectual Property*, 5 (2007), 265, 275, available at http://papers.ssrn.com/sol3/papers.cfm?abstract_ id=1021027.

also adopted United Copyright Conventions on January 21, 1958, Convention on Protection Producers of Phonograms on February 12, 1975, Universal Copyright Convention was entered by India on April 7, 1988, and finally India ratifies TWO on January 1st 1995.

GLOBAL RECOGNITION AND PROTECTION OF NATIONAL COPYRIGHT WORKS

At several points in the text that follows, the words 'world-wide protection' or 'global' are occasionally used. This is not strictly accurate because not every single country in the world is a member of the Berne Convention. For example, a few countries in the globe such as a number of small island nations situated in the Pacific Ocean are not Berne Union members. Two populous Middle-Eastern countries, Iran and Iraq, are also not Berne Convention members. But 'world-wide protection' is a helpful phrase to describe the impact and sweep of the Berne Convention because, as of November 2009, a total of 164 countries became the Berne Union members and most of the major countries in the globe are members.[32] 'Global protection' and 'global restrictions' means protections and restrictions which include all 164 Berne Union members. The discussion of other international copyright agreements giving international protection in certain aspects such as the WIPO Copyright Treaty 1996 etc. has not been made as India still has not signed those International instruments. Another leading international copyright agreement formulated as a substitute of Berne Convention, the Universal Copyright Convention (UCC), 1952. This also encourages the 'national treatment' concept by which the creation of one country shall be equally treated and protected by any member-countries of UCC, like their own[33].

RELATION BETWEEN INTERNATIONAL AND NATIONAL COPYRIGHT LAW

In a strict legal sense, there is no such thing as 'International

32. For the list of Berne Convention member-countries, see http://bit.ly/4Dddvo.
33. S. Ricketson and J. Ginsberg, International Copyright and Neighbouring Rights—The Berne Convention and Beyond (Oxford: Oxford University Press, 2nd edition, 2006) 1203.

or global copyright law'. National copyright law such as the Indian Copyright Act, 1957 for example called the national and territorial in nature and scope. This means that such laws cover a single political unit or territory, usually a self-governing country. Each national law has sovereignty or jurisdiction over that sole particular political unit. Just as the rape laws of Pakistan have no binding impact on or legal power over neighbouring Bangladesh, it might appear that Pakistan's copyright laws (or those of other countries) by themselves would have no power to regulate Bangladesh's copyright affairs. Moreover, copyrights are created within a single national territory and the national copyright laws of that country, whether those of India, Pakistan or Bangladesh, are supreme in most circumstances.

In fact, Indian copyright laws are only seemingly supreme and independent of the laws that exist in other countries and the rest of the world generally. Legislatures and parliaments operate under strict legal constraints as to what they can and what they cannot include in their own domestic copyright laws. This is somewhat unusual though not unique in international law. In the case of copyright, a number of international agreements, treaties and conventions establish binding standards or constraints which provide the framework within which all national governments must operate. When passing and amending their own laws regulating copyright on their own national terrain, countries must follow, without significant deviation, the international rules such as those found in the international laws like Berne Convention on all major issues.[34] In short, the International Union operates much like an international copyright cartel.[35] To be a member, a country must not only obey all of International Copyright's tightly worded rules with few exceptions but also establish its own national laws which collude in propagating the International Convention's restrictive copyright ideology. This ideology provides the legal basis for the

---

34. The Berne Convention has a number of "central content or core" sets of protections which must be included in the copyright laws of all Berne Convention members. Sam Ricketson, The Berne Convention for the Protection of Literary and Artistic Works: 1886-1986, (London: Centre for Commercial Law Studies, Queen Mary College & Kluwer, 1987), 206.
35. The Oxford English Dictionary defines a cartel as "an agreement or association between two or more business houses for regulating output, fixing prices, etc.; also, the businesses thus combined; a trust or syndicate".

huge revenue streams and cultural power that flow to global copyright owners. In brief, international copyrights' central operating assumption is that all countries and their citizens have essentially the same copyright interests.

The obvious consequences of this strict international regime and the associated 'cartel-like' or insiders' club mentality is that, to be clear, no country in the world is absolutely forced to join the cartel by signing up to any of these international agreements such as the Berne Convention. A few countries in the South world still have not joined and hence they are not bound by its provisions. Yet, to join or not join the international instruments like Berne 'club' is actually quite a hollow choice. If a country wants to become a member of the 153-member (August, 2009) World Trade Organisation and become an active world trader, it must also sign the other leading international agreement regulating copyright, the 1994 TRIPs Agreement.[36] TRIPs, which is administered by the WTO also regulates other forms of intellectual property rights. By signing up to the TRIPs Agreement a country also agrees to abide by Articles 1 to 21 of the Berne Convention as well as its Appendix; this is one exception.[37] These global treaties and conventions mark out the field of play; they define all of the important rules and they establish what are called the mandatory 'minimum standards' in national copyright law.

Additionally, agreements such as TRIPs are having an increasingly influential effect over the terms of national laws because, among other reasons, these international treaties have required countries to modify, read and tighten copyright restrictions over users. TRIPs gave new legal rights and freedoms to copyright owners such as the inclusion of new categories of protected/restricted works and new restrictions on users. Copyright users across the globe did not, by comparison, gain a

36. A copy of the TRIPs Agreement can be found at http://www.wto.org/english/docs_e/legal_e/27-TRIPs.pdf. A WTO overview of main contents of TRIPs is available at http://www.wto.org/english/tratop_e/TRIPs_e/intel2_e.htm. Some countries have had the choice of joining the WTO made for them. The United States has blocked Iran's full membership in the World Trade Organisation more than 20 times.

37. Article 9(1) of the TRIPs Agreement, Chiefly as a result of pressure from the US, countries signing TRIPs are permitted to ignore the non-economic (moral) rights provisions found in Article 6 *bis* of the Berne Convention.

single new right in the TRIPs Agreement. The situation has now become even worse. Not satisfied with its major 1994 victory in the signing of TRIPs[38], certain countries chiefly the United States and those of the European Union have put new coercive pressures on other countries to enact even stricter copyright laws than are required by the Berne Convention or the TRIPs Agreement. TRIPs itself required countries to add new copyright enforcement laws to their statutes; the fact that copyright infringement now must be treated as a potential criminal offence by all countries is also a direct result of TRIPs.[39] These new rights awarded to owners and related legal pressures have had a major global impact in the past decade because, copyright over products created in one country are often automatically valid rights in many other countries as well. The overall conclusion is the purported independence of national copyright laws and their supposed flexibility is mostly a myth; the objective is global harmonisation.[40]

INTERNATIONAL, NATIONAL COPYRIGHT LAW AND COMMUNICATION SYSTEM

There are three main consequences of the Berne Convention for individual member-countries, for the copyright goods produced within them, and, of course, for users:

> (a) There is automatic world-wide protection for most copyrighted works; (b) Foreign (non-national) copyright holders must receive the same level and type of protection as local (national) copyright holders receive; the technical legal term is 'national treatment'; and (c) Copyright laws in all countries must protect copyrighted expressions at a level above what are called

38. As the World Bank concluded, the TRIPs agreement, which incorporated much of Berne, decidedly shifted the global rules of the game in favor of rich countries. Global Economic Prospects and the Developing Countries (New York: World Bank, 2002), 129.
39. Article 61 TRIPs.
40. Christophe Geiger *et al.*, Declaration on a Balanced Interpretation of the Three-Step Test in Copyright Law, IIC 39 (2008), 707, 708: This article concludes, 'international harmonisation primarily serves the interests of copyright-exporting countries in a secure and predictable trade environment'.

'minimum standards'. Let's look at these three consequences which are interlinked and reinforce each other:

Automatic World-wide Protection

Acquiring copyright in one product in one country is relatively easy. But in addition, a product that gains copyright in one country which is member of the Berne Union also acquires copyright protection in all other member-countries. This global copyright stretch means that a poem, play or computer software program written in India or the England gets legal protection in USA and Switzerland as well as in their country of creation. The potent overall result is the following:

- Legal rights to copyright in one country become world-wide rights in more than 160 other countries. And they gain this protection without the creator or owner having to take any legal action, without carrying out any foreign or domestic government registration requirements, without having to spend any further money or indeed, without informing anyone. And legally, these properties like protections or legal claims as well as restrictions on users are established automatically and immediately.
- In the case of books, the owner's claim to global copyright, which also acts as a copyright infringement warning to users can be found on its copyright page. Such notification is often located on the reverse side of a book's title page.[41] Hence, the words **'Copyright Burdwan University Press 1994'** found within a book informs the reader that starting in 1994 and continuing on for many decades, this book is copyright protected in every other Berne Convention country in addition to the country, The India, where the copyright was first acquired. At the same time, this same notice informs all readers that it is illegal for anyone to infringe copyright in this book in either in India or any other Berne Union countries, this legal stranglehold will remain in place for many decades until its copyright expires.

It perhaps takes a few minutes to completely grasp the potency of the global power which this geographic stretch

41. In a film, one of its final frames usually contains its copyright notice.

creates. At a stroke it establishes both immense money earning capacity and immense cultural power. This stretch is, for example, at the very core of the reason why Bill Gates and Ajim Premji became a multi-billionaire with Microsoft's and Wipro's copyrighted software programme respectively.[42] Multi-billionaire media owners throughout the globe are rewarded. Few other legal rights operate in a similar global fashion and these provisions are undoubtedly the most important global consequences of the Berne Convention, the TRIPs Agreement and other similar copyright agreements. What has happened requires us to update the pithy conclusion reached by Macaulay in 1841 that copyright's main principle acts as:

> "a tax on readers for the purposes of giving a bounty for writers".[43]

Today, 170 years later, copyright has become an international tax on readers (and listeners and viewers and Internet surfers) for the purposes of primarily giving a bounty to publishers (and film and software multinationals). Certainly few other commodities acquire such a global protective legal sheath so easily and at such a low, in fact non-existent, cost. For a start, these agreements make copyrighted products potentially very valuable and very profitable globally, especially digital products such as music, books and films which can be cheaply delivered over the Internet.[44] It is not an easy matter to precisely calculate the specifics of how much some countries benefit from this global expansion of enforceable legal copyrights but one conclusion is indisputable; those countries and corporations which are the

---

42. Alan, Story, Intellectual Property and Computer Software: a Battle of Competing Use and Access Visions for Countries of the South, Issue paper #10, International Centre for Trade and Sustainable Development/United Nations Conference on Trade and Sustainable Development, Geneva (May 2004), The electronic copy of the article is available at http://www.iprsonline.org/unctadictsd/docs/CS_Story.pdf
43. Macaulay was speaking in the British House of Commons against a bill to increase the duration of copyright. His speech is worth reading in its entirety, available at http://www.chaos.org.uk/~eddy/politics/Macaulay.html.
44. The word "potentially" is important here because such products must also be globally marketed and sold, though the Internet often takes on a delivery and revenue-collection function as well.

biggest copyright producers and exporters are the largest beneficiaries of this one sided system based on the primarily one way traffic in cultural and technical goods. This guarantee of automatic global protection is not explicitly stated anywhere in the text of the Berne Convention or any other international instruments. It is, however, the direct result of the operation of the two other basics of international copyright, namely, national treatment and minimum rights. It should be noted that every copyrighted product created in one country is not necessarily protected in all other countries on the globe.

National Treatment in International Community

Essentially, the legal concept of national treatment means that national copyright holders and non-national (in other words, foreign) copyright holders must be treated, for copyright purposes, in exactly the same fashion. Established as a cardinal principle of the Berne Convention in 1886, national treatment has remained essentially unchanged since that date. It is sometimes labelled a rule of non-discrimination. It means, for example, that the laws of Country A must treat non-nationals (those from Country B) and the copyrighted works they produce as if they were produced by its own nationals (in Country A). In other words, the works of both nationals (from Country A) and foreigners (from Country B) must be protected equally in Country A, that is, on the same legal basis and without any discrimination against those from Country B. Put another way, an author's and an owner's rights are protected in another country as if the author and the owner actually were nationals or citizens of the protecting country and *vice-versa*. This same national treatment rule means that within India the Indian government must treat the works of an Indian author on the same basis of the works of an author from England. National treatment also means that if a country increases its duration of copyright or adds new categories of products which can be copyrighted, the copyright for all goods, whether national or foreign must be treated in the same or non-discriminatory manner within its borders.

National treatment provisions create one of the bases for the automatic global protection of copyright products explained in the previous section. Here is how these two features of Berne work in cycle. Corporations located in Country B may export their copyrighted products to Country A. Corporations located in Country A may also own copyright products which are sold within the borders of Country A. If the laws of Country A state that owners of a work are the only ones who can allow the translation of copyrighted work into another language (and the Berne Convention requires that such a privilege must be included in the copyright laws of all member-states),[45] works produced in Country B and Country A (or anywhere else for that matter) must get the same protection within the borders Country A. And because the laws of Country B must also include the same Berne Convention translation privileges found in Country A (and everywhere else), here is the end result: works produced within Country A get automatic protection against unauthorised translation not only in Country A, but also in Country B and in all other 160 Berne Convention member-countries. This is another concrete example of how automatic global protection works.

Establishing Mandatory Minimum Standards

The Berne Convention's third main requirement is that all members must establish and enforce a wide number of minimum copyright standards within their own borders. There are various mandatory minimum standards in the Berne Convention. They include the following:

All countries must include national treatment protections in it's own domestic law.[46]All countries must protect a broad variety of expressions and products.[47]All countries must not require any formal registration requirements for a work to become copyrighted; protection must commence as soon as a work is created. All countries must ensure that authors, actually owners, of copyrighted works get a number of exclusive rights, such as the right to copy their works and related rights, including those related to translations, which have just been mentioned in

---

45. Berne Convention, Article 8, Right of Translation. Article 8 states: "Authors of literary and artistic works protected by this Convention shall enjoy the exclusive right of making and of authorizing the translation of their works throughout the term of protection of their rights in the original works".
46. Berne Convention, Article 5.
47. For a complete list, see Article 2 of the Berne Convention.

the previous section.[48] The personal or non-economic rights of authors, more commonly called "moral rights", must be also protected for all authors.[49] And all countries must establish a minimum copyright term of protection of the life of the author, plus 50 years, or an alternative term of 50 years from the date of first publication or release, for example, in the case of a book•or film respectively.[50]

If these are some examples of the fixed and mandatory minimum copyright legal standards included in the Berne Convention, the 1994 TRIPs Agreement added several others in the field of copyright. TRIPs states that all countries must protect computer software as a copyrighted literary work.[51] As well, new requirements protecting databases regulating the rental of computer programs, films and requiring the strict enforcement of copyright laws were also added.[52] Taken together, it is these Berne and TRIPs minimum standards which, when linked with the national treatment, ensure automatic global protection. As a result, owners of copyrighted works in Country A can feel totally confident that the works they own in Country A will be legally protected in the domestic laws of all other countries because all other countries must establish the same minimum standards that exist in Country A. In reality then copyright ownership rights established in one country expand dramatically to become global ownership rights or property like rights that are enforceable, at least in theory, anywhere in the world.

In the current era, it is the linking of these two legal threads, national treatment and minimum standards, 'Trips Plus' which also give an additional impetus to rich copyright exporting countries to both spread and extend the 'Trips Plus' agenda, mentioned above.[53] When a country such as the United States was able to put enough pressure on a country such as Chile to tighten its own copyright laws and create even higher standards

48. Berne Convention, Article 9.
49. Article 6 *bis* of the Berne Convention.
50. Article 7 of the Berne Convention.
51. Article 10 (1) of the TRIPs.
52. Articles 11-14 and Articles 41-62 of the TRIPs.
53. Only two countries in the world, the United States and the United Kingdom, are net exporters of copyrighted goods, meaning they are the only two countries which export, in total, more copyrighted goods than they import. For graphic representation of the global flows of royalties for all types of intellectual property look at http://bit.ly/1jiejW.

than the already high minimum standards of the Berne Convention, the United States was ensuring that the world's largest copyright exporter, namely itself, would be a prime beneficiary. If such new Chilean laws favoured Chilean copyright owners or restricted gains to non-Chileans, they would be declared discriminatory as offending national treatment principles. All copyright owners everywhere must receive the equal potential benefit of the law; the most powerful ones, such as those located in rich industrial countries, receive the greatest real benefit. Conversely, all users everywhere must pay and some users have far more ability to pay than others. In short, ratcheting up copyright laws in one location in the name of 'Trips Plus' or the prevention of piracy ratchets up potential benefits to all copyright owners involved in this subsidised monopoly system.[54]

During the 1980s and early 1990s some countries such as the United States, Japan and the United Kingdom, decided that software should be a copyrighted product. Other countries, especially in the global south, where cheaper software was (and is) badly needed, disagreed with this approach. So these countries did not explicitly protect software in their own national copyright laws. And they were not ignoring or breaking any laws when they took this decision. At that time there was no international treaty or agreement such as the Berne Convention which placed software in the category of a protected work. Consequently, while software became a copyrightable commodity in the above three rich countries and some others which was not necessarily protected everywhere on the globe because the Berne Convention did not include computer software in its list of protected works, proprietary software corporations such as Microsoft could not take legal action under copyright law against some countries in the world that choose to copy this software or to develop their own. This was one infrequent case where global protection was not automatic although since, 1995 copyright's

54. Peter Drahos and John Braithwaite, Information Feudalism: Who Owns the Knowledge Economy? (London: Earthscan, 2002), electronic copy available at http://www.thecornerhouse.org.uk/item.shtml? x=85821#fn038ref.; Boldrin, Michele and K. Levine, David, Economic and Game Theory: Against Intellectual Monopoly, electronic copy available at http://www.dklevine.com/general/intellectual /againstfinal.htm.

control over software has been guaranteed everywhere.[55] This past and relatively brief absence of world-wide protection for software is another reason why countries which are the main exporters of both software and of the materials sent out using this software are so anxious that all countries sign up to the WIPO Copyright Treaty, this treaty deals with communication and information technology and places restrictions on Internet use.[56]

POSITION OF NATIONAL ELECTRONIC COPYRIGHT UNDER INTERNATIONAL COPYRIGHT LAWS

So far this primer has mostly examined laws that controlled traditional copyrighted products, such as printed books and CDs and films. In other words, it has concentrated on the situation in the pre-Internet era. This era, it should not be forgotten, still remains the norm in most parts of the world. In the United Kingdom, for example, 79.8 percent of the population has Internet access compared to only 23.4 percent in India and many countries in Africa have an even smaller percentage.[57] Yet, the rapid global increase in the number of computers in the past 15 years, the communication possibilities by which digitalisation opened up and the spread of the Internet created new challenges for traditional copyright doctrine to use the neutral sounding language of policy papers. We perhaps forget the Internet and the World Wide Web were created as tools for the global sharing of knowledge and for collaboration. But corporate copyright interests soon grasped that the Internet could also become a tool for the advertising, sale and delivery of their copyrighted products.[58]

Would traditional copyright doctrine continue to protect the interest of the copyright owners in this new Internet era? No, absolutely not and considering the fact only in the international

55. Article 10(1) of the TRIPs Agreement which makes copyright protection of software a new minimum standard for all WTO members.
56. Till August, 2009, less than 50% of WTO and Berne Convention members have signed the 1996 WIPO Copyright Treaty. http://www.wipo.int/treaties/en/ip/wct.
57. These are the statistics as of 30 June 2009 found at *http: //*www.internetworldstats.com/stats.htm.
58. Paul Przemyslaw Polanski, Chapter 10 of the Internationalisation of Internet Law, IUS Gentium 2 (2008)191.

scenario, international body drafted two new international treaties, i.e. WCT and WPPT, commonly known as WIPO Internet Treaties. At present (September 2009), 70 countries have signed the WCT. Many countries signed as result of free trade agreements with the US and others have joined voluntarily. In many African countries which have signed, less than 2 percent of the population even has Internet access.[59]

The preamble to the WCT states that the contracting parties recognise the profound impact of the development and convergence of information and communication technologies on the creation and use of literary and artistic works. It is perhaps a hint that the Berne Convention of 1886 has passed its sell by date. But any hope that things were perhaps moving ahead is quickly dashed when another preamble concludes that the Berne Convention already reflects a balance between the rights of authors and the larger public interest, particularly education, research and access to information. The real aim becomes even clearer when the first section of the first article of the WCT states that this Treaty is a special agreement within the meaning of Article 20 of the Berne Convention. Article 20 of the Berne Convention gives Berne members the authority *solely to increase,* but not decrease in any way, the rights of rights holders.[60] And so we are right back on the same old Berne Convention territory; this 1996 Internet treaty merely takes the 1886 elevator up another floor for the 21st century. The most important preamble states that countries recognise the need to introduce new international rules and clarify the interpretation of certain existing rules in order to provide adequate solutions to the questions raised by new economic, social, cultural and technological developments.

Carrying out the basic purpose of copyright law, namely to stop people from doing things, the WCT imposes two new main rules on countries and, in turn, on users:

1. Countries must bring in "adequate legal protection"

---

59. Internet usage statistics for three African members of the WCT: a total of 1.8 percent of people in Benin uses the Internet. In Mali and Burkina Faso, the figure is 0.9 percent. Found at *http://www.internetworldstats.com/stats1.htm.* : Brazil and India are two of the more prominent countries not signed, but China signed in 2007.
60. Article 20 of the Berne Convention.

which will stop people who try to avoid or evade or otherwise find a way around what are known as technological protection measures (or TPMs);[61] and

2. Countries must bring in "effective legal remedies" against any person who deliberately tries to remove or interfere with or disable such technological protection measures.[62]

Technological Protection Measures (TPMs), sometimes called anti-circumvention devices because they attempt to stop people circumventing copyright restrictions, are technical features or devices inserted into digitalised (and copyrighted) products. A system itself may be designed with the same anti-circumvention objectives in mind. TPMs attempt to prevent uses of a product in any fashion which the owner does not want the user to do, primarily sharing with other people or changing the format for one to another for own personal use. TPMs may also act as a tool of surveillance against users, as an evidence gathering device for later prosecution, and can even disable products or set a time span during which that product can be accessed. When time is up the product, such as a music file, may no longer be playable. And consumers may not even be aware that the product they have purchased contains such a TPM. Examples of TPMs include digital watermarking, content scrambling devices, root-kits, DVD region codes, encryption and a wide range of other devices and systems.[63]

The idea of copyright though began in a domestic perspective but flourished rapidly and very quickly became the subject matter of international community. The domestic treatment of a law is highly influenced by the character of the national environment but getting international recognition and protection of a national creation obviously has added multi-dimensional features to the copyright system. It brings recognition and uniformity to this law and moreover, added special economic value and cultural weight to the creators or authors or

---

61. WCT Article 11, Obligation concerning Technological Protection Measures.
62. WCT Article 12, Obligations concerning Rights Management Information. It must also be a crime to distribute copyrighted products in which TPMs have been removed or import such anti-TPM equipment.
63. The forms of TPMs are changing regularly and which ones are legal and illegal obviously depends on the particular laws in a country.

producers of the copyright-related matters. Specially, after the advent of WTO, the universal principles enunciated by the international conventions, like Berne, UCC, WCT and WPPT, etc. really supplemented momentum in the task of contributing not only to the knowledge and information world but forward a world of economic renaissance in the copyright-related industry after which the real booming has been observed in the field of copyright and related aspects throughout the globe. If the national laws providing protection to the creative works, international law obviously providing international recognition and impulse to provide more protection to that works and moreover encouraging creativity in the domestic as well as international level.

Despite the fact that the present international copyright law has taken the position to become international law in its nature, it is important for the global processes to critically consider local circumstances. Despite this anxiety to protect copyright, it is also important to understand and be aware of the danger that copyright law may inflict upon the area of knowledge distribution. In the knowledge-based economy, the understanding of intellectual property rights, particularly copyright, is important in order to make a well-informed policy decision on various aspects of human development. Further research should aim to contribute to the development of international copyright system by providing possible mechanisms or instrument that could be used to improve our current international copyright laws to suit the need for erudition-based advancement in the digital age, especially in the developing countries. This is imperative in the way to ensure that copyright law will not deviate from its original intention of promoting learnings and creations of beneficial knowledge for the public good.

4

POSITION OF COPYRIGHT LAW IN INDIA

Western concept of Intellectual property rights involves creating restrictive monopoly of knowledge which is quite contrary to the age old Indian belief where 'knowledge' has always been in public domain and 'Copyright' is not an exception to this general rule. The epics, the fables, the story of panchtantras had been shared freely without creating any monopoly rights in favour of anyone. The transition of the knowledge management system of ancient India to the modern India was strongly influenced as usual by two hundred years of British rule. Therefore, it is necessary to trace the genesis of present Copyright law in India right from the advent of the Britishers.

In India, ancient record of the laws never indicated about the presence of any Copyright law before the English Copyright Act, 1842 in its history but lots of valuable works had been created from century to century in this country. Like Shakespeare, Wordsworth and Keats in the foreign literature India had also 'Ram Charit Manas', 'Shakuntale' 'Arthasastra', etc. the few of the worthy creations by Tulsi Das, Kalidas and Koutilya without giving any monopoly of rights over their creations. The protection of these creations was not available in the sense of copyright, only non-enforceable moral obligations were experienced in our ancient creations.

India, like most developing countries, received modern Copyright Law as a gift from its colonial rules.[1] Prior to the 1957 Act, the colonial India had the Copyright Act of 1847, the first Copyright Act[2] for Indian and then the Act of 1914 which was heavily tilled towards the UK Copyright Act of 1911 and known as replica of the British Copyright Act of 1911, textually as well as principle-wise, though with a few suitable modification. This new statute, the imperial Copyright Act, 1911, was the next in the historical pipe made applicable to the Indian polity as it existed during the Queen's regime.

On this Copyright Act of 1911, the Supreme Court of India opined[3] that:

> "it seems to us that the fundamental idea of violation of copyright or imitation is the violation of the Eighth Commandment *'thou shall not steal'* which forms the moral basis of the protective province of the Copyright Act of 1911. It was a free law operating in an enslaved regime as the Indian Legislature had very limited power of amendment by way of modification or addition which was conferred by Section 27[4] of the Act".

Again Lal's commenting on the Imperial Copyright Act, 1911 was that:

> "Prior to Indian enactments on the subject the law in force was the Imperial Copyright Act, 1911 which, with slight modification, was made applicable to this country by the Indian Copyright Act (Act No. III of 1914). The Imperial Copyright Act, 1911 either operating as *proprio vigore* or as applied by the Indian Copyright Act, 1914, was 'a law in force in the territory of India immediately before the commencement of the Constitution', and, it,

1. Dr. Mira T. Sundarajan, Digital Learning in India: Problems and Prospects, available at *htpp:cyber.law.harvard.education/ home/ dl_india*
2. Raju, K.D., Intellectual Property Law, WTO and India, 229, New Era Law Publication (2005).
3. *R.G. Anand Vs. M/S Dlux Films,* AIR 1978 SC 1613 (1619).
4. Sec. 27 of Imperial Copyright Act, 1911 stated as :
   "The Legislature of any British possession to which this Act extends may modify or add to any of the provisions of this Act in its application to the possession, but except so far as such modifications and additions relate to procedure and remedies, they shall apply only to works the authors whereof were, at the time of the making of the work, resident in the possession and to works first published in the possession."

therefore continued to be in force as the law of the land by virtue of Article 372(1) of the Constitution."[5]

The Bombay High Court has observed that the applicability of the Copyright Act of 1911 depends upon the provisions of the Constitution of India[6] which makes this Act applicable even after the commencement of the Constitution.[7]

In this context, it is relevant to note that the copyright is a territorial concept though international repercussion, development and amendments of an Act in independent India, is a constitutional guarantee. This Act could hardly stand the test of time and was subsequently repealed by the Copyright Act, 1914. The preamble of this last pre-independent statute, on the species of civil law, also specifically indicated the application of British Copyright Act, 1911 in British India whereas, it is expedient to modify and act to the provisions of the Copyright Act, 1911.[8] Undoubtedly, the preamble was the key to open the mind of the legislature[9]; the same was forced to apply a foreign law on a foreign land. This law continued to be the law of the land until 1957,[10] when the need was felt to enact our own statute on copyright not only because of the change in the constitutional status of India but also in the light of growing public consciousness about rights.

The passive area of intellectual property law in India received a jolt by advancement in the technique of reprography, audio-visual technologies and the exponential growth of personal computers with capacities unheard of in the past.[11] World opinion in defence of the human rights in terms of intellectual property laid the foundation of international

---

5. Lal's Commentary on the Copyright Act, 1957 (Act 14 of 1957) with the copyright rules, 1958 and Neighbouring Rights, 4th edn., 99, Delhi Law House.
6. Article 372 of the Constitution of India.
7. *N.T. Raghunathan Vs. All India Reported Limited*, AIR 1971, Bom. 48(51).
8. Preamble to the Copyright Act, 1914.
9. *Jagjit Kumar Vs. Jagdish Chandra*, AIR 1982 M.P. 144(145): *Tribhuwan Prakash Nayyer Vs. Union of India*, AIR 1970 SC 540.
10. Quote Article 372(2) of the Constitution of India which permits next the pre-independent statute operative even after India has been liberated of colonial clutches. Also *N.T. Raghunathan Vs. All India Reported Limited*, AIR 1971, Bom. 48(51).
11. D.P. Mittal, Law relating to copyright, patent and trademark and GATT, 4, Taxmann Allied Services.

conventions, municipal laws, commissions, codes and organisation, calculated to protect works of art, literature, etc., and India responded to this universal need by enacting the Copyright Act, 1957.[12]

A GLIMPSE OF INDIAN COPYRIGHT LAW

In India, the Copyright Act, 1957 (as amended up-to-date), the Rules made thereunder and the International Copyright Order, 1999 govern the facets of copyright, related rights and neighbouring rights. The Act was originally divided into 15 Chapters with 79 sections. Moreover, the Central Government by virtue of Sec. 78 of the Copyright Act, is empowered to make rules by its notification in the Official Gazette for carrying out the purposes of this Act. The Copyright is granted and protected as per the provisions of the Act and there exists no common law right.[13] Under the Constitution of India, the matter of Copyright fall under Entry 49 of List-I[14] which is the Union list and it is a subject of Central law. Thus, the parliament has the exclusive right to frame laws on this subject. On the international plan, India is a part of the Berne Convention for Protection of Artistic and Literary Works (1886), the Universal Copyright Convention (1952) and the Agreement on Trade and Related Aspects of Intellectual Property Rights (TRIPs). However, India has not ratified the WIPO Copyright Treaty, 1996 and WIPO Performances and Phonogrammes Treaty, 1996, till date.

THE OBJECTS AND REASON OF PASSING COPYRIGHT ACT, 1957

The objects and the reasons for the passing Copyright Act of 1957 were stated in the Parliament as follows:

> "the existing law relating to Copyright is contained in the Copyright Act, 1911 of the UK as modified by the Indian Copyright Act, 1914 apart from the fact that the UK Act does not fit in with the changed constitutional status of India, it is necessary to enact an independent,

12. *Indian Performing Right Society Limited Vs. Eastern Indian Motion Pictures, Assam*. AIR 1977 SC 1443 (1453).
13. *Manojah Cine Production Vs. A. Sudarshan*, AIR 1976 Mad 22.
14. Schedule 7, List I, Entry 49, Patent, inventions and design; copyright, trade-marks and merchandise marks.

> self-contained law on the subject of copyright in the light of growing public consciousness and the rights and obligations of authors and in the light of experience gained in the working of the existing law during the last 50 years. New and advanced means of communication like broadcasting, lithography, etc., also call for certain amendments in the existing law. Adequate provision has also to be made for fulfillment of international obligations in the field of copyright which India might accept. A complete revision of the Law of Copyright, therefore, seems inevitable".[15]

The intention of the legislature behind enacting the copyright legislation was to regulate the commercial monopoly and competing interests of the person concerned. Notwithstanding, in our independent Copyright Statute we have extensively borrowed the principles from new Copyright Act, 1956 of the UK. Indeed, we respect the erudite views of Justice Deshmukh of the Bombay High Court who observed that:

> "the interpretation of the statute must be based on the law of the land and English statutes may be used as an aid to thinking if some roots of the copyright law bear historical significance to the law of the English soil, however, it must stated that the Indian Judiciary extensively refers to English cases in deciding cases relating to copyright".[16]

Actuality, not just the judiciary but even the legislature extensively borrowed from British laws and foreign Constitutions while drafting the Constitution of India. At this juncture, the noble words of Dr. Ambedkar, Chairman, Constituent Assembly can be recalled, when the Draft Constitution was being described as 'lacking in originality' and a copy of the Government of India Act, 1935 and other Constitutions. He stated that:

> "As to the accusation that the Draft Constitution has reproduced a good part of the provisions of the Government of India Act, 1935, I make no apologies. There is nothing to be ashamed of in borrowing. It

15. As referred in Law if Copyright & Industrial Designs, P. Naraynan, 7, Eastern Law House, IInd Edn., 1995.
16. *J.N. Bagga Vs. All India Reporter Limited*, AIR Bom. 302(308).

involves no plagiarism. Nobody holds any rights in fundamental ideas of a Constitution".[17]

We share the similar view as that of the great architect of the Constitution and we must consider that settled laws as well, not for saving time and labour, but for learning from the erudite views of our predecessor officers of legal standing, whether they be Indian or Foreign for even in delivering a judgment, the judge relies on the previous body of knowledge where such 'knowledge' comes from the public domain of settled principles of law grounded in case laws.

Furthermore, the jurisprudential foundations of the position of copyright were internationally sensitive and where no precedent existed, it was considered wise to affirm the view of a Court of a foreign nation. This was a matter relating to the copyrightability of case law reported as to whether the legal protection was wide to cover entire report itself or was limited to parts of it such as headnotes, marginal notes, etc.[18] Since judgments happen to be in the public domain[19] vide section 17 and section 52 of the Indian Copyright Act, 1957. The Court had referred to the English case of *Sweet Vs. Benning*[20] which decided the same facts and situation but on the English soil and read the dictum of that decision in this case before it. However, the 1957 Act has introduced a number of new provisions also.

In real sense of the term the first 'independent' statute of India was the Copyright Act of 1957 which kick started the modern copyright law in conformity with the Berne and the Universal Copyright Convention. The Act is both a substantive as well as procedural in nature and provided for legal remedies to enforce the right. Thus, it can be drawn that any country wishing to stimulate or inspire its own authors, composers or artists and thus augment its cultural heritage, must provide for effective copyright protection.[21]

---

17. CAD Volume IV.
18. *N.T. Raghunathan Vs. All India Reported Limited*, AIR 1971, Bom. 48(51).
19. *Eastern Book Company Vs. Navin J. Desai*, AIR 2001 DEL 185: Anu Tiwary & Shruti S. Rajan, Proprietary Rights or Common Property? The Dilemmas of Copyright Protection if Case Law Reporters, Vol. II, JIPR 33 (39), January, 2006.
20. (1855) 139 ALL ER 838.
21. S. Alikhan, 'The Role of the Berne Convention in the Promotion of Cultural Creativity and Development: Recent Copyright Legislation in Developing Countries', *Journal of the Indian Law Institute* 28, (1986), 423 (429-430).

On the first hand, it gives the definition of words to be understood in copyright parlance such as an 'author' would not be merely an author of a literary piece for the purposes of copyright but an author, as understood in copyright parlance is one who is the creator of the work. Similarly other terms such as 'reproduction', 'artistic work', 'work', 'reprography', etc. has been ascertained a definite connotation and scope, to be understood within the parameters of copyright coinage. It further defines the various categories of copyrighted works[22] and spells out the exclusive rights which constitute copyright in such different categories of copyrighted works[23], including term of copyright, such as literary, dramatic work, artistic work, sound recording, etc.

AMENDMENTS

Due to the global problem of piracy caused by the advanced technology the Berne and United Copyright Conventions were revised in 1971 at Paris, special concessions were drawn in favour of the developing countries for the larger interests of the public to have access to foreign works. Thus, to make the Indian Law at par with international one the Copyright Amendment Act, 1983 came in operation in conformity with the international developments as India is party to it.

However, the above amendment failed to cope up with the challenges of piracy which was the need of the hour and consequently to combat the new issues of emerging technological advancement, the amendment Act of 1984 was passed. It was the first initiatives of the government to recognise piracy as a grave threat to copyright industries of billions.

After this the Copyright Act has been amended several times i.e. 1992, 1994 and finally in 1999 to counter the challenges thrown by the technological advancement, comply the TRIPs requirements, to prevent the piracy-related problems and regulate the cases of infringement of copyright of domestic as well as foreign creations.

22. Section 2 of Indian Copyright Act, 1957.
23. Section 14 of Indian Copyright Act, 1957.

The amendments of Copyright Act, 1957 are discussed in details under the following heads:

Indian Copyright Law and Amendment Act, 1983

India is a member of the Berne Convention and the United Copyright Convention. The Copyright Act, 1957 conforms to these two conventions but both the convections were revised at Paris in the year 1971 enabling developing countries to grant compulsory licences for translation and reproductions of works of foreign origin, required for the purpose of research or teaching or for the purposes of systematic instructional activities, if these rights could not be obtained on freely negotiated terms and conditions enabling their publications or ensuring their availability at prices reasonable in their context, the object of the international community shall not be feasible. In persuasion of the international development the amendments of Indian Copyright law was also effected in order to avail these benefits. Provisions are also made for publication of unpublished works where the author is either dead or unknown, as the owner of the copyright cannot be traced. Further, the Copyright Board has been empowered to decide disputes arising out of such assignment which may extend to permitting the author to withdraw from the assignment. Broadcasting authorities are now permitted to translate foreign works for broadcasting for the purpose of systematic instrumental activities. Provisions have also been made for copyright in lectures, address, etc. delivered in public and for the publication of the entries made in copyright register.[24]

Indian Copyright Law and Amendment Act, 1984

After few months to the Copyright Amendment Act, 1983, more remarkable technological challenges appeared before the owners or authors and to cope up with those challenges once again parliamentary amendment was made to the Act of 1957. This amendment was also to make the Indian copyright laws at par with the international copyright laws. This amendment was related to inclusion of video film, introduction of duplication equipment, protection of computer programme, empower the

24. The object of the Copyright (Amendment) Act, 1983.

police to search without warrant, enhancement of punishment and declaration of the infringement of copyright and related rights as an economic offence, etc.

Indian Copyright Law and Amendment Bill (Cess) 1992

A Bill in the name of 'The Copyright Cess Bill, 1992' was introduced for the purpose of imposing a levy and collection of a cess on copying equipment and for the transfer of them to the owners of rights. The bill was not passed by the parliament and subsequently lapsed.

Indian Copyright Law and Amendment Act, 1992

A very small but important amendment was made by the parliament in the year 1992 by which the term of the copyright was extended for a period of ten years which raised the term of copyright protection and total period of copyright become life plus 60 years in general.

Indian Copyright Law and Amendment Act, 1994

This amendment was the major amendment of the Copyright Act, 1957. This amendment was to bring the Indian Copyright law in conformity with TRIPs agreement. This amendment brought lots of changes in the main Act. It changes the definition of the term 'adaptation' and 'author' in terms of cinematograph film, reconstitution of 'Copyright Board' and its power, changes made in the rights of the owner of the copyright and the assignments and licences of the copyright, brought 'Copyright Societies' in place of Performing Rights Societies, introduction of the 'special rights to performers', 'Broadcasting rights', identifying the act not constituting the infringements, introduction of 'author's special rights', changes in offences relating to use of infringing copy of a computer programme and changes in the rule-making powers of the Central Government.

Indian Copyright Law and Amendment Act, 1999

The Amendment in the year 1999 was also to conform to the principles of TRIPs agreement in India. This amendment was mainly related to some sections like sections 38, 40A, 42A and 52, etc. Under these sections parliament brought certain changes to cope with the changes brought throughout the world by the TRIPs agreement. The performer rights that were protected for 25 years previously, extended to 50 years in this amendment. Second important amendment was the power of the Central Government to apply Chapter-VIII of the Act to broadcasting organisations and performers in certain other countries, has been inserted by this amendment of Copyright Act. On the same platform if it appears to the Central Government that a foreign country does not give or has not undertaken to give adequate protection to rights of broadcasting organisations or performers, the Central Government may, by order published in the Official Gazette, direct that such of the provisions of this Act shall not apply to broadcasting organisations or performers.

Indian Copyright Law and Amendment Act, 2012

After a decade of last amendment **in** the year 1999 and lapse of time coupled with scientific, electronic and digital development in the field of literary work and in conformity with WIPO Copyright Treaty and WIPO, present Copyright Amendment Bill, 2010 was introduced in the Rajya Sabha by the Minister of Human Resource Development Shri Kapil Sibal on April 19, 2010 which was referred to the Department related Standing Committee on HRD under the Chairmanship of Shri Oscar Fernandez, which was finally passed from the Rajya Sabha on 17th May, 2012 and thereafter passed from the Lok Sabha on 22th May, 2012 after a long wait for about 2 years.

The Bill has proposed lot of amendments considering the abovementioned factors and to catch the momentum of international nature but following are the most remarkable and important amendments which have been incorporated **in** the said Act which will certainly encourage literary works.

- Three important definitions 'commercial rental', 'Rights Management Information' and 'Visual Recording' have been incorporated for the first time and existing definition of 'author', (cinematograph film', 'Communication to the public', infringing copy', 'performer' and ' joint/authorship' have been amended to cope with the change of the time;
- The author of a work to be the first owner of copyright which empowers the author with the right

of reproduction of a literary or dramatic work, or computer programme or artistic work;

- The definition of 'copyright' also includes artistic work, cinematograph films and sound recording to be saved in the electronic form;
- In case of the cinematographic films the Producer and Principal Director shall be the joint first owner of the copyright. Term of copyright for the Principal Director will be 70 years and for the Producer it will be 60 years;
- Recognized organization working for the disabled may apply to the Copyright Board for compulsory licensing of any copyrighted works for the benefit of the disabled.
- System of registration of Copyright Societies by authors and other owners has been introduced in order to protect the interest of the author and the convenience of the people seeking licenses.
- Special arrangements have been made for those whose work is used in films or sound recording such as Lyricists or Composed. Right to get royalties from such work, when used in media other than films or sound recording, shall rest with the creator of the work and can only be assigned to heirs or Copyright Societies which act in their interests.
- Production of copyrighted work in special formats like Braille, for the use of disabled without infringing copyright has been introduced;
- A list of activities which does not constitute infringement of copyright has been included which excludes copying of computer programme and includes reporting of current events and non-commercial libraries; and
- A higher penalty of imprisonment upto 2 years has been incorporated for any person who infringes a technological measures applied for protecting rights in the law.

The analysis of the Law relating to Copyrights in the light of the TRIPs agreement, 1994 as it forms the base, has set the standards concerning the availability, scope and use of Intellectual Property Rights. It provides the parameters for the range of works that fall within the copyright regime along with the rights that can be claimed by the copyright owner and stipulates the term of protection and the limitations and exceptions in exercising these rights.[25] The Indian Copyright law is not beyond the reach of the policies and principles adopted in the TRIPs agreement. The above amendments of the Indian copyright law were made firstly, to keep the Indian copyright law on the same footage as the international copyright law and secondly, to protect the intellectual property from flouting by the use of modern mechanism developed due to the technological advancement of the time. It not only checks the technological gap but also tried to enforce the treaty obligations by honouring its international commitments in furtherance of Article 253 of the Indian Constitution. The present Copyright Law, subsequent to the 1999 Amendments finds itself in complete compliance with TRIPs and other international instrumental compliance.

SUBJECT MATTER OF PROTECTION

Now-a-day the subject matter of protection of Copyright is same throughout the globe because copyright is become of international nature and due to advancement of technology any one can violate the rights of others from any part of the world. As per different sub-sections of section 2 of Copyright Act, 1957 and judicial interpretations from time to time many matters are eligible to get the protection. Analysing all the classifications and categorizations of the works as provided under different sub-Sections of Section 2 of the Copyright Act, 1957 and taking reference from the judicial views of different High Courts and the Supreme Court of India, the following heads of copyrighted and related works will enjoy the copyright protection under the current uptodate amended legislation:

- Literacy works;
- Dramatic works;
- Musical works;

25. Articles 9 to 14 of TRIPS agreement, 1994.

- Artistic work including sculpture, painting, engraving, architect and all works where artistic craftsmanship is involved;[26]
- Cinematograph film;
- Sound recording;
- Literary, dramatic works or musical works in the form of computer programming or computer generated programme including computer software;
- Adaptation, Translation and Reproduction of work;
- Creating unpublished works;[27]
- Foreign works including the works of International Organisation;
- Literary works such as poems, articles, works of fiction, factual works such as encyclopedias as dictionaries, etc.;
- Thus, question papers set for the examination;[28]
- Research theses and dissertations prepared by students;[29]
- Compilation of a book on household and accounts and domestic arithmetic;[30]
- School textbooks;[31]
- Guide books;[32]
- Dictionary;[33]
- A book of scientific questions and answers;[34]
- Questionnaire for collecting statistical information;[35]
- Head notes of a judgment;[36]
- Lecture notes have all come under the class of literary works entitles for copyright protection;
- Musical work such as songs operas, instrumental music, etc.;

---

26. Section 2(c) of Indian Copyright Act, 1957.
27. Copyright is the protection of expression and thus protection starts as soon as the works is given a shape by giving expression.
28. *Jagdish Prasad Vs. Parmeshwar Prasad*, AIR 1966 Pat. 33.
29. *Fatesh Singh Mehta Vs. Singhal*, AIR 1990 Raj. 8(14).
30. *Manohar Lal Gupta Vs. State of Haryana* (1977) 79 Punj. LR 181 (Del).
31. *Shaikh Ghafoor Bakhsh and Sons Vs. Jwala Prasad Singhal*, AIR 1921 ALL 95.
32. *E.M. Foster Vs. A.M. Parasuram*, AIR 1964 M ad. 331.
33. *Givinddan Vs. Gopalkrishnan*, AIR 1955 Mad. 319.
34. *Joral Vs. Houlston* (1857) 3 Kay & J 708.
35. *Interfirm Comparison (Australia) Pty Ltd. Vs. Law Society of New South Wales* (1977) RPC 149.
36. *N.T. Raghunathan Vs. All India Reporter*, AIR 1971 Bom. 48.

- Works of art and architecture;
- Photographs, technical drawings, motion picture (Cinematograph film), computer programme, etc.; and
- Live performance of a drama fixed in a storage devise such as a compact disk etc.

In *Blackwood Vs. Parasuraman*[37], Madras High Court held that:

> "translation of literary work is itself a literary work and is entitled to copyright protection; reproduction of publication of translation without consent or license of the owner of copyright in the original would amount to infringement."

Originality

The basic premise to be protected by copyright is originality. The work should be original and not infringing any other's copyrighted material to enjoy one's copyright status under the Copyright Act. At the same occasion it is submitted that originality does not imply literary merit or accuracy standing in the same manner as 'an artistic work is protected even if it lacks artistic quality'.[38] The copyright criteria is that the work should not constitute unauthorised reproduction from another existing source in substantial terms so as to constitute infringement as per provision of the Act,[39] obviously considering the concessions in favour of public interest[40] and the constitutional guarantee of freedom of speech and expression.

RIGHTS BESTOW BY THE INDIAN COPYRIGHT ACT, 1957

Copyright is a bundle of rights arising out of statute itself and judicial interpretations of copyright and related laws. It confers a set of rights upon the authors or creators in order to protect their moral, economic and material interests:

---

37. AIR 1959 Mad. 410.
38. Section 2(c)(i) of the Indian Copyright Act, 1957.
39. Section 51 of the Indian Copyright Act, 1957.
40. Section 52 of the Indian Copyright Act, 1957.

Economic Rights

The copyright subsists in original literary, dramatic, musical and artistic works; cinematographs films and sound recordings.[41] The authors of copyright in the aforesaid works enjoy economic rights.[42] The rights are mainly, in respect of literary, dramatic and musical works, other than computer program, to reproduce the work in any material form including the storing of it in any medium by electronic means, to issue copies of the work to the public, to perform the work in public or communicating it to the public, to make any cinematograph film or sound recording in respect of the work and to make any translation or adaptation of the work.[43] In the case of computer program, the author enjoys in addition to the aforesaid rights, the right to sell or give on hire or offer for sale or hire any copy of the computer program regardless, whether such copy has been sold or given on hire on earlier occasions.[44] In the case of an artistic work, the rights available to an author include the right to reproduce the work in any material form including depiction in three dimensions of a two dimensional work or in two dimensions of a three dimensional work, to communicate or issues copies of the work to the public, to include the work in any cinematograph work and to make any adaptation of the work.[45] In the case of cinematograph film, the author enjoys right to make a copy of the film including a photograph of any image forming part thereof, to sell or give on hire or offer for sale or hire, any copy of the film, and to communicate the film to the public.[46]These rights are similarly available to the author of sound recording.[47] In addition to the aforesaid rights, the author of a painting, sculpture, drawing or of a manuscript of a literary, dramatic or musical work, if he was the first owner of the copyright, shall be entitled to have a right to share in the resale price of such original copy provided that the resale price exceeds rupees ten thousand.[48]

41. Section 13 of the Indian Copyright Act, 1957.
42. Section 14 of the Indian Copyright Act, 1957.
43. Section 14(a) of the Indian Copyright Act, 1957.
44. Section 14(b) of the Indian Copyright Act, 1957.
45. Section 14(c) of the Indian Copyright Act, 1957.
46. Section 14(d) of the Indian Copyright Act, 1957.
47. Section 14(e) of the Indian Copyright Act, 1957.
48. Section 53A of the Indian Copyright Act, 1957.

Copyright is not a single statutory right. It extends multiple rights comprising of a bundle of different rights in the same work. It is seldom that the author of a copyright work himself exploits the work for monetary benefit. It includes all ways and means through which the copyright owner can normally exploit the work. Ordinarily, it is not possible for copyright holder to exploit all the rights. Therefore, it is in his interest that he should transfer his rights by way of assignment or license to those, whose business is to exploit the rights of the creator so that the work enjoys market coverage and the copyright holder secure his fair share of profits for his intellectual, labour, investment and time.

The transfer of the copyright, fully or partially, can be done either by assignment or licensing. Assignment and Licenses are the functional equivalent of 'Lease' and 'Sale' for the transfer of tangible property.[49] Both acts involve economic rights, apart from other rights, of the authors/owners.

Moral Rights

France was the founder of not only the *'droit d'auteur'* or 'moral rights' vested in a copyright but the duration of copyright extending to 50 years after the death of the authors/owners. The Indian statute on the subject recognises 'moral rights' as an inalienable right[50] under the head of the author's 'special rights'. Copyright law in Indian was thus, brought at the same footing with the Berne Convention in conformity with article 6 *bis* of the Berne Convention. Section 57 of the Copyright Act, 1957 protects the author's right of paternity as also the right of integrity. Distortion, mutilation or modification which established to be prejudicial to the author's reputation or honour is actionable.[51]

In case of *Smt. Manu Bhandari Vs. Kala Vikash Pictures Ltd.,*[52] it was observed, in respect of Section 57 of the Copyright Act, 1957:

> "Section 57 is a special provision for the protection of author's moral rights. The object of it is to put the Copyright on a higher footing than normal matters of

49. Joseph Richard Falcon, Managing intellectual Property Rights: The cost of innovation, 6 Duq Bus LJ 241(2004).
50. Though it has been used in the contractual sense.
51. *Amar Nath Sehgal Vs. Union of India,* 117(2005) DLT 717: 2005(30) PTC 253(DEL) 263.
52. AIR 1987 DEL 13(17); *Ganapati Prasad Vs. Paranandi,* AIR 1992 AP 230.

> right, the language of Section 57 is of widest amplitude. It cannot be restricted to literary expressions only. Audio-visual manifestations are also directly covered under it".

Thus, Section 57 of the Copyright Act, 1957 defines the two basic moral rights of an author. These are:

(i) Right of paternity; and

(ii) Right of integrity;[53]

Right of paternity: The right of paternity refers to a right of an author to claim authorship of work and a right to prevent all others from claiming authorship of his work.

Right of integrity: Right of integrity empowers the author to prevent distortion, mutilation or other alterations of his work, or any other action in relation to said work, which would be prejudicial to his honour or reputation.

The proviso to section 57(1) provides that the author shall not have any right to restrain or claim damages in respect of any adaptation of a computer program to which section 52(1)(aa) applies (i.e. reverse engineering of the same). It must be noted that failure to display a work or to display it to the satisfaction of the author shall not be deemed to be an infringement of the rights conferred by this section.[54] The legal representatives of the author may exercise the rights conferred upon an author of a work by section 57(1) rather than the right to claim authorship of the work.[55]

Creative expressions are as old as human societies.[56] Copyright and the Related Rights cover protection for the broadest range of innovative works.[57] It provides a framework for the protection of creative works that's expressions fixed in any medium. Copyright by its very nature interfaces with the publishing, photography, computer generated works, entertainment including films, drama, architectural, works of artistic craftsmanship, audio recordings, dance forms, educational, transmission/broadcasting, art including industrial

53. Dalal, Praveen, A work analysing the law pertaining to copyright in India.
54. Explanation to Section 57(1) of the Indian Copyright Act, 1957.
55. Section 57(2) of the Indian Copyright Act, 1957.
56. Intellectual Property, A Powerful Tool for Economic Growth WIPO Publication No. 888, Chapter 6, pp. 190-236.
57. Professor Ganguli, Prabuddha, Advisor, VISION-IPR Relevance of Copyright and Related Rights for SMEs.

drawing, sculpture, painting, lectures, etc. There is thus, copyright of the creators in literary, dramatic, musical and artistic works and neighbouring rights or related rights for those who produces sound recordings, films, broadcasts, cable casts and published editions.

Fundamental to copyright are the recognition of the creator and the owner of the work. Hence, documentation and establishment of the author, the time and place of creation of the work, the nature of the creative work and the circumstances under which the work is created are of paramount importance. Based on these parameters, the work qualifies for a copyright or neighbouring and related rights (in some texts also defined as entrepreneurial copyrights). Accordingly, the copyright law has provisions for ownership, nature of the right, the duration of the right and scope of monopoly.[58]

For example, it is reported that an author and a government-owned publisher have settled their copyright infringement litigation, the Vietnam investment Review has reported. ***Nguyen Thi Thu Hue,*** an author of popular love stories had sued the Literature Publishing House, a government-owned company for publishing 10 of her stories without her permission or paying her for them.[59]

In India, the case of *Amar Nath Sehgal Vs. Union of India,*[60] is illustrative and leading in the contention of moral rights. In the present case, the Plaintiff Amar Nath Sehgal received a proposal in 1957 from the Government of India to create a bronze mural for display in the Vigyan Bhawan, to which he readily agreed, the plaintiff produces a bronze mural sculpture which was placed at the entrance of Vigyan Bhawan and in the words of the learned Judge:

> "it symbolised a delicate balance between culture and material aspects in national perspective and science of rural and modern India being its theme".

The mural was pulled down and consigned to the store room belonging to the Union of India in the year 1979. This act of destruction was established to be without the permission,

58. Intellectual Property by W.R. Cornish, Universal Law Publishing Co Pvt Ltd, Delhi, India, 3rd ed., 1st Indian Reprint 2001, pp. 330-31.
59. Managing Intellectual Property, p. 6, March 2003.
60. 2002 IV AD (DEL) 349; 2002(2) ARBLR 130 (DEL) 97; (2002) DLT 439; 2002 (63) DRJ 558.

consent or authorization of the plaintiff. As a result, the plaintiff moved to the Court under Section 57 of the Copyright Act, 1957. Union of India defended the suit by urging that it was the owner of mural and had a right to consign the same to a store room. It further contended that the Plaintiff was paid the price for the work. Defence of limitation was also set-up. It was averred that the mural was removed in the year 1979 and the suit being filed after 13 years which attracting the Limitation Act. In response, the plaintiff stated that since suit was one for violation of his moral rights which would last for his lifetime and having not waived the same, suit could not be said to be barred be limitation. Unlike other forms of IPR, copyright subsists as soon as the work is created and fixed in a tangible medium and the moral and other rights begins from that very date of bringing the idea into creative existence.

Publication

'Publication' under the Copyright Act has been defined as making a work available to the public by issue of copies or communicating the work to the public. In order that there shall be an 'issue of work', not only the copies are to be made but the copies must be issued to the public, more clearly, issue for the purposes of sale is not essential, although no doubt, its reproductions are issued for such a purpose which would amount to a publication of work.[61]

The question, whether the copies of the work or the record have been issued to the public in sufficient quantities, will, in each case, depend upon its own facts and circumstances and the nature of the work. It is a question of fact and can be decided by the Copyright Board under the jurisdiction conferred upon it by virtue of the provision of the copyright law.[62]

'Publication' refers to the circumstances under which a work ceases to fall within the class of unpublished work and becomes a published work. A work cannot be orally published. There can be no publication of a literary, dramatic, musical or artistic work, or of record, if they exist in a single copy thereof. To constitute

61. *White Vs. Geroch*, (1819) 2 B & Ald 298 as reff in Lal's, Commentary on the Copyright, 1957 (Act 14 of 1957) with the Copyright Rules, 1958 & Neighbouring Rights, 4th Edn., Delhi Law House at p. 83.
62. Section 11 f the Copyright Act, 1957.

publication, not only the copies of the work or record must be made but they must be issued to the public for any purposes whatsoever, whether for sale or for any other purposes.[63] A private circulation of copies does not amount to publication.[64] Communication of the work can take place when the work is heard, seen or otherwise enjoyed.[65] Copyright, neighbouring rights and related rights are therefore of immense significance to all sectors including the Small and Medium Size Enterprises (SMEs) involved in traditional businesses and electronic businesses of creative arts, crafts, technologies.

Copyright Office and Registration

Copyright in India arises as soon as the work is 'fixed' in a tangible medium. The Nation adheres to the principles of 'automatic' protection and registration of works is not mandatory to avail the protection of copyright. The Act has established a Copyright Office[66] under the immediate control of the Registrar of Copyrights, an administrative authority who shall act under the superintendence and directions of the Central Government. Such a facility exists at the Copyright Office at New Delhi or other regional offices where the Registrar of Copyrights, headed by the Registrar of Copyright maintained to provide registration for all types of works. There exists a set procedure for registration of a work under the Copyright Rules, 1958 which has been suitably amended from time to time and registration is provided for both published and unpublished works.[67]

However, registration of works is not a condition precedent to avail copyright protection. Registration serves as a *prima facie*

---

63. *White Vs. Geroch,* (1819) 2 B & Ald 298 as *Novello Vs. Ludlow* (1952) 12 CB 177 as reference in Lal's Commentary on the Copyright, 1957 (Act 14 of 1957) with the Copyright Rules, 1958 and Neighbouring Rights, 4th Edn., Delhi Law House at p. 83. T.R. Srinivasa Iyengar, The Copyright Act, 1957, 36, 5th Edn, Law Book Company, 1985.
64. *Prince Albert Vs. Strange,* (1894) 1 M&G 25 as reference in T.R. Srinivasa Iyengar, *The Copyright Act, 1957,* 36 5th Edn., Law Book Company, 1985.
65. Ashwani Kumar Bansal, Economic Rights of the Copyright owner with special reference to the Right to Communication in Law of Copyright: From Gutenberg's Invention to Internet, 45, Prof. A.K. Koul, V.K. Ahuja eds., Faculty of Law , University of Delhi, 2001.
66. Section 9 of Indian Copyright Act, 1957.
67. Chapter X of the Indian Copyright Act, 1957 and Form IV of Copyright Rules are relevant for the registration process.

evidence of copyright ownership in the Court of Law. In the case of *Asian Paints (I) Ltd. Vs. Jaikishan Paints & Allied Products*,[68] the High Court of Bombay has observed:

> "Registration under the Copyright Act is optional and not compulsory. Registration is not necessary to claim a copyright. Registration under the Copyright Act merely raises a *prima facie* presumption in respect of the particulars entered in the Register of Copyright. The presumption is however not conclusive. The Copyright subsists as soon as the work is created and given a material form even if it is not registered".

In the case of *International Association of Lions Clubs Vs. National Association of Indian Lions*,[69] the same Court held that registration thereof, is only a *prima facie* evidence of a ownership of such a Copyright and Design.

Non-Compulsory Registration

Section 44 of the Copyright Act, 1957 provides for registration of a work in which copyright subsists but it is not necessary to claim copyright. Copyright sunbursts as soon as the work is created and given a material form.[70]

In *R.G. Anand's Case*,[71] the Supreme Court rejected a contrary view which had been taken by a Division Bench of the Madhya Pradesh High Court terming it as being 'wrongly decided'. It was the case of *Mishra Bandhu Karyalaya Vs. Section Koshal*[72] in which the High Court held that:

> "under the Act of 1957, the registration of the work with the Registrar of Copyright is a condition precedent for acquiring copyright in respect of it, and that the author has no right or remedy unless the work is registered."

The Apex Court held to the contrary, that registration of works is not mandatory for availing copyright protection.[73] Therefore, through the catena of cases, the Courts in India have upheld the principle of 'automatic protection' and that registration in not a condition prerequisite for availing copyright

68. 2002 (6) Bom CR 1: (2002) 4 Bom LR 941: 2002(4) MAH LJ 536.
69. 2006 (33) PTC 79 (BOM) 91.
70. Marihuana, P., *'Law of Copyright and Industrial Design'*, 3rd edition.
71. AIR 1978 SC 1613.
72. AIR 1970 MP 261.
73. AIR 1978 SC 1613.

protection which inheres in the work upon its creation from the mind and manifestation in a tangible medium. Section 45 of the Copyright Act, 1957 read with Rule 16 of The Copyright Rules, 1958 prescribes detailed procedure for registration of copyright in India.[74] The copyright is conferred only upon authors or those who are natural person form whom the work has originated, or the authors may be legal persons to whom copyright has been assigned in accordance with law, by the authors from whom the work had originated.[75]

Copyright Board

The Copyright Act of India provides dual legal machinery to the right holders for enforcing their rights. The enforcement is possible through (1) the Copyright Bard, and (2) the Courts.[76]

The Act has established a quasi-judicial body called the Copyright Board[77]entrusted with the task of adjudication of disputes pertaining to copyright registration, assignment of copyright, grant of licenses in respect of works withheld from public, unpublished Indian works, production and publication of translations and works for certain specified purposes. It also hears cases in other miscellaneous matter instituted before it under the Copyright Act, 1957.[78] The Registrar of Copyrights is to perform the secretarial functions of the Board and thus has been statutorily designated as the Secretary of the Copyright Board[79] who is duty bound to perform under the direction and control of the Chairman of the Copyright Board.

Copyright Board is a quasi-judicial body constituted by the Central Government. The constitution of the Board has been clearly laid down in the Copyright Act, 1957. The Board shall consist of a Chairman and other members. The person to be appointed as a Chairman of the Copyright Board should be

---

74. Dr. M.K. Bhandari, Lae Relating to Intellectual Property Rights, 38, Central Law Publications, Ist Edn., 2006.
75. *Camlin Pvt. Ltd. Vs. National Pencils Industries*, 96 (2002) DLT 8.
76. Committee Report (Chapter II), Copyright Piracy in India, available at Manupatra.
77. Section 11 of Indian Copyright Act, 1957. An order made under section 3 of the Act is quasi-judicial in nature. Also *Gramophone Company of India Ltd. Vs. Birendra Bahadur Pandey*, AIR 1984 SC 667 point 40 of the last page.
78. http:/ / www.copyright.gov.in/ mainboard.asp
79. http:/ / www.copyright.gov.in/ cpr.asp

qualified to hold the office of a judge of a High Court or could be holding such position or must have held. The members as aforesaid shall be eligible for reappointment. The Copyright Board shall be deemed to be a Civil Court for the purpose of sections 345 and 346 of the Code of Criminal Procedure, 1973 and all proceedings before the Board shall be deemed to be judicial proceedings within the meaning of sections 193 and 228 of the Indian Penal Code, 1860.[80]

As regards the power and procedure of the Copyright Board, it is pertinent to note that the Board is autonomous as in the sense that it shall have the power to regulate its own procedure including the fixing of places and times of its sitting.[81] Further, it has been expressly provided that the Board shall hear any proceeding instituted before it under this Act within the zone in which, at the time of the institution of the proceeding, the person instituting the proceeding actually and voluntarily resides or carries on business or personally works for gain.[82] The disputes which the Board is empowered to decide shall be through a Bench comprising of not less than three members constituted by the Chairman of the Board from amongst its members. In exceptional cases which involve decision on any matter of importance, the matter can be referred by the Chairman to a Special Bench comprising of five members. The Act also stipulates the dictate that 'no person shall be a judge of his own cause or decide a matter in which he has personal interest',[83] by application of which no member of the Copyright Board shall take part in any proceedings in which he has a personal interest.

The Board comprises of people with legal standing since copyright itself is a specialized branch of Intellectual Property Law. The terms and conditions of service of the Chairman are prescribed in Rule 3 of the Copyright Rules, 1958. Moreover, the Board has been entrusted with the powers of a Civil Court[84] and its proceedings are deemed to be judicial proceedings. The Board also enjoys appellate jurisdiction by virtue of section 72(1) of the Copyright Act, 1957. The decisions of the Copyright Board can be

---

80. Section 12(7) of the Indian Copyright Act , 1957.
81. Section 12(1) of the Indian Copyright Act, 1957.
82. Proviso to section 12(1) of the Indian Copyright Act, 1957.
83. Section 12(5) of the Indian Copyright Act, 1957.
84. Section 12(7) of Indian Copyright Act, 1957.

challenged in the Higher Courts.[85] As per explanation to section 12 of the Indian Copyright Act, 1957 read with Section 15 of the States Reorganisation Act, 1956, India has been divided into five zones to ascertain the jurisdiction of the Copyright Board.[86]

Copyright Society

The Copyright Society is such a legal entity which safeguards the interests of owners of the work in which a copyright subsists.[87] Chapter VII of the Copyright Act (Sections 33 to 36A) deals with the Copyright Societies. The Copyright (Amendment) Act, 1994 made the working of Performing Rights Societies wider in respect of rights relating to granting licences for the performance in India.[88]

The Copyright Society is empowered to do the following acts in furtherance of administration of copyrights in India:

(i) To issue licenses under section 30, in respect of any rights under this Act;
(ii) To collect fees in pursuance of such licences;
(iii) To distribute such fees among owners of rights after making deductions for its own expenses;
(iv) To pay remuneration to individual copyright owners;
(v) To submit returns and reports to the Registrar of Copyrights; and
(vi) To perform any other functions consistent with the provisions of section 35 of the Act.

Limitations on Copyright

There are three types of limitation identifiable in the Copyright statute which can be broadly classified under the heads of limited duration of copyright, permitted uses and non-voluntary licenses (statutory or compulsory licenses). The Act intends to advance the welfare of the society by disseminating

---

85. Section 72(2) of Indian Copyright Act, 1957.
86. In this sub-section 'Zone' means a zone specified in section 15 of the States Reconstructions Act, 1956 (37 of 1956).
87. B.L. Waddhera, Law Relating to Patent, Trademarks, Copyrights, Designs and Geographical Indications, 420, Universal Law Publishing Co., 3rd ed., 2004.
88. D.P. Mittal, Law Relating to Copyright, Patents and Trademark and GATT, 235, Taxman Allied Services (P.) Ltd.

ideas, schemes, etc. to maximize availability of literature, music, arts or the technological knowledge to the public.[89]

In the case of *Penguin Books Ltd. Vs. M/s India Book Distributors,*[90] Justice Rohtagi observed:

> "Copyright is a property right, throughout the world retarded as a form of property worthy of special protection in ultimate public interest. The law starts from a premise that protection must be as long as broad possible and should provide only those expectations, limitations which are essential in public interest."

Therefore, it is imperative that the law must be prepared to respond in order to ensure both a continued creation of intellectual and cultural works and the availability of such works to the public.[91] The twin goal seeks to achieve this through a set of statutory limitations in public interest. The practice to encourage the public access to works under Indian copyright law is essentially managed by two methods: copyright licensing and extensive provisions on exceptions to copyright protection. Interestingly, the Indian Copyright Act rejects the terminology of 'exceptions', instead making reference to acts that are "not to be infringement of copyright".[92]

Duration of Copyright

The Berne Convention provides for a minimum terms which applied uniformly to all signatory nations which is 50 years after the life terms of the author, however, the signatories are free to increase the terms of protection, but not to reduce less than the agreed international consensus. For example, in Europe and United States, the term of protection is life plus seventy years. Copyright in India, subsists for a period of 25 to 60 years, depending upon the nature of the work.[93] The Act provides a copyright for works whether published or unpublished for a lengthy though limited period of 60 years excluding the life of the author which shall commence to run after the death of the

---

89. *K. Kumari Vs. Muppala Ranganayakamma*, 1987 (2) ALT 699 (709).
90. AIR 1985 DEL 29(35).
91. *K. Kumari Vs. Muppala Ranganayakamma*, 1987 (2) ALT 699 (710).
92. Dr. Mira T. Sundararajan, Digital Learning in India: Problems and Prospects, available at http://cyber.law.harvard.edu/ home/dl_india.
93. Poorva Chothani, Managing Copyright in the Digital Era, available at http://www.managingip.comarticle.aspx?

author.[94] The municipal statute provides a longer term of 60 years *post mortem auctoris* which is 10 years more than the international requirement under the Berne or the TRIPs agreement. However, in cases where the work falls under the category of a cinematograph film, sound recording, photograph, posthumous publications, anonymous organisations, the 60 years period is counted from the date of publication.

Permitted Applications

Indian Copyright law specifies permissible uses under Section 52 of Copyright Act, 1957. This happens to be the longest section of the Copyright Act and refers to a set of exceptions to copyright law. These provisions enable legitimate use of new copyrighted works for the educational, scientific, cultural advancement of the society which is the implied objective of copyrights law as could be derived from the first copyright law of this country.[95] The permitted applications under the aforesaid section can be broadly classified as acts constituting 'fair dealing' and acts, 'other than fair dealing' which do not amount to infringement of copyright.

Fair Dealing

Fair dealing is permitted for private use including for the purpose of educational study or research[96] or criticism[97]or review.[98] Such a 'fair dealing' provisions also extends to reproduce literary, dramatic, musical or artistic work for the purposes of reporting current events in a newspaper, magazine or similar periodical[99] or by broadcast[100] or even in a cinematograph film or by means of photographs[101] or using

94. The term of Copyright protection has increased with the Amendments to the Copyright Act in 1992 before which is the Berne requirement of 50 years.
95. T.C. James, Copyright Law of India and the Academic Community, Vol. 9, JIPR 207(211), May 2004.
96. Section 52(a)(i) of the Indian Copyright Act, 1957 as substitute by Act 38 of 1994, section 17 (w.e.f. 10-05-1995).
97. In the US it is called 'Parody'.
98. Section 52(a)(ii) of the Indian Copyright Act, 1957.
99. Section 52(b)(i) of the Indian Copyright Act, 1957.
100. The word 'broadcast' has been substituted by Act 23 of 1983, section 2, for "radio-diffusion" (w.e.f. 09-08-1984).
101. Section 52(b)(ii) of the Indian Copyright Act, 1957.

excerpts of a performance or of a broadcast in the reporting of current events or for *bona-fide* review, teaching or research.[102] Further, it has been inserted through an amendment in 1994 that the act of making copies or adaptation or a computer programme by the lawful possessor of such copy constitutes fair use if the use is to utilize the programme for the purpose for which it was supplied or as a means to offer temporary protection against loss, destruction or damage of the programme.

In the case of *Civic Chandran Vs. Ammini Amma,*[103] the court observed:

> "The terms 'fair dealing' has been not defined as such in the Act. But section 52(1)(a) and (b) specifically refers to 'fair dealing' of the work and not to reproduction of the work. Accordingly, it may be reasonable to hold that the re-production of the whole work or a substantial portion of it as such will alone be permitted even as 'fair dealing'. Further the court held that 'in a case like the one on hand, court will have to take into inconsideration; (1) the quantum and value of the matter taken in relation to the comments or criticism; (2) the purpose for which it is taken; and (3) the likelihood of competition between the two works' similar to the four factor test of the U.S. fair use doctrine."

The same court quoting Denning L.J. held that—

> "It is impossible to define what is 'fair dealing'. It must be a question of degree. The 'Fair Dealing' provisions can be said to reflect the notions which were instrumental in shaping the Berne Three-Step-Test".

In fact, *Senftleben*[104]opines that in so far as the making of quotations for criticism and review and the reporting of current events are concerned, the fair dealing provisions automatically constitute a special case in sense of the three-step test. Fair dealing is not a license to violate the exclusive right of the copyright owner. One cannot copy from another and claim protection under the garb of fair dealing. Simply giving the credit

---

102. Section 39(b) of the Indian Copyright Act, 1957 as substituted by Act 38 of 1994, section 15 (w.e.f. 10-05-1995).

103. 1996 PTC 670 (Ker HC) 675-77.

104. Martin Senftleben, Copyright, Limitations and Three-Step Test—An Analysis of the Three Step Test in International And EC Copyright Law, 165, Prof. P. Bernt Hugenholtz ed., Kluwer Law International, 2004.

to the original author would not help either. Even where the user has copied a substantial part of the work, it would be considered as 'fair' and 'legitimate' since copyright protection requires reseanable skill and labour to reach the threshold of originality and quality for protection. Nevertheless, in the case of fair dealing, the British concepts somewhat narrower than the US doctrine of 'fair use' which may not be entirely relevant to the Indian copyright statute.[105] Notwithstanding, there has been applicability of 'fair use' in at least one case law.

In one case before the High Court of Andhra Pradesh, involving an appeal where the trial court had held that the film was an adaptation of the novel and since copyright permission had not been obtained, the act constituted piracy. The Court read the four-factor-test as an important criteria in adjudging where the cinematographic film infringes the copyrighted literary work and arrived at the conclusion that if the person, infringing the copyrighted work obtains, a direct pecuniary benefit from the use of the copy in its stream of commerce, then it would be considered to be an unfair use for profit.[106]

Assignment

Provision relating to assignment is located under section 18 of the Copyright Act and Section 19, 19A relates to the modes of assignment. The Statute stipulates that the owner of the copyright can assign the entire copyright or make the partial assignment of the rights on certain terms and conditions for a limited period or for the whole term of copyright. In order to safeguard the interest of the assignor and the assignee, the Act stipulates that the assignment, which is in the nature of the contract, shall be in writing. Assignment of a copyright is valid only if it is in writing[107] and signed by the assignor or by his duly authorised agent. Prime importance is the fact that the assignment of copyright in any work shall identify such work and shall specify the rights assigned and the duration and territorial extent of such assignment.[108] It is important and in the

105. Dr. Mitra T. Sundararajan, Digital Learning in India: Problems and Prospects, available at http://cyber.law.harvard.edu/home/ dl_india.

106. *K. Kumari Vs. Muppala Ranganayakamma*, 1987 (2) ALT 699 (718).

107. *K.A. Venugopal Setty Vs. Dr. Suryakantha U. Kamath*, AIR 1992, KER 1.

108. Secction 19(2)of the Indian Copyright Act, 1957.

larger interest of the contracting parties in relation to the assignment of the work that they observe the legal stipulation as stated above. In case, they do not follow any reason, be it by positive act or ignorance of law, the period of assignment shall be deemed to be five years from the date of assignment and the territorial extent shall be presumed to be within India.

In the case of *Sunil Agarwal Vs. Kumkum Tandon,*[109] it was observed that Section 18 of the Copyright Act, 1957 confers ownership rights in a copyright on the assignment.

Licensing

The term 'Licence' has been derived from the Latin term *'licentia'* which means 'freedom' or 'liberty'.[110] The Licence does not transfer ownership; it only grants a right to use the licensor's property.[111] Once the license comes to an end the licensee may be subjected to an action for infringement just like the rest of the world.[112] The licensee must remember that the right to use the Copyright is permitted only to the extent described in the license agreement because a license is construed as reserving all other rights.[113]

Sections 30-32B of the Copyright Act, are concerned with provisions related to licensing. Section 30 of the Copyright Act, 1957 empowers the owner of copyright to grant an interest in the right by a license in writing. The section also purports that license can be granted in relation to the copyright which shall vest in a future work and can only take effect once the work comes into existence. A license is granted by the right holder to any person in pursuance of a contract in writing. The contract specifies as to what rights have been licensed and for what duration.

109. 1995 II AD (Del) 627: 1995 (33) DRJ 599.

110. Compact Oxford Dictionary, Thesaurus, and Wordpower Guide (Indian Edn.) as referred in, Gitanjali Mehlwal, Intellectual Property Licensing: Discovering its Facets, Vol. 10, May 2005, 214(214).

111. Intellectual Property Licensing: Discovering its Facets, Gitanjali Mehlwal, JIPR, Vol. 10, May 2005, 214 (215).

112. Intellectual Property Licensing: Discovering its Facets, Gitanjali Mehlwal, JIPR, Vol. 10, May 2005, 214 (216).

113. Intellectual Property Licensing: Discovering its Facets, Gitanjali Mehlwal, JIPR, Vol. 10, May 2005, 214 (217).

The role of copyright is to harmonise the relationship and balance the conflicting interest of the society and the copyright industry/creator at the same time not to lose foresight that the bargain between the authors, the intermediaries and the industries with which copyright is destined to get involved is to make a successful commercial product of intellect and here comes the role of the law to ensure that in getting the works to the public, the entrepreneurs do not indulge in unhealthy market practices nor the belt of the law is tied so tight that legitimate returns on investment cannot be reaped.

Thus for the above reason the provisions for licensing under the Indian Legislation on Copyright can be broadly classified into two category, Voluntary licensing and Compulsory licensing.

Voluntary Licensing

Chapter 6 of Indian Copyright Act, 1957 deals with the licensing of copyrighted work. Licensing ordinarily involves a contractual agreement to exploit the exclusive right which is conferred to the creator of the work by the process of contractual bargaining between the creator and the entity/organisation which shall be responsible in getting the work across to the public. In the process, the author gets his returns from the sales of his work by way of royalty and the responsible entity earns its share of investment from the profits. Indeed, the author has to exercise due care and caution in licensing of his rights to get a fair share of his intellectual efforts and not bent to the bargaining pressure of the entrepreneur.

In the case of *Deshmukh and Co. (Publishers) Pvt. Ltd. Vs. Avinash Vishnu Khandeka,*[114] High Court of Bombay has aptly described the features of a 'Licence' in the context of copyright contracts:

> "The copyright comprises of schedule rights which can be exercised independent of each other. The licence is a personal right which cannot be transferred except in certain circumstances. Licence is a right to do some positive act. Licence is a personal right and creates no more than personal obligation between a licensor and licensee. The licence is generally revocable at the will of the grantor. There are different kinds of licences. A

114. 2006 (2) Bom CR 321; 206 (32) PTC 358 (Bom); 2005 (3) Mah LJ 387.

> Licence may be exclusive or non-exclusive; exclusive licence means a licence which confers on licensor or licensee and persons authorised by him to the exclusion of all other persons (including the owner of the copyright) any right comprised in the copyrighted work. In the case of non-exclusive licence the owner of copyright retains the right to grant licenses to more than one person or to exercise it himself. Licence is a personal right and licensee may not always be entitled to make alternations to the terms. These are broad guidelines."

Compulsory Licensing

The Indian Copyright Act has its scales inclined in favour of access to knowledge and wider diffusion of Indian works. Though, it seeks to protect the rights of the authors in the best possible manner, nevertheless, it has elaborate statutory provisions to encourage public access to works through the system of compulsory licensing. The system comes into operation in the circumstances when the work which has been previously published or performed in public is not available in the market and the owner of the copyright has refused to allow republication, public performance or communication of the work by way of broadcasting. To simplify, in case where the copyright holder has refused to grant the public, the right to access the work, a complain can be filed before the quasi-judicial body, i.e. the Copyright Board.

Compulsory licence is granted to produce and publish a translation of a literary or dramatic work in any language after a period of seven years (three years if the translation is a non-Indian work) for the purpose of teaching, scholarship or research and one year if such a translation is in a language not in any general use in any developed country from the first publication of the work under certain conditions.[115] The royalty paid at the rate prescribed by the Board is required to be kept in the public account of India or such other account which may be claimed by

115. D.P. Mittal, Law Relating to Copyright, Patent and Trademark and GATT, 485, Taxman Allied Services (P.) Ltd.

the copyright owner or his legal heirs, executors or legal representatives at any time.[116]

In the case of *Phonographic Performance Ltd. Vs. Music Broadcast (P) Ltd.,*[117] the learned counsel submitted the provision under Article 27 of the Universal Declaration of Human Rights.[118] It is submitted that compulsory licence is provided to ensure that the members of the public are not deprived of the enjoyment of the copyright work. At the same time, rights of the owner of the copyright cannot be put in jeopardy and the scheme of the Act is that a compulsory licence is granted only when such work is withheld from the public.

Section 31 of the Indian Copyright Act, 1957, also empowers the Board to conduct the necessary enquiry into the complaint with a co-relative duty to hear the owner of the copyright, in furtherance of natural justice principles. If the Board is satisfied upon the facts and circumstances of the particular case that such refusal is not reasonable, then it shall direct the Registrar of Copyrights to grant a license to the complainant to republish the work. However, such a license shall not be issued, by prejudicing the rights of the owner of copyright and towards the end the provision mandates that the compulsory license to republish the work shall be granted to the complainant, after the Board determines among the terms and conditions, the suitable compensation which should be given to the owner of copyright by the complainant and it is only after this, the Registrar of Copyright is empowered to grant the license to the complainant in accordance with the directions of the Copyright Board.

In the case of *Super Cassette Industries Ltd. Vs. Entertainment Network (India) Ltd.,*[119] The Delhi High Court observed:

---

116. Kala Thairani, How Copyright works in Practice-The Copyright Act, 1957 and Judicial Interpretation (A case law study in perspective) 24, Popular Prakashan, 1996.
117. 2004 (29) PTC 282 BOM (286).
118. Article 27 of UDHR:
    (i) Everyone has the right freely to participate in cultural life of the community, to enjoy the arts and to share in scientific advancement and its benefits.
    (ii) Everyone has the right to the protection of the moral and material interests resulting from any scientific, literary or artistic production of which he is the author.
119. AIR 2004 DEL 326 (344).

> "It is clearly incorporated in the language of this section that the case of the complainant for grant of compulsory licence can be considered if the work has been withheld from public and after giving reasonable opportunity to the owner of the copyright, upon holding an enquiry and, arriving at, the conclusion that grounds of refusal are not reasonable. Once the copyright is in the public domain, refusal has to be on reasonable and valid grounds."

It has further observed:

> "The Board while adjudicating the application for compulsory licence must also determines that the parties before the Board have their competing commercial interest. The public interest can only be safeguarded by the Board. This indeed is the main duty and obligation of the Board. Any decision which is taken by the Board must be taken while keeping larger public interest in view. The Board has carefully maintained the balance between creations of monopoly which is generally considered opposed to public interest and protecting intellectual property rights as a measure to encourage creativity in the respective fields."

Thus, it can clearly be observed that the Indian law reflects the concerns about the access to knowledge/information by the citizen of the country and elaborately provides for the compulsory licensing of works in public interest. Indeed, one can say that, the statutory instrument of licensing reflects the loss of control for the owner of copyright and deprives him of his power to negotiate the terms of his publication, however, that shall not deter this Quasi-Judicial Board[120] to grant a compulsory license to meet the larger goal of copyright which is to provide the public access to copyrighted works. However, this provision[121] applies only to 'works' which is first published in the country or the author of which is a citizen of India. Compulsory licensing provisions do not apply to licensing reproduction of foreign works. But the copyright statute enlists provisions for compulsory license to translate foreign literary and dramatic

---

120. *State of Himachal Pradesh Vs. Raja Mahindra Pal*, AIR 1999 SC 1786: (1999) 4 SCC 43. (It was submitted that the power of the Copyright Board under section 31 of the Act is quasi-judicial in nature.

121. As per explanation to section 31 of the Indian Copyright Act, 1957.

works in certain circumstances and under certain terms and conditions. Thus, the provision of compulsory licensing is a control mechanism which would ensure that the society is not deprived of their access to creative works and the copyright owner is not unjustly deprived of his fair returns.

Compulsory License in Translation of Foreign Works

The statute enlists detailed provisions on licensing wherein any person may apply to the Copyright Board to produce and publish a translation of a literary or dramatic foreign work, in any language, but after a specified period of seven years from the first publication of such work. Where the application concerns itself with the translation of foreign works and it is for the purpose of teaching, scholarship or research,[122] any person may apply to the Copyright Board, after three years from the date of first publication circumstance that such a language is not in general use in any 'developed country'[123] and entitles any person to apply to the Copyright Board in this regard for a license to produce and publish a translation of a literary work in any language,[124] subject to the condition that the copyright owner has denied authorisation to produce and publish such translations[125] and such work has not been published in such a language or if the work though published, is out of print. The scope of this provision extends to the translation, being produced and published by way of printed or analogous forms of reproduction.

INTERNATIONAL COPYRIGHT

Copyright being territorial, the statutes protecting copyright are applicable within the territorial boundaries of a nation state. However, the same statute protects foreign works as well. Section 40 of the Copyright Act confers the power on the Central Government to extend the provision of the Copyright Act to foreign works. The Act read with the International Copyright Order, 1999 affords protection to works of all Berne and UCC

---

122. Such 'purpose' has been defined in the explanation clause of section 32 of Chapter VI of the Indian Copyright Act, 1957.
123. 'Developed Country' has been defined in the explanation clause of section 32 of Chapter VI of the Indian Copyright Act, 1957.
124. Section 32(1) of the Indian Copyright Act, 1957.
125. Proviso 3(b) to Section 32(4) of the Indian Copyright Act, 1957.

signatories.[126] The same protection as if a work shall not exceed that which is enjoyed by it in its country of origin. The benefits granted to foreign works will not extend beyond what is available to the works in the home country and that to only on a reciprocal basis, i.e., to say the foreign country must grant similar protection to works entitled to copyright under the Act.[127]

India follows the principle of reciprocity in granting protection to foreign authors whose work is first published in India. It can also be noted that where the foreign country does not give adequate protection to works by Indian authors, the Government of India may by order deny protection to works first published in India whose author is a citizen of a foreign country.[128] Thus, it is through the principle of national treatment that foreigners enjoy the same rights as nationals except in terms of protection which may vary, but it cannot be less than the Berne standard set out by the Berne Convention.

ON-LINE COPYRIGHT ISSUE IN INDIA

The reference to on-line copyright issues can be found in the following two major enactments:

(1) The Copyright Act, 1957, and

(2) The Information Technology Act, 2000.

The Copyright Act, 1957 and On-line Copyright Issues

The following provisions of the Copyright Act, 1957 can safely be relied upon for meeting the challenges of advanced technology, etc.:

(a) The inclusive definition of computer is very wide which includes any electronic or similar device having information processing capabilities.[129] Thus, a device storing or containing a copyrighted material cannot be manipulated in such a manner as to violate the rights of a copyright holder.

(b) The term computer programme has been defined to mean a set of instructions expressed in words, codes, schemes or in any other form, including a machine

126. Appendix to the International Copyright Order.
127. P. Narayan, Intellectual Property Law, IVth edn., Eastern Law House, 2004.
128. *Ibid.*
129. Section 2(ffb) of Copyright Act, 1957.

readable medium, capable of causing a computer to perform a particular task or achieve a particular result.[130] It must be noted that Section 13(a) read with Section 2(o) confers a copyright in computer programme and its infringement will attract the stringent penal and civil sanctions.

(c) The inclusive definition of literary work includes computer programmes, tables and compilations including computer databases.[131] Thus, the legislature has taken adequate care and provided sufficient protection for computer-related copyrights.

(d) The copyrighted material can be transferred or communicated to the public easily and secretly through electronic means. To take care of such a situation, the Copyright Act has provided the circumstances which amount to communication to the public. Thus, making any work available for being seen or heard or otherwise enjoyed by the public directly or by any means of display or diffusion other than by issuing copies of such work regardless of whether any member of the public actually sees, hears or otherwise enjoys the work so made available, may violate the copyright.[132] The communication through satellite or cable or any other means of simultaneous communication to more than one household or place of residence including residential rooms of any hotel or hostel shall be deemed to be communication to the public.[133]

(e) The copyright in a work is infringed if it is copied or published without its owner's consent. The Copyright Act provides that a work is published if a person makes available a work to the public by issue of copies or by communicating the work to the public.[134] Thus, the ISPs, BBS providers, etc. may be held liable for copyright violation if the facts make out a case for the same.

(f) The copyright in a work shall be deemed to be infringed when a person, without a licence granted by the owner

130. Section 2(ffc) of Copyright Act, 1957.
131. Section 2(o) of Copyright Act, 1957.
132. Section 2(ff) of Copyright Act, 1957.
133. Explanation to Section 2(ff) of Copyright Act, 1957.
134. Section 3 of Copyright Act, 1957.

of the copyright or the Registrar of Copyrights under this Act or in contravention of the conditions of a licence so granted or of any condition imposed by a competent authority under this Act:

(i) Does anything, the exclusive right to do which is by this Act conferred upon the owner of the copyright, or

(ii) Permits for profit any place to be used for the communication of the work to the public where such communication constitutes an infringement of the copyright in the work, unless he was not aware and had no reasonable ground for believing that such communication to the public would be an infringement of copyright.[135]

(g) The Copyright Act specifically exempts certain acts from the purview of copyright infringement. Thus, the making of copies or adaptation of a computer programme by the lawful possessor of a copy of such computer programme from such copy in order to utilize the computer programme for the purpose for which it was supplied or to make back-up copies purely as a temporary protection against loss, destruction, or damage in order only to utilize the computer programme for the purpose for which it was supplied, would not be copyright infringement.[136] Similarly, the doing of any act necessary to obtain information essential for operating inter-operability of an independently created computer programme with other programmes by a lawful possessor of a computer programme is not a copyright violation if such information is not otherwise readily available.[137] Further, there will not be any copyright violation in the observation, study or test of functioning of the computer programme in order to determine the ideas and principles, which underline any elements of the programme while performing such acts necessary for the functions for which the computer programme was supplied.[138] The Act also makes it clear that the making

135. Section 51(a) of Copyright Act, 1957.
136. Section 52(1)(aa) of Copyright Act, 1957.
137 Section 52(1)(ab) of Copyright Act, 1957.
138. Section 52(1)(ac) of Copyright Act, 1957.

of copies or adaptation of the computer programme from a personally legally obtained copy for non-commercial personal use will not amount to copyright violation.[139]

(h) If a person knowingly makes use on a computer of an infringing copy of a computer programme, he shall be held liable for punishment of imprisonment for a term which shall not be less than seven days but which may extend to three years and with fine which shall not be less than fifty thousand rupees but which may extend to two lakh rupees. However, if the computer programme has not been used for gain or in the course of trade or business, the court may, for adequate and special reasons to be mentioned in the judgment, not impose any sentence of imprisonment and may impose a fine which may extend to fifty thousand rupees.[140]

It must be noted that copyright can be obtained in a computer programme under the provisions of the Copyright Act, 1957.[141] Hence, a computer programme cannot be copied, circulated, published or used without the permission of the copyright owner. If it is illegally or improperly used, the traditional copyright infringement theories can be safely and legally invoked.

Information Technology Act and Copyright Issue

The following provisions of the Information Technology Act, 2000 are relevant to understand the relationship between copyright protection and information technology:

(a) Section 1(2) read with Section 75 of the Act provides for extra-territorial application of the provisions of the Act.[142] Thus, if a person (including a foreign national) violates the copyright of a person by means of computer, computer system or computer network located in India, he would be liable under the provisions of the Act.

(b) If any person without permission of the owner or any other person who is in charge of a computer, computer

---

139. Section 52(1)(ad) of Copyright Act, 1957.
140. Section 63B of Copyright Act, 1957.
141. Section 13(1)(a) read with Section 2(o) of Copyright Act, 1957.
142. Praveen Dalal and Shruti Gupta: The Unexplored Dimensions of Right to Privacy (May-04 issue of IJCL).

system or computer network accesses or secures access to such computer, computer system or computer network[143] or downloads, copies or extracts any data, computer data base or information from such computer, computer system or computer network including information or data held or stored in any removable storage medium,[144] he shall be liable to pay damages by way of compensation not exceeding one crore rupees to the person so affected. Thus, a person violating the copyright of another by downloading or copying the same will have to pay exemplary damages up to the tune of rupees one crore which is deterrent enough to prevent copyright violation.

(c) While adjudging the quantum of compensation, the adjudicating officer shall have to consider the following factors:
   (i) The amount of gain or unfair advantage, wherever quantifiable, made as the result of the default;
   (ii) The amount of loss caused to any person as a result of the default; and
   (iii) The repetitive nature of the default.[145]

Thus, if the copyright is violated intentionally and for earning profit, the quantum of damages will be more as compared to innocent infringement.

(d) A network service provider (ISP) will not be liable under this Act, rules or regulations made thereunder for any third party information or data made available by him if he proves that the offence or contravention was committed without his knowledge or that he had exercised all due diligence to prevent the commission of such offence or contravention.[146] The network service provider under section 79 means an intermediary and third party information means any information dealt with by a network service provider in his capacity as an intermediary.[147]

143. Section 43(b) of the Information Technology Act, 2000.
144. Section 43(b) of the Information Technology Act, 2000.
145. Section 47 of the Information Technology Act, 2000.
146. Section 79 of the Information Technology Act, 2000.
147. Explanation to Section 79 of the Information Technology Act, 2000.

(e) The provisions of this Act shall have overriding effect notwithstanding anything inconsistent therewith contained in any other law for the time being in force.[148]

Internet and Established Body Responsible for Copyright Issue

The advent of information technology has made it difficult to apply the traditional theories to various cyberspace entities and organizations. These cyberspace players can be grouped under the following headings:

(1) Internet Service Providers (ISPs),

(2) Bulletin Board Services Operators (BBSO),

(3) Commercial Web Page owner/operators, and

(4) Private users.

Internet Service Providers (ISPs)

Internet Service Providers most often provides Internet access and he may be held liable for copyright infringement. But in India neither under Copyright Act, 1957 nor under Information Technology Act, 2000, ISP has made unconditional liable instead a flexible conditional liability has been imposed. As per I.T. Act ISP shall be made liable only if it has previous knowledge about the materials and it has not taken appropriate steps to protect the interest of the authors/owners.[149] The provision for liability has been clearly provided under US copyright law. In the case of *Religious Technology Center Vs. Netcom On-Line Communication Services, Inc*[150] a former minister uploaded some of the copyrighted work of the Church of Scientology to the Internet. He first transferred the information to a BBS computer, where it was temporarily stored before being copied onto Netcom's computer and other Usenet computers. Once the information was on Netcom's computer, it was available to Netcom's subscribers and Usenet neighbours for downloading for up to eleven days. The plaintiffs informed Netcom about the infringing activity; nonetheless, Netcom refused to deny the subscriber's access because it was not possible to prescreen the subscriber's uploads, and kicking the subscriber off the Internet meant kicking off the rest of the BBS

148. Section 81of the Information Technology Act, 2000.

149. Section 79 of I.T. Act, 2000.

150. 907 F. Supp. 1361 (N.D. Cal. 1995).

operator's subscribers. Thus, plaintiffs sought a remedy against Netcom for infringement under all three theories: direct, contributory, and vicarious. The Court first analyzed whether Netcom directly infringed plaintiff's copyright. Since Netcom did not violate plaintiff's exclusive copying, distribution, or display rights, Netcom was held not liable for direct infringement. The court then analyzed the third party liability theories of contributory and vicarious infringement. The court held that Netcom would be liable for contributory infringement if plaintiffs proved that Netcom had knowledge of the infringing activity. The court then analyzed whether Netcom was vicariously liable. Here, once again the court found that a genuine issue of material fact supporting Netcom's right and ability to control the uploader's acts existed. The court found that Netcom did not receive direct financial benefit from the infringement. Thus, the court found that the Netcom was not liable for direct infringement, could be liable for contributory infringement if plaintiffs proved the knowledge element, and was not liable for vicarious infringement.

Bulletin Board Services

The BBSs are more vulnerable to copyright infringement litigations than the ISPs because they can operate independent of the World Wide Web. The first case in this category was *Playboy Enterprises, Inc. Vs. Frena.*[151] In this case, the defendant operated a subscription BBS that allowed the subscribers to view, upload, and download material. The court held that Frena had violated Playboy's exclusive distribution right and their exclusive display right. Because Frena supplied a product containing unauthorized copies of copyrighted work, he has violated the distribution right. Moreover, because Frena publicly displayed Playboy's copyrighted photographs to subscribers, he violated the display right. The court concluded that Frena was liable for direct infringement, though Frena himself never placed infringing material on the BBS and despite his arguments that he was unaware of the infringement. The court relied upon the strict liability theory and held that neither intent nor knowledge is an essential element of infringement.

151. 839 F. Supp. 1552 (M.D. Fla. 1993).

In *Sega Vs. Maphia*[152] the BBS was providing services to numerous subscribers who upload and downloaded files to and from the BBS. The evidence clearly showed that the BBS operator knew that subscribers were uploading unauthorized copies of Sega's video games to and downloaded from his BBS. The court held that since the BBS operators only knew and encouraged uploading and downloading, but did not upload or download any files himself, he was not liable for direct infringement. The court, however, found the BBS operator contributory liable. Regarding the knowledge element, the BBS operator admitted that he had knowledge of the uploading and downloading activity. The court rejected the BBS operator's asserted fair use defense since their activities were clearly commercial in nature.

Commercial Web Sites

The Web Page owners must be cautious of the things they post on their Web Pages so that they do not violate the stringent provisions of the copyright laws. A Web Page owner cannot successfully plead and prove that they were unaware about the copyrighted material because copyright notices are prominently given in authorized software. They also have the controlling power over the content of their pages. The owners are usually the parties that actually perform upload to their pages.

Private Users

A computer user who uploads copyrighted material to the Internet is liable for direct infringement. This liability could be avoided only if he can prove the fair use doctrine. Thus, an Internet user should not post copyrighted material on the Internet in a casual manner.

INFRINGEMENT OF COPYRIGHT

Right to reproduction is the core of all economic rights. It occupies the central importance amongst the bundle of copyrights. To establish the case of infringement, the copyright owner must show only that he or she (1) owns a valid copyright, and (2) the defendant exercise one or more of the owner's

152. 948 F. Supp. 923 (N.D. Cal. 1996.

exclusive rights to reproduce, to publicly distribute, to publicly perform, to publicly display or to adapt the copyrighted work.[153]

Section 51 of the Indian Copyright Act, 1957 discussed in detailed that when Copyright in a work shall be deemed to be infringed, in particular clause (b) states that Copyright shall be deemed to be infringed when any person:

(i) makes for sale or hire, or sells or lets for hire or by way of trade displays or offers for sale or hire, or
(ii) distributes either for the purpose of trade or to such an extent as to affect prejudicially the owner of the copyright, or
(iii) by way of trade exhibits in public, or
(iv) imports (except for the private and domestic use of the importer) into India, any infringing copies of the work.

Opinion of Justice S. Murtaza Fazal Ali quoting from American Jurisprudence in the case of *R.G. Anand Vs. Deluxe Films*[154] can be referred here:

> "Infringement of a copyright is a trespass on a private domain owned and occupied by the owner of the copyright, and, therefore, protected by law, and infringement of copyright, or piracy, which is a synonymous term in this connection, consists in the doing by any person, without the consent of the owner of the copyright, of anything the sole right to do which is conferred by the statute on the owner of the copyright."

Section 2(m) defines 'infringing copy' to mean:

(i) In relation to a literary, dramatic, musical or artistic work, a reproduction thereof, otherwise that in the form of a cinematographic film;
(ii) In relation to a cinematographic film, a copy of the film made on any medium by any means;
(iii) In relation to a sound recording, any other recording embodying the same sound recording, made by any means; and
(iv) In relation to a programme or performance in which such a broadcast reproduction right or a performer's right subsists under the provisions of this Act, the sound

153. Ashly Aull, Fair Use and Educational Uses of Content available at http://cyber.law.harbard.edu/home/dl_fairuse
154. AIR 1978 SC 1613.

recording or a cinematographic film of such programme or performance, if such reproduction, copy of sound recording is made or imported in contravention of the provisions of this Act.

The infringer invades a statutorily defined province guaranteed to the copyright holder alone. But he does not assume physical control over the copyright; nor does he wholly deprive its owner from its use.[155]

Modes of Copyright Infringement/ Piracy in India

Nowadays, copyright infringement is a prevalent phenomenon throughout the globe and India is not an exception to this menace. Infringement means unauthorised reproduction, importation or distribution either of the whole or of a substantial part of works protected by copyright. The author of a copyrighted work, being the owner, enjoys certain exclusive rights with respect to his or her works. These include right to reproduce, to publish, to adopt, to translate and to perform in public. The owner can also sell, assign, license or bequeath the copyright to another party if he wishes so. If any person other than the copyright owner or his authorised party undertakes any of the above mentioned activities with respect to a copyrighted product, it amounts to infringement of the copyright. Copyright infringement is thus like any other theft which leads to loss to the owner of the property. Besides economic loss, infringement also adversely affects the creative potential of a society as it denies creative people such as authors, artists or creators from their legitimate dues.

There are different ways through which infringement of copyright takes place. Book piracy takes place when a book is reproduced by someone other than the real publisher and sold in the market. A performer's right is violated when a live performance of an artist is recorded or telecasted live without his/her permission. In a cinematographic work, infringement generally takes place through unauthorised reproduction of the film in video forms and/or displaying the video through cable networks without taking proper authorisation from the film producer (the right holder). Computer software is pirated by simply copying it onto another machine not authorised for its

155. *US Vs. La Macchina*, 871 F Supp 535.

use. In fact, there are numerous other ways through which infringement of copyrighted works takes place. The nature and extent of infringement also vary across the segments of the copyright industry. It is, therefore, necessary to discuss the nature and extent of the problems of infringement segment-wise.

The study of infringement of copyright can be discussed under two major categories: (1) The manual or traditional modes of infringement; and (2) The electronic or non-traditional modes of infringement.

Manual or Traditional Modes of Infringement

This includes those modes of infringement which have been recognised as elementary case of infringement. The history of infringement shows that this practice is available since the introduction of copyright and related rights in the globe. These are as follows:

Literary Works

Piracy of literary works means illegal reproduction of books and other printed materials and distribution/selling of these for profit. In India, the journals/magazines and other periodicals are not pirated much. Here piracy of literary works generally takes place in three principal ways: (1) wholesale reprinting of text and trade books, (2) unauthorised translations, and (3) commercial photocopying of books/journals. Many a time piracy takes the form of publishing fake books. Book piracy, in India, primarily depends on two factors, namely, the price of the book and its popularity. These two factors have positive contribution to acts of infringement of copyright in this area. Infringement is generally confined to foreign and good indigenous books because these books are demanded in large quantities and are also priced high. The types of books pirated mostly are medical, engineering and other professional books, encyclopedia and popular fictions. The pirates first identify the books to be pirated and then get the same printed in large numbers through unscrupulous printers. The pirated books are normally sold with other (legitimate) books by usual retailers identified by the pirates. The number of printers/sellers involved in the process of infringement is generally less. The infringement is also seasonal in nature. The entire process of printing through selling gets over within one or two months generally.

Besides the above, piracy in the form of mass photocopying of books is largely prevalent in India, especially in and around educational institutions. Students borrow books from libraries and then get these photocopied from the photocopier kept at the institution where from the books are borrowed. While copyright law permits photocopying of literary works for limited private uses such as research, review or criticism but what happens many a time is that the entire book is photocopied including the cover pages. In this process student community and the photocopy operators gain but the publishers lose huge revenue. Unfortunately, the institutions turn a blind eye to this. Sometimes even some renowned publishers involve themselves in piracy by way of selling books beyond the contract period. This happens when an Indian publisher buys reprint rights from some foreign publishers and keeps on selling books even after the expiry of the period mentioned in the agreement. This is done in the pretext of clearing old stock. Thus, an impression is created that books are printed during the contract period but in reality and are sold beyond the contract period just to exhaust the old stock.

The other way through which piracy takes place is printing/ selling of books meant for review. Many foreign publishers send books to India for review. The pirates somehow get access to such books and make quick prints to sell in Indian market. All these happen much before the authorised Indian distributors get their copies for selling of original books in India. Naturally, the distributors' sales get affected adversely.

Sound Recordings

The sound recording industry faces three types of infringement. First, there is a simple way by which songs from different legitimate cassettes/CDs (and thus different right-holders) are copied and put in a single cassette/CD. These are then packaged to look different from the original products and sold in the market. Second, there is counterfeiting, when songs are copied into and packaged to look as close to the original as possible using the same label, logos, etc. These products are misleading in the sense that ordinary end users think that they are buying original products. The third form of music piracy is bootlegging, where unauthorised recordings of performance by artists are made and subsequently reproduced and sold in the market. All these happen without the knowledge of the performers, composer or the recording company.

Earlier the music piracy was confined to cassette tapes only. With the advent of CDs in the eighties it was thought that infringement of copyright of sound recordings would become things of the past. But in reality CD piracy is the greatest threat to today's music world. In fact, CDs piracy has got an international vigour. Fortunately or unfortunately, CD industry is still in its nascent stage in India. At present CD market is just 2 to 3 percent of the overall music market in the country. CDs have not taken off mainly because of high prices. In India CDs are sold on an average price ranging between Rs. 150 to Rs. 550. Considering price of cassettes, the price differential (between cassettes and CDs) is quite high and prohibitive for ordinary music lovers. Cassette piracy in India is as old as the cassette industry itself. Government policy put music industry in the small scale category and volume of a record company's cassette production was restricted to 300,000 units per annum. This led to a wide gap in the demand supply front which was ultimately bridged by the pirates. Even if music piracy percentage has declined from a high of 30% in 1995 to about 27% in 2005, India is the world's sixth largest pirate market in value terms but third in volume terms.[156]

The popularity of Indian music has gone beyond the national boundaries. There is large demand for Indian music in the neighbouring countries such as Pakistan, West Asia as well as far off countries like USA, Canada and the UK. Indian music is also pirated in some of these foreign countries, the notable among these being Pakistan and the West Asia. Similarly, foreign audio products are also subject to piracy in Indian soil.

Cinematographic Works

Copyright in cinematographic works is more complex in nature as there is a variety of copyrights exist in a single work and many a times these rights are also overlapping. The first right in a film is the 'theatrical right', i.e. the right to exhibit films

156. According to a survey conducted jointly by Business Software Alliance (BSA) and NASSCOM in May 2006.

in theatres. The producer is the copyright holder. The distributors buy theatrical rights from producers and then make some arrangements with the theatre owners for actual exhibition to the public. The theatrical rights are limited by territory and time. Films are also released in video cassettes. In fact, these days viewing film at home has become more popular than seeing the same at theatres. The producers sell the video rights to another party who makes video cassettes for sale in the market. These cassettes are meant for 'home viewing' only, i.e. one can buy a copy of it for seeing at home with family members and friends. Such cassettes cannot be used for showing the film in cables or through satellite channels because showing films in cables or satellite channels require acquisition of separate sets of rights namely, 'cable rights' and 'satellite rights', etc. A cable network is generally limited to local areas as it requires receivers (viewers' TVs) which are to be physically connected through cable wire to the operators. In case of satellite channels, however, there is no such physical limit as transmission takes place through air and received at the users end by dish antenna(s). Interestingly, in India satellite transmissions, in most of the cases, reach to end-users through cable networks only. The cable networks in India works in a two-tier system. At the top there are main operators who transmit their programmes through numerous small local operators on a franchise basis. The programmes of satellite channels reach to the viewers through cable networks. The (main) cable operators do not pay anything to satellite channels for showing latter's programmes in the network except for pay channels (e.g. ESPN, Zee Cinema, Movie Club, etc). The small cable operators, however, share their incomes with their respective main operators. The revenue for small operators comes from the subscription of viewers.

Music is an integral part of any cinematographic work. In India, film sound tracks account for almost $3/4^{th}$ of the total music market. Even if film producer has the copyright in the film, the music included in the film is the outcome of efforts undertaken by a separate group of creative people such as the composer, lyricists, etc. each of them is a rightholders of its own right.

Infringement of copyright of cinematographic works takes two principal forms, namely, 'video piracy' and 'cable piracy'.

However, infringement of copyright in one form can spill over and affect the revenues of the other. 'Video piracy' takes place when a film is produced in the form of video cassette without taking proper authorisation from the right holder, i.e. producer. Two types of video piracies are common in India. One, where video right for films has not been sold at all (by the producer) but video cassettes are available in the market for buying or borrowing. And two, when video right is (legally) sold to a party but cassettes are made and sold by others (pirates) as well.

Cable piracy is unauthorised transmission of films through cable network. As mentioned above, showing a film in a cable network requires acquisition of proper authorisation from the rightholders. But many a time, films, especially the new releases, are shown through cables without such authorisation, which tantamount to infringement of copyright.

Infringement of copyright is a rare phenomenon in satellite channels because such channels are organised and generally do not show films without buying proper rights. But there are cases where right of one channel operator is violated by others.

Electronic or Non-Traditional Modes of Infringement

This includes such modes of infringement which have been entered in the field of piracy business after the development of technology. Electronic machine, digital technology and instruments are rampantly used to infringe the copyright of the authors/owners here and there because most of the countries in this world are lacking in laws for the protection of copyright from electronic or on-line modes of infringement. These are as follows:

Software Piracy

The infringement of copyright in computer software simply means copying and distribution of computer programmes without the copyright holder's permission. The software industry, generally, consists of creation and distribution of computer programmes. Creation of computer programme is similar to writing a novel or other literary works and it requires intellectual skill and training in software programming. Though a software can be written by individual programmer, most of the major softwares are the outcome of group efforts, where medium to large sized teams spend months or even years to write a complete programme.

Distribution of computer programmes in most of the developed countries occurs through a two-tiered system of wholesalers and dealers, similar to that of many other industries. The software publishers make a substantial amount of their shipments to a small number of distributors in any given country, who maintain well-stocked warehouses and can respond quickly to orders from hundreds or thousands of individual retail dealers or resellers. The dealers market and provide the software products directly to end-users of computers. The end-users can be individuals, commercial enterprises, educational institutions and government establishments. Sometimes, software publishers also deal directly with a small number of the larger dealers or resellers in an individual country. Licensing is a common practice in software industries. The publisher of software generally authorises its end-users through the mechanism of the shrink-wrap license contained in the package.

Like other copyright-based industries, the software industry also faces several forms of piracy. In fact, infringement of copyright in software is more than in others because it is relatively easy to copy software in computers especially in PCs and for all practical purposes the pirated version looks and performs in an identical manner as the original. The five principal types of software piracy involve (1) counterfeiters, (2) resellers, (3) mail order houses, (4) bulletin boards, and (5) end-user piracy. Counterfeiters are relatively new phenomenon in the software industry and most flagrant software counterfeiters produce disks, documentation and packaging that look very similar to those of the software publisher. Reseller infringement of copyright occurs in the software distribution channel, when distributors or dealers either make copies of software onto floppy disks, or the internal storage device or the 'hard disk' of computers that they are selling, without authorisation from the software publisher.

Identifying pirated software is not an easy task. This is primarily for two reasons. First, as mentioned earlier there is hardly any difference between original software and pirated software, once it is copied onto hardware. Second, detection of infringement of copyright requires access to software or hardware or both, which may not be feasible in many cases. However, there are some ways through which an unauthorised copy of software can be identified. Many a times publishers supply softwares in packaged form which contain software on diskettes with printed labels giving manufacturer's name, full product name, version number, trade mark and copyright notices. Besides these, the packages also typically, contain professionally printed documentation, a keyboard template, end-user license and registration cards and other printed materials pursuant to a standard bill of materials that would apply to all packages of that particular product. In such cases, the simplest pirated copies may be spotted easily on 'black-disks', which do not contain manufacture's label but rather type written, hand-written or crudely printed labels indicating the programmes contained on the diskettes. In case of installed software it is more difficult to identify a pirated copy. Once a computer is searched, the programmes copied onto it can be found and identified. Then users can be asked to produce the proof of original possession (e.g. original packages, documentation, purchase record, license cards, etc.) of such programmes. If users fail to do so, there is a *prima facie* case of infringement. In some cases even test purchases can be made to secure evidence of infringement of copyright. In India software piracy is costing the IT industry quite dear. Total losses due to software piracy in India stood at a staggering figure of about Rs. 500 crores (US$ 151.3 million) showing about 60 per cent piracy rate in India.[157]

Internet or On-Line Infringement

Internet activities like caching, browsing, mirroring, scanning, uploading, downloading or file swapping may result in:

(a) Transmission of information from one computer system or network to another, involving temporary storage (RAM) of the information;

(b) An unauthorised storage of such information is a violation of the copyright owner's exclusive right to make copies, i.e. to reproduce the copyrighted work;

157. According to a survey conducted jointly by Business Software Alliance (BSA) and NASSCOM in May 2006.

(c) A violation of the copyright owner's exclusive distribution right;
(d) An appearance of a copyright image in a web browser infringing the copyright owner's public display right; and
(e) An infringement of the copyright owner's exclusive right to make adaptation, (re-arrangement or alteration).

Hence, the Copyright Act, in the present form, has no provision against those who violate the copyright owner's statutory 'exclusive' right to fix (store), reproduce, distribute, public display (perform) and/or re-arrangement (adaptation),[158] when cache, browse, upload, download, scan or transmit any information (copyright material) in the Internet without seeking authorisation from the copyright owner. Even section 52 of the Copyright Act containing provisions on fair dealing, is silent on internet-related activities like caching, browsing, uploading, downloading, etc.

Moreover, by extending section 51(a)(ii) of the Act, to include network service provider within its ambit would make the service provider liable for copyright infringement on account of its caching and/or mirroring activities. Its role to provide access service to download, transit (distribute or swap files), exhibit (public display), someone else' copyrighted work would amount to copyright infringement. The immunity offered to the service providers under the said section is rather limited. For assistance, one may also take cognizance of Section 79 of Information Technology Act, 2000 which speaks about the Network Service Provider not to be made liable in certain cases:

> "For the removal of doubts, it is hereby declared that not person providing any service as a network service provider shall be liable under this Act, rules or regulations made hereunder for any third party information or data made available by him if he proves that the offence of contravention was committed without his knowledge or that he had exercised all due diligence to prevent the commission of such offence or contravention."[159]

158. Section 14 of the Copyright Act, 1957.
159. Section 79 of The Information Technology Act, 2000.

Whereas, it also defines the NSP and TPI which is given under the explanation for the purpose of the above Section of the Information Technology Act, 2000, this provides:

(a) 'network service provider' means an intermediary; and
(b) 'third party information' means any information dealt with by a network service provider in his capacity as an intermediary.

Thus, the abovesaid section expresses the legislative intent of granting immunity to the network service provider. The said immunity is absolute if and only if the ISP proves for any third party information that:

(i) he had no knowledge that the information content transmitting is unlawful; or
(ii) he had exercised all due diligence to prevent transmission (or publication) of unlawful information content.

But case should be taken, as Section 15(a)(ii) of the Copyright Act pertains to 'communication is the work to the public where such communication constitutes an infringement of the copyright in the work' whereas Section 79 of the Information Technology Act, 2000, is silent about any infringement of the Copyright for any third party information or data. Copyright is the relevant law dealing with these sorts of protection by bringing the software and other internet-related matters under the premise of the Copyright Act.

Infringement in Playing Television Channel

The concept of 'Communication to Public' is central theme to Copyright and a subject of copyright protection. The question as to what constitutes communication to public depends on the particular act of communication. The exhibition of any copyrighted work in a closed circle of family or friends or personal viewing is outside the purview of infringement. However, when such an exhibition is made to an audience who avail the facility in hotels, etc., it amounts to communication to public which if done without licence or permission of copyright holder may invite infringement proceedings.

Recently, the present issue has been analysed by the Apex Court in the *Super Cassette Industries Limited Vs. Entertainment*

Network (India) Limited Case[160], where the plaintiff Super Cassette Industries Limited is copyright holder of an array of literary and musical works, sound recordings, music videos and cinematographic videos and manufacture, and sells VCDs, DVDs and Cassettes containing these works. It also licenses the right to exploit its works. The defendants are engaged in the business of hotels/restaurants. The plaintiff alleged infringement of its copyright in musical works by the defendant by exhibiting the musical works to its guests in their restaurant/ hotels and sought interim injunction against them which was granted by the court. Plaintiff contended that titles in which it had copyright were being played in the hotel rooms, without a proper licence. Such usage would amount to public performance, or communication to public, of the work, the exclusive rights to which were granted only to the copyright holder or a duly licensed person under the Act. The explanation to Section 2(ff) of Copyright Act, 1957 inserted in 1995 specifically mandates that making a work available by simultaneous means of communication in hotel rooms would amount to a communication to the public. Plaintiff relied on Sections 14 and 51 of the Copyright Act to make out a case of infringement. It was submitted that guests in the defendant's hotel rooms would amount to a distinct public audience, since, the defendant and not the cable operator provides the service directly to the customers. The television sets installed in the rooms by the defendant are the means through which electronic signals are converted into audio and video signals and therefore constitute a separate act of communication to the public distinct from the act of the cable operator. He relied on the judgment delivered in *Performing Right Society Vs. Hammonds Bradford Brewery Co. Ltd.,*[161] where it was held that the hotel which through its wireless set makes available to its guests acoustic presentations was in fact communicating it publicly. He also cited the judgment of the *Garware Plastics and Polyester Ltd. Vs. Telelink,*[162] where the Court held that broadcasting of content through cable channels to various households, etc. amounts to public performance. The defendant in its written statement demanded rejection of plaint stating therein absence of a cause of

---

160. AIR 2004, DEL. 326.
161. (1934) Ch. 121.
162. AIR 1989 Bom 331.

action as required by CPC.[163] They averred that the broadcast itself and the receiving of such broadcast would not amount to infringement under section 51 of the Act. He submitted that he was merely receiving the signals transmitted by the cable operator and because the plaintiff does not dispute the legality of the cable operator's content, the defendant itself could not be held liable for infringement of the work through communication to the public, since it has obtained the consent of the cable operator to receive such content.

The issue here is whether communication via playing a television channel, the contents of which were broadcasted by the cable operator or the channel itself could be held as infringement of the copyright? The court decided this issue in the affirmative and held that such a communication being in the control of the defendant was an infringement of copyright by virtue of the provisions of Copyright Act.[164] The Parliamentary intention was to exclude commercial establishments from the benefit of non-infringement, thus, the court would also not extend the law beyond its meaning to take care of any perceived broader legislative purpose. The court also considered the question of proportions saying that:

> "the placing of a common television in a motel reception, accessible to all but without keeping a television set, in each hotel room, or placing such a set in a grocery shop for the recreation of the owner, or a wayside restaurant, may not fall within the mischief of the definition of infringement. Proportion in this context, would necessarily imply the nature of the activity of the establishment and the integral connection, the infringement complained of has with it."

The plaintiff was thus, able to prove copyright infringement in that defendants were using cable connection and extending facilities of television to their patrons in the hotel rooms for payments received. *Prima facie*, the content of songs and videos broadcast were communications to the public.

163. Order 8, Rule 11 of the CPC.
164. Section 52 and 2(ff) of Indian Copyright Act, 1957.

REMEDIES FOR THE INFRINGEMENT

Taking reference from Copyright Act, 1957 and recent development through judicial response the remedies can be discussed under the following heads:

- Civil Remedies
- Criminal Remedies
- Administrative Remedies
- Other Remedies

Civil Remedies

Copyright Act provides different types of civil remedies available under the civil court of justice.[165] The owner of the copyright shall, except as otherwise provided by this Act, be entitled to all such remedies by way of above mentioned modes of remedy as they are conferred by law for the infringement of a copyright.[166] The provisions for the civil remedies in India are provided from Sections 54 to 62 of the Copyright Act, 1957. Further the civil remedies under the Copyright Act are also divided into two categories: **Preventive Civil Remedies** and **Compensatory Civil Remedies.**

Preventive Civil Remedies

This again includes the Anton Pillar Order and Injunctions. These types of remedies are preventive in nature which prohibits the offender from doing something. These remedies also advocates about the negative rights of the owner over the infringement or to be infringed copyrights.

Anton Pillar Order: This form of order actually made under the court's inherent power. It was invented and used for the first time by English exponent, Lord Denning in *Anton Pillar K.G. Vs. Manufacturing Process Limited*.[167] Presently, it has got recognition in the provision of TRIPs also.[168] Where there is a possibility of the defendant destroying or disposing of the incrimination material, the Court may take an order in order to inspect the

165. Sections 54-62 of the Indian Copyright Act, 1957.
166. Section 55 of the Indian Copyright Act, 1957.
167. (1976) Ch. 5 (Known as Anton Piller Order), Dr. J.K. Das, Intellectual Property Rights, p. 212, 2008, Ist Edn, 2008, Kamal Law House, Kolkata.
168. TRIPs Agreement, Para 2 of Article 50.

premises of the defendant on an ex-parte application by the plaintiff without giving notice of the application to the defendant. It is not a search warrant. It only authorise entry and inspection of the defendant, by permission, in the absence of which the act would tantamount to the tort of trespass.[169]

Injunction: The main remedy sought in most copyright suits is an injunction to restrain the defendant from continuing to do acts which constitute infringement.[170] It is granted to safeguard the interests of the copyrights owner of his legitimate benefits where there is a likelihood that irreparable harm shall be caused to the copyright holder. It is an interim relief granted during the pendency of the proceedings. The injunctions can be temporary and permanent which may depend upon the situation and circumstances of the case. The laws relating to injunction are contained in the Specific Relief Act, 1963.

Compensatory Civil Remedies

This includes Damages, Accounts of Profit and Delivery of infringing copies. These sorts of remedies are curative in nature and compensate the owner or the creator to save him from pecuniary/economic loss which may arises from the act of infringement.

Damages: Apart from the injunction, Copyright Act also provides remedies by means of Damages.[171] The Copyright owner can either claim for damages or accounts of profit and not both since the spirit behind this legal remedy is that the plaintiff must be compensated and he cannot be compensated twice for the same violated act. However, the remedy of injunction can be joined either with that of damages or accounts, but the remedies of accounts and damages can in no case be joined.[172]

Account of Profit: This kind of remedy is available to the owner of the copyright generally along with damages but sometimes along with injunctions also. Thus, in case of suit of infringement of copyright the owner may seek the relief in form of accounts as well as of damages. Further, since damages were

---

169. Prof. A.K. Koul, Dr. V.K. Ahuja, Law of Copyright: From Gutenburg's Invention to Internet, in Law of Copyright, 16-17.
170. Section 55(1) of the Indian Copyright Act, 1957.
171. Section 55 of the Indian Copyright Act, 1957.
172. *Pillalamari Lakshmikant and others Vs. Ramkrishna Pictures*, AIR 1981 AP 224.

awarded and the decree of damages became final, the publishers were not entitled to the relief of accounts. Thus, the court held that the remedies of damages and accounts are remedies in the alternative and the two reliefs are incompatible.[173]

Delivery of infringing copies: If any infringing copy of the copyrighted materials has been ceased or collected from any place or custody of any person infringing the rights of the owner than the infringing copies of the copyrighted materials should be delivered to the original copyright owner or creator.

Criminal Remedies

This is another kind of remedy available to the owner/ holder of the copyright under the Indian Copyright Act, 1957. Sections 63 to 70 of the above the Copyright Act deals with the provision of criminal remedy in India. When any person knowingly infringe (a) the copyright in a work, or (b) any other right conferred by the Copyright Act, (viz. broadcasting, reproduction, special rights) or knowingly to abet such infringement.[174]

Punishment: It is further added that the work of infringement shall be punishable with imprisonment for a term which may extend to three years.

Fine: Along with the punishment a fine which shall not be less than fifty thousand rupees but which may extend to two lakh rupees can also be imposed.

Though, the court has been empowered to impose a lesser punishment or fine for adequate and special reasons to be mentioned in the judgment. It also provides that the punishment increases for the second or further conviction.[175]

It is however, clarified that the construction of a building or other structural work infringes or which, if completed would infringe the copyright in some other work is not an offence under the Act.[176] The amendment Act has also widened the powers of the police, it empowers any police office, not below the rank of a sub-inspector, if he satisfied that an offence of infringement of copyright in any work has been or is being or is likely to be committed, to seize without warrant, all infringing copies of the

173. *Ibid.*
174. Section 63 of the Indian Copyright Act, 1957.
175. Section 63 of the Indian Copyright Act, 1957.
176. Explanation to section 63 of the Indian Copyright Act, 1957.

work 'wherever found' and he is thereupon required to produce before a magistrate all copies and plates so seized as soon as practicable.[177]

Administrative Remedies

Except the abovementioned remedies another kind of remedy is known as administrative remedy. This is also known as quasi-judicial remedy available under the Copyright law in India.[178] The copyright owner can prevent importation of such copies in the Indian Territory which would infringe the copyrights of a work made in India. The Registrar of Copyrights can make an order to that effect upon receipt of such application by the owner of the copyright (or his agent) and after conducting due inquiry. Further the Registrar or any person authorised by him on his behalf is empowered to enter into any ship, dock, premises where any such copies may be found and can examine such copies. The copies so confiscated shall not vest to the Government, but shall be delivered to the owner of the copyright in the work. An appeal under section 72 of the Copyright Act lies to the Copyright Board against the order of the Registrar.

The journey of the Copyright law from the Pre-WTO to the Post-WTO era clearly emanates the position of copyright in India especially in the age of technological and electronic advancement. A crafting effort has been made to transparently deal with various aspects of this unique Intellectual Property Rights, Copyright, with special emphasis on its influence on the various stakeholders of 'creativity' down the ages. Historically, India's stands on the international level has been to strike an equitable balance and ensured that the copyright monopoly is responsibly restricted in public interest. Again we refer to Senftleben who quoted Singh, (a part of the delegation which represented India at 1967 Stockholm Conference for the revision of the Berne Convention) who pointed that 'protection of the author's rights could not be considered apart from the rights of users'.[179] India historically has placed reliance on the primacy of

177. Section 64 of the Indian Copyright Act, 1957.
178. Section 53 of the Indian Copyright Act, 1957.
179. Plenary of the Berne Union, Records, 1967, 807 as reference in Martin Senftleben, Copyright, Limitations and the Three-Step Test—An Analysis of the Three Step Test in International and EC Copyright Law, 70, Prof. P. Bernt Hugenholtz ed., Kluwer Law International, 2004.

the public interest and continues to do so in the milieu of its socio-economic development. The infringement in the context of the online, electronic and digital uses have been a real challenge before India where the protections really lacking. The broadcast and telecast areas are also out of reach of the present law in India where the rights of the performers and producers, etc. are grossly infringed. These areas are to be taken seriously by the authority concerned in the process of making or amending the laws relating to copyright in India. There is need for statutory action on this subject and we need to act fast. Delay can only mean denial.

5

CASE STUDY AND ANALYSIS OF COPYRIGHT LAW

The importance of Judiciary in a democratic set-up for protection of personal and proprietary rights can hardly be overestimated. The principal function of Judiciary is to provide legal protection and remedies against infringement of personal and property rights of persons.

The copyright for their effectiveness depend upon the speed with which they can be enforced by the courts. The statutory provisions provide only a modicum of direction as regards the nature of remedies and the procedure for safeguarding them, leaving a large extent of free play within the province of judges.

Infringement of copyright is a tortuous invasion of property in general. The common law has developed several heads of liability constituting the economic torts. 'Their general characteristics are that the defendant must be acting intentionally or recklessly; that the plaintiff must suffer or be about to suffer damage; and that they will not apply if some ground of justification is open to the defendant'.[1] Before statutory provisions in respect of these rights were enacted the remedy was the award of damages by the common law courts, and, remedy by way of injunction was developed by the equity courts.

1. W.R. Cornish, Intellectual Property: Patents, Copyright, Trade Marks and Allied Rights, (Second Edition), p. 28.

Copyright is inchoate property when manifested in a legally recognizable way. Property right till the deletion of Article 19(1)(f) and Article 31 of the Constitution of India by 44th amendment, 1978, was a fundamental right for citizens, but now placed under Article 300-A, it is separately notified as a Constitutional right ensuring that no person can be deprived of his property save by the authority of law.

CONSTITUTIONAL MANDATE ASSURING EQUALITY

Even though certain important fundamental rights including right to carry on any trade or business are guaranteed only to citizens, all persons including non-citizens can claim equality before the law and equal protection of the laws.[2] Therefore, any arbitrary discrimination against a person, who is a non-citizen qua his claim to be treated equally as others before the law, can be challenged before the Courts.

Recourse to Court by law is a well recognized concept world over and firmly entrenched in the Constitutional and other laws of India. Therefore, any person can claim a statutorily or customarily recognized right to property. In case of infringement of a legally recognized right recourse to law cannot be denied and the rule of law enshrined in Article 14 of the Constitution will enable any person including a non-citizen to approach the legal forum of the country for redressal of his grievances. In India, as provided by Section 83 of the Code of Civil Procedure alien friends may sue in any Court otherwise competent to try the suit, as if they were citizens of India. The alien enemies residing in India or in a foreign country shall not be allowed to sue in any such Court without permission of the Central Government.

Ordinarily, infringement of copyright has a private dimension in as much as it affects the proprietary rights of individuals and may cause financial loss and loss of credit to the owner. Therefore, the question of national or public interest would rarely arise when redressal is sought by a non-citizen for violation of such proprietary rights by the infringer. The judiciary is under an obligation to implement the laws and redress grievances of all persons including aliens to uphold their common law or statutorily recognized rights.

2. Article 14 of the Constitution of India.

CONSTITUTIONAL DIRECTIVES ADMIRING INTERNATIONAL LAW

As provided by Article 51(c) of the Constitution of India, the State is under a constitutional directive to endeavour to foster respect for international law and treaty obligations in the dealings of the organized peoples with one another. Though the directive principles of State Policy are non-justiciable rights, nevertheless, they are fundamental in the governance of the Country. The definition of 'State' given in Article 12 of the Constitution relating to Fundamental Rights and incorporated in Article 36 which contains the Directive Principles of State Policy covers judicial and quasi-judicial authorities also. Therefore, the courts in India are obliged to endeavour to foster respect for international law and obligations under the international treaties.

The constitutional concern for respecting international laws including international treaties and conventions is also reflected under Article 253 which, notwithstanding the distribution of legislative powers between the Federal Union and the States, empowers the Parliament to make law for the whole or any part of the territory of India for implementing any treaty, agreement or convention with any other Country or Countries or any decision made at any international Conference, association or other body. The Parliament is under Article 246 read with entry 14 of the Union List of subjects on which it can legislate contained in Schedule VII of the Constitution, empowered to legislate with respect to the subject of entering into treaties and agreements with foreign countries and implementing of treaties, agreements and conventions with foreign countries. However, barring treaties which require legislation to be made, the international agreements entered into by the Union in exercise of its executive power under Article 73 which are not contrary to law are required to be recognized by the Municipal Courts. For entering into treaty or bringing it in force for India, it is not a Constitutional requirement that the executive should have the support of Parliamentary legislation.[3] The copyright along with other intellectual properties like inventions, patent, trademarks, design and merchandise marks is assigned to the Parliament under entry 49 of the Union List for the purpose of legislation.

3. *Maganbhai Vs. Union of India*, AIR 1969 SC 783.

INDEPENDENT INTEGRATED JUDICIAL SYSTEM

India has a highly developed judicial system with the Supreme Court having plenary powers[4] to make any order for doing complete justice in any cause or matter and a mandate in the Constitution,[5] to all authorities, Civil and Judicial, within the territory of India to act in aide to the Supreme Court. The scope of Writ Jurisdiction of the High Courts[6] is wider than traditionally understood and the judiciary is separate and independent of the executive to ensure impartiality in the administration of justice. The judiciary has a central role to play in this thriving democracy and shuns arbitrary executive action. The higher judiciary has been empowered to pronounce upon the legislative competence of the law-making bodies and the validity of a legal provision. The range of judicial review recognized in the higher judiciary in India is the widest and most extensive known to any democratic set-up in the world.

The Civil Courts have jurisdiction to try all suits of a civil nature excepting suits of which their cognizance is either expressly or impliedly barred.[7] The exclusion of jurisdiction of a Civil Court to entertain civil causes is not readily inferred and there is a presumption in favour of the jurisdiction of a Civil Court. As noted above aliens may sue in any court as if they were citizens of India[8]. Therefore, in respect of violation of any property rights including intellectual property rights any aggrieved person can resort to remedies available under the Indian law in any court which has jurisdiction in the matter affected. Aliens and Foreign Corporation can invoke the principle of equality before the law enshrined under Article 14 of the Constitution of India which applies to 'any person' and is not limited to citizens. This should allay any doubts in the International Community about the protection of the legitimate interests of their nationals who may have to seek redressal in this country, of their grievances against violation of their legal rights.[9]

4. Article 142 of the Constitution of India.
5. Article 144 of the Constitution of India.
6. Article 226 of the Constitution of India.
7. Section 9 of the Code of Civil Procedure.
8. Section 83 of the Code of Civil Procedure.
9. Role of Judiciary in the Effective Protection of Intellectual Property Right, by Justice R.K. Abichandani, High Court of Gujarat, at http://www.gujarathigh court. nic.in/Articles/roleofjudicary.htm

COURT'S POWER UNDER THE PRESENT COPYRIGHT LAW

The Courts in India are empowered under the municipal laws to grant reliefs against violation of Intellectual Property rights including copyright, and the parameters reflected in Part III of the TRIPs agreement are already adopted enabling the courts to protect these private rights. This can be briefly outlined:

> The civil proceedings in respect of the infringement of copyright or any other rights conferred by the Copyright Act can be instituted in the District Court having jurisdiction.[10] The civil remedies available for the infringement of the copyright are by way of injunction, damages, accounts of profit and otherwise as are or may be provided by law for such infringements.[11] There is a rebuttable presumption that the person, whose name appears on the work or the copies of the work, as published, is the author or the publisher of the work, as the case may be.[12] Independently of his copyright, the author of a work has a special right to claim authorship of the work and to restrain or claim damages in respect of any distortion, mutilation, modification or other act which is done before the expiration of the term of copyright if such deviation would be prejudicial to the honour or reputation of the author.[13] The infringing material (copies and plates) will be deemed to be the property of the owner of the copyright.[14] Remedy in the case of groundless threat of legal proceedings, is by way of a declaratory suit that the infringement alleged was in fact not infringement of any legal rights of the person making such threats. The court can grant an injunction against continuance of groundless threats and award damages for the loss sustained by the owner by reason of such threats, except where the person making such threats with due diligence commences and prosecutes an action for infringement of the copyright claimed by

10. Section 62 of the Copyright Act, 1957.
11. Section 55 of the Copyright Act, 1957.
12. Section 55(2) of the Copyright Act, 1957
13. Section 57 of the Copyright Act, 1957.
14. Section 58 of the Copyright Act, 1957

him.[15] Though, no copyright can be claimed except as provided by the Act, it is specifically provided that there will be no abrogation of any right or jurisdiction to restrain a breach of trust or confidence.[16]

The Central Government by Section 40 of Copyright Act, 1957, is empowered to direct that all or any of the provisions of the Copyright Act shall apply to foreign works. The government has made the International Copyright Order, 1991 applying the provisions of the Copyright Act as indicated in paragraph 3 of the Order, except those of Chapter VIII relating to Rights of Broadcasting Organisation and of Performers and the provisions which apply exclusively to Indian Works, to the Bern Conventions Countries and the Universal Copyright Convention Countries.

Indian Judiciary is proactive one and benevolently responded to avert any sort of injustice or malpractices, etc. It has rightly reacted in the area of copyright also. It has not only taken the books of law but also considering the social demands in discharging their responsibility for protection of national property, bestowed to them in terms of protection of the dynamic nature of law. The Courts are not only protecting the rights of the owners or authors but also providing splendid mechanism for the protection of the copyright from infringers. The analysis of the following cases as decided by different Higher Courts in respect to the infringement of copyright will show the real development on law regarding copyright protection:

ANALYSIS OF CASES

Macmillan & Another Case[17]

Facts and Analysis of the Case

Macmillan and Company had published a book called 'The Golden Treasury of the Best Songs and Lyrics' which was a selection made by Professor Palgrave from the poems of numerous English authors of various periods. This book was very popular and there were several editions to this book. It was alleged that the defendants published a similar book containing

15. Section 60 of the Copyright Act, 1957.
16. Section 16 of the Copyright Act, 1957.
17. *Macmillan and Another Vs. Suresh Chunder Deb*, ILR (1890) 17 Calcutta 951.

the same poems. In this case the Court dealt with the question whether the Court can grant a copyright for the selection of original works?

Analysis of Case

The Court held:

> "In the case of works not original in the proper sense of the term but composed of or compiled or prepared from materials which are open to all, the fact that one man has produced such a work does not take away from anyone else the right to produce another work of the same kind, and in doing so to use all the materials open to him. But, as the law is concisely stated by Hall, V.C., in *Hogg Vs. Scott* (1), "the true principle in all these cases is that the defendant is not at liberty to use or avail himself of the labour which the plaintiff has exerted for the purpose of producing his work, that is, in fact, it would amount to taking away a man's labour, or, in other words, his property".

Thus, anyone can use the publicly available materials to develop new ideas or creations. In doing new things by taking the assistance of the materials which are open to all, no question of copyright infringement will arise. The person who has invested labour and idea to create a new thing by taking resources available for open use will, of course, get the monopoly right over his creation.

University of London Case[18]

Facts and Analysis of the Case

It was held that the papers set-up by the examiners were literary work within the meaning of the Copyright Act, 1911. The court in this case was concerned with the question as to whether the question paper set-up by the examiners was original work of the plaintiffs in that case.

According to the Court, the word 'original' did not in that connection meant that the work must be the expression of original inventive thought. Copyright Acts are not concerned

18. *University of London Press Limited Vs. University Tutorial Press Limited*, 1916 (2) Chancery Division 601.

with the originality of ideas but with the expression of thought, and, in the case of literary work, with the expression of thought in print or writing. It was held that the plaintiffs in that case had proved that they had thought out the questions which they set and that they made notes or memoranda for future questions which they set. The papers which they prepared originated from themselves and were within the meaning of the Act, the original creator is countering the arguments that the questions in the elementary papers are of common type, the Court held that most elementary books of mathematics may be said to be a common type, but that fact would not give impunity to a predatory infringer. The book and the papers alike originate from the author and are not copied by him from another book or other papers. After all, there remains the rough practical test that what is 'worth copying is *prima facie* worth protecting'.

Thus, the main theme here is that the copyright law has nothing to do with the original idea, moreover, it dealt with the concept of original expression of ideas. If the expression is original one by taking the existing idea, in that case also the creator will certainly come within the umbrella of copyright protection and shall be entitle to get copyright for his creation. In this case British Court held that the literary work, with original expression of thought in print or writing medium is the domain of the copyright law no further.

Ladbroke (Football) Limited Case[19]

Facts and Analysis of the Case

The respondents were well known bookmakers who had done business for many years in fixed odds football betting sending out to their clients each week during the football season a fixed odds football coupon. The coupon was a sheet of paper on which sixteen lists of matches to be played each week were printed; each list was headed with an appropriate name and offered a variety of wagers at stated odds and contained explanatory notes. One of the lists contained the full list of matches to be played at the end of the week this list being determined by the Football League who owned the copyright in

19. *Ladbroke (Football) Limited Vs. William Hill (Football) Limited*, (1964) 1 All ER 465: (1964) 1 WLR 273 (HL).

it. The other lists were shorter lists of matches selected by the respondents from the full list. Altogether the coupon offered 148 varieties of wages at widely differing odds. A great deal of skill, judgment, experience and work had gone into devising the coupon for the respondents had to select from the very great variety of possible wagers those that would appeal to the punter while being profitable to the respondents, and had then to arrange and describe the selected wagers in an attractive way on the coupon. The respondents had not altered their coupon since 1951, though the selection of matches in the lists was necessarily changed each week. Some of the wagers offered by the respondents were commonly offered by other bookmakers. The appellants, who were also well-known bookmakers, decided to enter the field of fixed odds football betting in 1959, and in developing their coupon for the 1960-61 season they copied from the respondents coupon fifteen out of the sixteen lists arranging them in the same order as they appeared in the respondents coupon, in many cases with the same headings and almost identical varieties of wager, and with similar explanatory notes. They did not copy the odds offered by the Respondents but worked these out for themselves and since the respondents and the appellants coupons were published simultaneously each week there was not copying of matches selected by the respondents. The respondents claimed copyright in their coupon and alleged infringement by the appellants. As per the Section 2(12) of the Copyright Act, 1957, copyright subsists in every 'original' literary work; a literary work includes, by virtue of section 48(1), a compilation.

Under section 2(5) (a) and section 49(1) copyright holder is given the exclusive right to reproduce a substantial part of the work in any form. Though the appellants admitted copyright in the respondent's selection of matches and statement of adds (neither of which they had copied) they denied copyright in the rest of the coupon. It was not disputed that, as regards a compilation (such as the coupons), the originality requisite to render a work original for the purpose of section 2(1) was a matter of degree depending on the amount of skill, judgment or labour that had been involved in making of the compilation.

On these facts, the House of Lords held that the correct approach in deciding if there was infringement of copyright in literary compilation first was to determine whether the work as a whole was entitled to copyright, and, second, to enquire whether the part reproduced by the defendant was a substantial part of the whole; but it was not the correct approach to dissect the work into fragments and, if the fragments were not entitled to copyright, to deduce that the whole compilation could not be so entitled.

Shyamlal Pacharia Case[20]

Facts and Analysis of the Case

It was held that the expression literary work means not only such work which deals with any particular aspect of literature in prose and poetry but also indicates a work which is literary i.e. anything in writing which could be said to come within the ambit of literary work. A compilation derived from a common source falls within the ambit of literary work. In this case, the mistakes appearing in the plaintiff's book were also appearing in the defendant's book and commenting on that aspect of the case, it was held that it was true that the mere fact that the defendants had the plaintiffs book with him will not by itself lead to an irresistible inference that he had copied the calculations from the plaintiff's work. But from the fact that the mistakes committed by the plaintiffs in certain calculations in his book were found in the defendant's book in similar calculations, clearly shows that the defendants had copied the calculations from the plaintiff's book and must be deemed to have infringed the copyright of the plaintiff with regard to such calculations.

An observation of the above judgment shows that the court has accepted that compilation of data required considerable skill and labour, which is exercised in producing the work.

In case, the publication of the plaintiffs is held to be their original literary work entitled to protection under the Copyright Act, defendants may have to be injuncted from reproducing the same. The only question, therefore, is whether the plaintiff's work is an original literary work and is entitled to protection under the Copyright Act. As already stated above, it is not denied that under Section 2(k) of the Copyright Act, 1957, a work which is made or published under the direction or control of any

20. *Shyam Lal Paharia and Another Vs. Gaya Prasad Gupta 'Rasal'*, AIR 1971 Allahabad 192.

Court, Tribunal or Judicial Authority in India is a Government work. Under Section 52(q), the reproduction or publication of any judgment or order of a Court, Tribunal or other Judicial Authority shall not constitute infringement of copyright of the Government in these works. It is thus, clear that it is open to everybody to reproduce and publish the government work including the judgment/order of a Court. However, in case, a person by extensive reading, careful study and comparison and with the exercise of taste and judgment has made certain comments about the judgment or has written a commentary thereon, may be such a comment and commentary is entitled to protection under the Copyright Act. It is in this background that the Court has to examine as to whether or not: (i) the work produced by the plaintiffs is an original literary work; and (ii) it is entitled to protection under Copyright Act, 1957. In term of section 52(1)(q) of the Act, reproduction of a judgment of the Court is an exception to the infringement of the copyright. The orders and judgments of the Courts are in the public domain and anyone can publish them. Being a Government work, no copyright exists in these orders and judgments but not one can claim copyright in these judgments and orders of the Courts merely on the ground that he had first published them in his book.

After examining the various decisions on this issue, the Court was of the opinion that there cannot be any monopoly in the subject matter which the author has borrowed from public domain. Others are at liberty to use the same material. Every person can take what is useful for them, improve and add so that the person can claim a copyright for his additions and improvements. Yet, under the guise of copyrights the plaintiff cannot ask the court to restrain the defendants from making the material available to the public. Therefore, the Court observed that the works published in the Law Reports is not an original work and the plaintiffs cannot claim any copyright over the judgments that are published in their Law Reports.

The Division Bench accepting the verdict of the single judge held that the same arrangement has to continue and the defendants were entitled to sell their CD ROMs with the text of the judgments of the Supreme Court along with their own head notes which should not in any way be copy of the head notes and text belonging to the plaintiff's work.

Indian Performing Rights Society Ltd. Case[21]

Facts of the Case

The Indian Performing Right Society Ltd. (hereinafter referred to for the sake of brevity as 'the IPRS'), the appellant before the Court, was incorporated in the State of Maharashtra on August 23, 1959, as a company limited by guarantee, for the purpose of carrying on business in India of issuing or granting licences for performance in public of all existing and future Indian Musical works in which copyright subsists in India. The incorporation of the IPRS was in terms of section 2(r) of the Copyright Act, 1957 (Act 14 of 1957).

The IPRS has amongst its members the composers of musical works, authors of literary and dramatic works and artists. In accordance with the provisions of section 33 of the Act, the IPRS published on September 27, 1969 and November 29, 1969 in the 'Statesman' and the Gazette of India respectively a tariff laying down the fees, charges and royalties that it proposed to collect for the grant of licences far performance in public of works in respect of which it claimed to be an assignee of copyrights and to have authority to grant the aforesaid licences. A number of persons including various associations of producers of cinematograph films who claimed to be the owners of such films including the sound track thereof and the Cinematograph Exhibitors' Association of India filed objections in respect of the aforesaid tariff in accordance with the provisions of section 34 of the Act repudiating the claim of the IPRS that it had on behalf of its members authority to grant licences for performance in public of all existing and future musical works which are incorporated in the sound track of cinematograph films in which copyright may subsist in India or the right to collect in relation thereto any fees, charges or royalties.

The association of producers averted *inter alia* that their members engaged composers and sound writers under contracts of service for composing songs to be utilised in their films; that

21. *Indian Performing Rights Society Ltd. Vs Eastern India Motion Picture Association and Others* (1977) 2 SCC 820: AIR 1977 SC 1443.

the musical works prepared by the composers of lyric and music under contract of service with their members-producers of the cinematograph films having been utilised and incorporated in the sound track of the cinematograph films produced by the latter, all the rights which subsisted in the composers and their works including the right to perform them in public became the property of the producers of the cinematograph films and no copyright subsisted in the composers which they could assign to and become the basis of the claim of the IPRS under section 33 of the Act; that their members, i.e. the producers of cinematograph films being the authors and first owners of the copyright in the cinematograph films produced by them had the exclusive right *inter alia* to cause the said films in so far as the same consisted of sounds (which include musical works) to be heard in public as also the exclusive right to make records embodying the sound track of the films produced by them (including any musical work incorporated therein) and to cause the said records to be heard in public; that in the making of a cinematograph film as contemplated by the Act a composer composes a lyric or music under a contract of service or for valuable consideration which is substantial a music director sets it to tunes and imparts music to it and a singer sings the same but nonc of them nor any one of their aforesaid works can and have any separate copyrights; that motion picture is the combination of all arts and music in the sound track which cannot be detached from the film itself; that the purpose of making a motion picture is not only to complete it but also to publicly exhibit it throughout the world; that having regard to the provisions of the Act the' copyright in the case of a cinematograph film vests in the owner of the film as defined in section 2(d)(v) of the Act; and that in the premises any assignment purporting to have been made in favour of the IPRS was void and of no effect and was incapable of conferring any rights whatsoever in such musical works on the IPRS. The Cinematograph Exhibitors' Association of India also filed objections challenging the right of the IPRS to charge fees and royalties in respect of performance in public of the musical works incorporated in the sound track of the films. Besides raising contentions identical to those raised by various associations of producers they averred that copyright in a cinematograph film which vested in the producers meant copyright in the entirety of the film as an integrated unit including the musical work incorporated in the sound track of the film and the right to perform the work in public; that in accordance with the agreement with the distributors of films the exhibition of cinematograph film includes the right to play in public the music which is an integral part and parcel of the film; that the producers lease out copyrights of public performance of the films vested in them to the distributors who give those rights to the exhibitors an agreement and that when an exhibitor takes a licence for exhibition, it is complete in all respects and a third party like the IPRS cannot claim any licence fee from the exhibitors.

On the aforesaid objections being referred to it for determination under section 35 of the Act, the Copyright Board expressed the view that in the absence of proof to the contrary, the composers of lyrics and music retained the copyright in their musical works incorporated in the sound track of cinematograph films provided such lyrical and musical works were printed or written and that they could assign the performing right in public to the IPRS. The Copyright Board further held that the tariff as published by the IPRS was reasonable and the IPRS had the right to grant licences for the public performance of music in the sound track of copyrighted Indian cinematograph films and it could collect fees, royalties and charges in respect of those films with effect from the date on which the tariff was published in the Gazette of India. Aggrieved by the decision of the Copyright Board, the objectors preferred an appeal under section 72 of the Act to the High Court which allowed the same holding that unless there is a contract to the contrary, a composer who composes a lyric or music for the first time for valuable consideration for a cinematograph film does not acquire any copyright either in respect of film or its sound track which he is capable of assigning and that under proviso (b) to section 17 of the Act, the owner of the film at whose instance, the composition is made, becomes the first owner of the copyright in the composition. The High Court further held that 'the composer can claim a copyright in his work only if there is an express agreement between him and the owner of the cinematograph film reserving his copyright'. The High Court also held that 'though section 18 of the Act confers power to make a contract of assignment, the power can be exercised only when there is an existing or future right to be assigned and that in the circumstances of the present case, assignment, if any, of the copyright in any future work is of no effect'. Dissatisfied with this decision, the IPRS has preferred this appeal to the Supreme Court by certificate granted under Article 133(1) of the Constitution by the High Court of Judicature at Calcutta which is directed against its judgment dated February 13, 1974, raises the following substantial question of law of general importance:

> "Whether in view of the provisions of the Copyright Act, 1957, an existing and future right of music composer, lyricist is capable of assignment and whether the producer of a cinematograph film can defeat the same by engaging the same person."

Analysis of the Case

The special feature of this case is that the Supreme Court has examined the rights over musical works and Justice Krishna Iyer has clearly pointed out that it is indeed an un-Indian feature that the Indian Copyright Act has failed to provide rights to the singer and to the artists who have rendered a musical performance and has sought right to a singer for his compositions.

'Musical work', as defined in Section 2(p) is as follows:

> S. 2(p): Musical work means any combination of melody and harmony or either of them printed reduced to writing or otherwise graphically produced or reproduced.

In the course of his judgment Justice Krishna Iyer stated that:

> "Copyrighted music is not the soulful tune, the superb singing, the glorious voice or the wonderful rendering. It is his melody or harmony reduced to printing, writing or graphic form. The Indian music lovers throng to listen and be enthralled or enchanted by the nada brahma, the sweet concord of sounds, the raga, the bhava, the laya and the sublime or exciting singing printed music is not the glamour or glory of it, by and large, although the content of the poem or the lyric or the song does have appeal. Strangely enough, 'author', as defined in Section 2(d) in relation to a musical work, is only the composer

and Section 16 confines copyright to those works which are recognised by the Act. This means that the composer alone has copyright in a musical work. The singer has none. This disentitlement of the musician or group of musical artists to copyright is un-Indian because the major attraction which lends monetary value to the musical performance is not the music-maker, so much as the musician. Perhaps, both deserve to be recognised by the copyright law. I make this observation only because art in one sense depends on the ethos and the aesthetic best of a people, and while universal protection of intellectual and aesthetic property of creators of 'work' is an international obligation, each country in its law must protect such right wherever originally is contributed. So viewed, apart from the music composer, the singer must be conferred a right. Of course, law-making is the province of Parliament, but the Court must communicate to the law-maker such infirmities as they exist in the law market."

The second important issue that was examined in this case relates to the ownership of the rights over a cinematographic film. The copyright Act protects the composite cinematographic film. It also protects the composite cinematograph work that is produced in collaboration with many talents. To begin with, the scheme of the Copyright Act as disclosed under Section 2(d) an author means (ii) in relation to a musical work, the composer, (v) in relation to a cinematograph film or song recording, the producer; and later the Section 2(m), it states that infringing copy means (i) in relation to a literary, dramatic, musical or artistic work, a reproduction thereof otherwise than in the form, a cinematographic film; (ii) in relation to a cinematographic film, a copy of the film made on any medium by any means and under section 14(d) the right that is granted to the producer includes (i) right to make a copy of the film; (ii) to sell or give on hire or offer for sale or hire any copy of the film; and (iii) of communicate the film to the public.

The above said legal provisions thus clearly state that the producer of a cinematograph film can claim the right of ownership over the film. The question that arises is whether the producer can defeat the right of the composer of music who has been engaged in composing the music for the film. The answer to this question is found in Section 17 of the Indian Copyright Act wherein Section 17(b) states that when the producer commissions a composer of music for reward or valuable consideration for composing the music or lyrics or for the sound-track associated with the film, he remains the owner over the music and no copyright can subsist in the composer of the lyrics or for the music so composed unless there is a contract to the contrary between the composer or the music director with the producer of the film.

The reason for granting sole rights to the producer has been described in a very significant manner by ***Justice V.R. Krishna Iyer***. In the course of his judgment he elaborated that:

> "A cinematograph is a felicitous blend, beautiful totality, a constellation of stars, if I may use these lovely imageries to drive home my point, slurring over the rule against mixed metaphor. Cinema is more than song strips of celluloid, more than miracles in photography, more than song, dance and dialogue and, indeed more than dramatic story, exciting lot, gripping situations and marvelous acting. But it is that ensemble which is the finished product of orchestrated performance by each of the several participants, although the components may, sometimes, in themselves be elegant entities. Copyright in a cinema film exists in law, be Section 13(4) of the Act preserves the separate survival, it its confluence in the film. This persistence of the aesthetic 'Personality' of the intellectual property cannot cut down the copyright of the film qua film."

Justice Iyer further contended that:

> "The film producer has the sole right to exercise what is his entitlement under Section 14(1)(c) qua film; but he cannot trench on the composer's copyright which does only if the 'music' is performed or produced or reproduced separately in violation of Section 14(1)(a). For instance, a film may be caused to be exhibited as a film but the pieces of music cannot be pocked out of the sound track and played in the cinema or other theatre. To do that is the privilege of the composer and that right of his is not drowned in the film copyright except where

> there is special provision such as in Section 17, proviso (c). So, beyond exhibiting the film as a cinema show if the producer plays the songs separately to attract an audience or for other reason, he infringes the composer's copyright. Anywhere, in a restaurant or aeroplane or radio station or cinema theatre, if music is played, there comes into play the copyright of the composer or the performing rights society. These are the boundaries of composite creations of art which are at once individual and collective, viewed from different angles. In a cosmic perspective a thing of beauty has not boundary and is humanity's property but in the materialist plane on which artist thrive, private and exclusive estates in art subsist. Man, the noblest work of the infinite artist, strangely enough, battles for the finite products of his art and the secular law, operating on the temporal level, guard material works possessing spiritual values. The enigmatic smile of Mona Lisa is the timeless heritage of mankind but, till liberated by the prescribed passage of time, the private copyright of the human maker says, 'hands off'.

The Supreme Court therefore, on an examination of the relevant provisions of the Copyright Act has held that the right of ownership over a film lies with the producer of the film and he can claim exclusive rights over a musical work that is rendered in the film unless there is a contract to the contrary between the composer and the producer.

R.G. Anand Case[22]

Facts of the Case

The appellant-plaintiff is a playwright, dramatist and producer of stage plays. The appellant had written and, produced a number of plays. The subject matter of the appeal however, is the play entitled 'Hum Hindustani'. This play was written by him in the year 1953 and was enacted in the year 1954 and thereafter the play proved to be popular one. In November 1954 the appellant received a letter from the second defendant, Mr. Mohan Sehgal requesting the appellant to supply a copy of the play so that he

22. *R.G. Anand Vs. M/S. Delux Films & Others*, AIR 1978 SC 1613; (1978) SCC (4) 118.

could consider the desirability of making, a film on it. Thereafter, the appellant and defendant No. 2 met at Delhi and heard the story from the plaintiff and depart with a word that he will inform his decision to the plaintiff after returning to Bombay. In May, 1955 the second defendant announced the production of a motion picture entitled 'New Delhi'. The picture was released in Delhi in September 1956. The appellant saw the picture and found that it is the production of his play 'Hum Hindustani' on screen in substantial form.

The appellant then filed a suit alleging that the film 'New Delhi' was entirely based upon the play 'Hum Hindustani', that the play was narrated by the appellant to defendant No. 2 and he dishonestly imitated the same in his film and thus committed an act of piracy as to result in violation of the copyright of the plaintiff. The appellant, therefore, filed the suit for damages, for decree for accounts of the profits made by the defendant and a decree for permanent injunction against the defendants restraining them from exhibiting the film. The suit was contested by the defendants. The defendants pleaded that defendant No. 2 is a film director and producer and director of Delux Films defendant No.1 that at the instance of a common friend Mr. Gargi the defendant No. 2 met the appellant and saw the script of the play, that the play was inadequate for the purpose of making of a full length commercial motion picture. The defendants contended that there could be no copyright so far as the subject of provincialism is concerned which can be used or adopted by anybody in his own way. The defendants further contended that the motion picture was quite different from the play both in contents, spirit and climax. The mere fact of some similarities between the films and the play could be explained by the fact that the idea, provincialism was the common source of the play as also of the film. The trial court raised several issues and came to the conclusion that the appellant was the owner of the copyright in 'Hum Hindustani' but there was no violation of copyright of the appellant. Thereafter, the appellant filed an appeal in the Delhi High Court. A Division Bench of the Delhi High Court upheld the decree dismissing the appellant's suit.

This appeal by special leave is directed against the judgment of the Delhi High Court dated 23rd May, 1967 affirming the decree of the District Judge, Delhi and dismissing the plaintiff's suit for damages against the defendants on the ground that they had violated the copyrighted work of the plaintiff which was a drama called 'Hum Hindustani'.

Analysis of the Case

The analysis may be stated with the contentions made by both the parties before the apex court. **The counsel for the appellant** contended that: (1) the principles enunciated and the legal inference drawn by the courts below are against the settled legal principles laid down by the courts in England, America and India. (2) The two courts have not fully understood the imports of the violation of copyright particularly when the similarities between the play and the film are so close that would lead to the irresistible inference and unmistakable impression that the film is nothing but an imitation of the play. **The counsel for the respondents submitted** that: (1) the two courts below have applied the law correctly. (2) This Hon'ble Court may not enter into the merits in view of the concurrent findings of fact given by the two courts. (3) Even on the facts found it is manifest that there is a vast difference both in the spirit and the contents between the play and the film.

In order to appreciate the argument of the parties the court discussed the law on the subject. At the time when the cause of action arose in the present suit, the Indian Parliament had not made any law governing copyright violation and therefore, the court relied on the old law passed by the British Parliament *viz.*, the Copyright Act of 1911. Section 1, Sub-Sec. (2)(d) defines copyright as including in the case of a literary, dramatic or musical work, to make any record, performed roll, cinematograph film, or other contrivance by means of which the work may be mechanically performed or delivered. S. 2(i) defines that copyright in a work shall be deemed to be infringed by any person who without the consent of the owner of the copyright, does anything, the sole right to do which is by this Act conferred on the owner of the copyright. The play written by the appellant falls within the definition of copyright. It is well settled principle of law that a mere idea cannot be the subject matter of copyright. In the present case the two courts, in fact, having considered the entire evidences, circumstances and materials before them have come to a finding of fact that defendants committed no violation of the copyright. The Supreme Court was slow to disturb the findings of fact arrived at by the courts below particularly when after having gone through the entire evidence the court finds that the judgments of the court below are absolutely correct.

On a careful comparison of the script of the plaintiff's copyright play with the film, although one does not fail to discern a few resemblances and similarities between the play and the film, the said resemblances are not material or substantial and the degree of similarities is not such as to lead one to think that the film taken as a whole constitutes an unfair appropriation of the appellant's copyright work. In fact a large majority of material incidents, episodes and dramatic situations portrayed by defendants 1 and 2 in their aforesaid film are substantially different from the plaintiff's protected work and the two social evils viz. caste system and dowry system sought to be exposed and eradicated by defendants 1 and 2 by means of motion film, do not figure at all in the appellant's play.

There has been no breach on the part of the defendants of the appellant's copyright. It appears from a comparison of the script of the play 'Hum Hindustani' and the script of the film 'New Delhi' that the authors of the film have been influenced to a degree by the salient features of the plot set forth in the play script. There can be little doubt from the evidence that the author of the film script was aware of the scheme of the play. But, the story portrayed by the film travels beyond the plot delineated in the play. The theme of provincial parochialism is illustrated only in the opposition to a relationship by marriage between two families hailing from different parts of the country. In the film the theme is also illustrated by the hostile attitude of proprietors of lodging accommodation towards prospective lodgers who do not belong to the same provincial community. The plot then extends to the evils of the dowry system which is a theme independent of provincial parochialism. There are still other themes embraced within the plot of the film. The question can arise whether there is an infringement of copyright even though the essential features of the play can be said to correspond to a part only of the plot of the film. In the attempt to show that he is not guilty of infringement of copyright it is always possible for a person intending to take advantage of the intellectual efforts and labour of another to so develop his own product that it covers a wider field than the area included within the scope of the earlier product and in the common area covered by the two productions to introduce changes in order to disguise the attempt at plagiarism. If a reappraisal of the facts in the present case were open to this Court, the Court perhaps would have differed from the view taken on the facts by the High Court but in view of the concurrent findings of the two courts below to the effect that the appellant's copyright has not been infringed this Court is extremely reluctant to interfere with the concurrent findings of fact reached by the Courts below. In another, and perhaps a clearer case for the Apex Court was to interfere and remove the impression which might have gained ground that the copyright belonging to an author can be readily infringed by making immaterial changes, introducing in substantial differences and enlarging the scope of the original theme. So that a veil of apparent dissimilarity is thrown around the work then produced. The Court looked strictly at not only blatant examples of copying but also took reprehensible attempts at colourable imitation.

The facts have been succinctly stated by the District Judge in his judgment and summarised by the High Court, and, therefore, the Supreme Court has not repeated the same all over again, however, a brief resume of some of the striking facts in the case which might be germane for the purpose of deciding the important issues involved in the appeal may not be out of place. It might mentioned here that the High Court as also the District Judge negatived the plaintiff's claim and *prima facie* the appeal appears to be concluded by finding of fact, but it was rightly argued by Mr. Andley, appealing for the appellant, that the principles of violation of copyright in the instant appeal have to be applied on the facts found and the inferences from proved facts drawn by the High Court which is doubtless, a question of law and more particularly, as there is no clear authority of the Court on the subject. The court agreed on the persuasion to go into this question without entering into findings of facts. After hearing counsel for the parties, the court felt that as the case is one of first impression and needs to be decided, as such the court entered into the merits, on the basis of the facts, found and inferences drawn by the High Court and the District Judge. Relying on the fact that both the District Judge and the High Court have relied upon some well established principles to determine whether or not in a particular case a violation of copyright has taken place, but learned counsel for the appellant has challenged the validity of the principles enunciated by the High Court.

The plaintiff is an architect by profession and is also a playwright, dramatist and producer of stage plays. Even before 'Hum Hindustani' the plaintiff had written and produced a number of other plays like 'Des Hamara', 'Azadi' and 'Election' which were staged in Delhi. The subject matter of the appeal, however, is the play entitled 'Hum Hindustani'. According to the plaintiff, this play was written by him in Hindi in the year 1953 and was enacted by him for the first time on 6th, 7th, 8th and 9th February, 1954 at Wavell Theatre, New Delhi under the auspices of the Indian National Theatre. The play proved to be very popular and received great approbation from the Press and the public as a result of which the play was restaged in February and September, 1954 and also in 1955 and 1956 at Calcutta. In support of his case the plaintiff has referred to a number of comments appearing in the *Indian Express, Hindustan Times, Times of India* and other papers. Encouraged by the success and popularity of the aforesaid play the plaintiff tried to consider the possibility of filming it. In November, 1954 the plaintiff received a letter dated 19th November, 1954 from the second defendant Mr. Mohan Sehgal wherein the defendant informed the plaintiff that he was supplied with a synopsis of the play by one Mr. Balwant Gargi, a common friend of the plaintiff and the defendant. The defendant had requested the plaintiff to supply a copy of the play so that the defendant may consider the desirability of making a film on it. The plaintiff, however, by his letter dated 30th November, 1954 informed the defendant that as the play had been selected out of 17 Hindi plays for National Drama Festival and would be staged on 11th December, 1954, the defendant should take the trouble of visiting Delhi and seeing the play himself in order to examine the potentialities of making a film, and at that time the matter could be discussed by the defendant with the plaintiff. However, some time about January, 1955 the second and the third defendants came to Delhi, met the plaintiff in his office where the plaintiff read out and explained the entire play to the defendants and also discussed the possibility of filming it. The second defendant did not make any clear commitment but promised the plaintiff that he would inform him about his reaction after reaching Bombay. Thereafter, the plaintiff heard nothing from the defendant. Sometime in May, 1955 the second defendant announced the production of a motion picture entitled 'New Delhi'. One Mr. Thapa who was one of the artists in the play produced by the plaintiff happened to be in Bombay at the time when the picture 'New Delhi' was being produced by the defendant and informed the plaintiff that the picture being produced by the defendant was really based on the plaintiff's play 'Hum Hindustani'. The plaintiff thereupon by his letter dated 30th May, 1955 wrote to the second defendant expressing serious concern over the adaptation of his play into a motion picture called 'New Delhi'. The defendant, however, by his letter dated 9th June, 1955 informed the plaintiff that his doubts were without any foundation and assured the plaintiff that the story treatment, dramatic construction, characters, etc. were quite different and bore not the remotest connection or resemblance with the play written by the plaintiff.

The picture was released in Delhi in September, 1956 and the plaintiff read some comments in the papers which gave the impression that the picture was very much like the play 'Hum Hindustani' written by the plaintiff. The plaintiff himself saw the picture on the 9th September, 1956 and he found that the film was entirely based upon the said play and was, therefore, convinced that the defendant after having heard the play narrated to him by the plaintiff dishonestly imitated the same in his film and thus, committed an act of piracy so as to result in violation of the copyright of the plaintiff. The plaintiff accordingly filed the suit for damages, for decree for accounts of the profits made by the defendants and a decree for permanent injunction against the defendants restraining them from exhibiting the film 'New Delhi'.

The defendants, *inter alia,* pleaded that they neither were aware that the plaintiff was the author of the play 'Hum Hindustani' nor were they aware that the play was very well received at Delhi. Defendant No. 2 is a film Director and is also the proprietor of defendant No. 1 Delux Films. The defendants averred that in November, 1954 the second defendant was discussing some ideas for his new picture with Mr. Balwant Gargi who is a playwright of some repute. In the course of the discussion, the second defendant informed Mr. Gargi that the second defendant was interested in producing a motion film based on 'provincialism' as its central theme. In the context of these discussions Mr. Gargi enquired of defendant No. 2 if the latter was interested in hearing the play called 'Hum Hindustani' produced by the plaintiff, which also had the same theme of provincialism in which the second defendant was interested. It was, therefore, at the instance of Mr. Gargi that the second defendant wrote to the plaintiff and requested him to send a copy of the script of the play. The defendant goes on to state that the plaintiff read out the play to the second defendant in the presence of Rajinder Bhatia and Mohan Kumar, Assistant Directors of the second defendant when they had come to Delhi in connection with the release of their film 'Adhikar'. The second defendant has taken a clear stand that after having heard the play he informed the plaintiff that though the play might have been all right for the amateur stage, it was too inadequate for the purpose of making a full length commercial motion picture. The defendants denied the allegation of the plaintiff that it was after hearing the play written by the plaintiff that the defendants decided to make a film based on the play and entitled it as 'New Delhi'.

The defendant thus submitted that there could be no copyright so far as the subject of provincialism is concerned which can be used or adopted by anybody in his own way. He further averred that the motion picture was quite different from the play 'Hum Hindustani' both in contents, spirit and climax. The mere fact that there were some similarities between the film and the play could be explained by the fact that the idea, viz., provincialism was the common source of the play as also of the film. The defendant thus denied that there was any violation of the copyright.

On the basis of the pleadings of the parties, the learned trial Judge framed the following issues:

1. Is the plaintiff owner of the copyright in the play 'Hum Hindustani'?
2. Is the film 'New Delhi' an infringement of the plaintiff's copyright in the play 'Hum Hindustani'?

3. Have defendants or any of them infringed the plaintiff's copyright by producing, or distributing or exhibiting the film 'New Delhi'?
4. Is the suit bad for mis-joinder of defendants and cause of action?
5. To what relief is the plaintiff entitled and against whom?

Issue No. 1 was decided against the defendants and it was held by the trial Judge that the plaintiff was the owner of the copyright in the play 'Hum Hindustani'. Issue No. 4 was not pressed by the defendants and was accordingly decided against them. The main case however turned upon the decision on issues No. 2 and 3 which were however decided against the plaintiff as the learned Judge held that there was no violation of the copyright of the plaintiff. The plaintiff then went up in appeal to the Delhi High Court where a Division Bench of that Court affirmed the decision of the District Judge and upheld the decree dismissing the plaintiff's suit. The findings of fact arrived at by the learned trial Judge and the High Court have not been assailed before the Supreme Court. The only argument advanced by the appellant was that the principles enunciated and the legal inferences drawn by the courts below are against the settled legal principles laid down by the courts in England, America and India. It was also submitted by Mr. Andley that the two courts have not fully understood the import of the violation of copyright particularly when the similarities between the play and the film are so close and sundry that would lead to the irresistible inference and unmistakable impression that the film is nothing but an imitation of the play. On the other hand, it was argued by Mr. Hardy counsel for the respondents that the two courts below have applied the law correctly and it is not necessary for this Court to enter into merits in view of the concurrent findings of fact given by the two courts. He further submitted that even on the facts found it is manifest that there is a vast difference both in the spirit and the content between the play 'Hum Hindustani' and the film 'New Delhi' and no question of violation of the copyright arises.

Thus, the position appears to be that an idea, principle, theme, or subject matter or historical or legendary facts being common property cannot be the subject matter of copyright of a particular person. It is always open to any person to choose an idea as a subject matter and develop it in his own manner and give expression to the idea by treating it differently from others. Where two writers write on the same subject similarities are bound to occur because the central idea of both are the single but the similarities or coincidences by themselves cannot lead to an irresistible inference of plagiarism or piracy. Take for instance the great poet and dramatist Shakespeare most of whose plays are based on Greek-Roman and British mythology or legendary stories like *Merchant of Venice, Hamlet, Romeo Juliet, Julius Caesar,* etc. But the treatment of the subject by Shakespeare in each of his dramas is so fresh, so different, and full of poetic exuberance, elegance and erudition and so novel in character as a result of which the end product becomes an original in itself. In fact, the power and passion of his expression, the uniqueness, eloquence and excellence of his style and pathos and bathos of the dramas become peculiar to Shakespeare and leaves precious little of the original theme adopted by him. It will thus be preposterous to level a charge of plagiarism against the great play-writer. In fact, throughout his original thinking, ability and incessant labour Shakespeare has converted an old idea into a new one, so that each of the dramas constitutes a master piece of English literature.

It has been rightly said that 'every drama of Shakespeare is an extended metaphor'. Thus, the fundamental fact which has to be determined where a charge of violation of the copyright is made by the plaintiff against the defendant is to determine whether or not the defendant not only adopted the idea of the copyrighted work but has also adopted the manner, arrangement, situation to situation, scene to scene with minor changes or super additions or embellishment here and there. Indeed, if on a perusal of the copyrighted work the defendant's work appears to be a transparent rephrasing or a copy of a substantial and material part of the original, the charge of plagiarism must stand proved. Care however must be taken to see whether the defendant has merely disguised piracy or has actually reproduced the original in a different form, different tone, and different tenor so as to infuse a new life into the idea of the copyrighted work adapted by him. In the latter case there is no violation of the copyright.

Thus, on a careful consideration and elucidation of the various authorities and the decided cases in various countries viz. England, America and India, etc. on the subject discussed above, the Apex Court emerged with the following propositions:

1. There can be no copyright in an idea, subject matter, themes, plots or historical or legendary facts and violation of the copyright in such cases is confined to the form, manner and arrangement and expression of the idea by tile author of the copyrighted work.
2. Where the same idea is being developed in a different manner, it is manifest that the source being common, similarities are bound to occur. In such a case the courts should determine whether or not the similarities are on fundamental or substantial aspects of the mode of expression adopted in the copyrighted work. If the defendant's work is nothing but a literal imitation of the copyrighted work with some variations here and there it would amount to violation of the copyright. In other words, in order to be actionable the copy must be a substantial and material one which at once leads to the conclusion that the defendant is guilty of an act of piracy.
3. One of the surest and the safest test to determine whether or not there has been a violation of copyright is to see if the reader, spectator or the viewer after having read or seen both the works is clearly of the opinion and gets an unmistakable impression that the subsequent work appears to be a copy of the original.
4. Where the theme is the same but is presented and treated differently so that the subsequent work becomes a completely new work, no question of violation of copyright arises.
5. Where however apart from the similarities appearing in the two works there are also material and broad dissimilarities which negative the intention to copy the original and the coincidences appearing in the two works are clearly incidental, no infringement of the copyright comes into existence.
6. As a violation of copyright amounts to an act of piracy it must be proved by clear and cogent evidence after

applying the various tests laid down by decided case laws.

7. Where however the question is of the violation of the copyright of a stage play by a film producer or a Director the task of the plaintiff becomes more difficult to prove piracy. It is manifest that unlike a stage play a film has a much broader prospective, wider field and a bigger background where the defendants can by introducing a variety of incidents give a colour and complexion different from the manner in which the copyrighted work has expressed the Idea. Even so, if the viewer after seeing the film gets a totality of impression that the film is by and large a copy of the original play, violation of the copyright may be said to be proved.

Following are some of the cases which have been analysed and found helpful in setting the abovementioned remarkable points. *Hanfstaengl Vs. W.H. Singh & Sons;*[23] *Bobbs-Merill Co. Vs. Isdor Straus and Nathan Straus;*[24] *Ladbroke (Football) Ltd. Vs. William Hill (Football) Ltd.;*[25] *N.T. Ragllunathan & Anr. Vs. All India Reporter Ltd., Bombay;*[26] *Mohini Mohan Singh & Ors Vs. Sita Nath Basak.*[27]

The Supreme Court then endeavoured to apply the principles enunciated above and the tests laid down by it to the facts of the present case in order to determine whether or not the plaintiff has been able to prove the charge of plagiarism and violation of copyright levelled against the dependant by the plaintiff. The learned trial Judge who had also had the advantage of seeing the picture was of the opinion that the film taken as a whole is quite different from the play written by the plaintiff. In order to test the correctness of the finding of the trial Court, the Supreme Court also got the play read to it by the plaintiff in presence of counsel for the parties and has also seen the film which was screened at C.P.W.D. Auditorium, Mahadev Road, New Delhi. This was done merely to appreciate the judgment of the trial Court and the evidence led by the parties and was not at all meant to be just a substitute for the evidence led by the parties. Bearing in mind the well recognised principles and tests

23. [1905] 1 Chancery Division 519.
24. 210 US 339; West Francis, (1822) 1 B & Ald. 737, 743.
25. (1964) 1 All. E.R. 465.
26. AIR 1971 Bom. 48.
27. AIR 1931 Cal. 238.

to determine whether there has been an infringement of the law relating to copyright in a particular case which were brought to the notice of the Supreme Court by the counsel on both sides and which have been elaborately considered and discussed by learned justice Murtaza Fazal Ali in the course of the judgment prepared by him, the Court proceeded at the request of the counsel to hear the script of the play 'Hum Hindustani' which as read out to it by the plaintiff himself in a dramatic style and to see the film 'New Delhi' produced by defendants 1 and 2, the exhibition of which was arranged by the defendants themselves. On a careful comparison of the script of the plaintiff's copyrighted play with the aforesaid film, although one does not fail to discern a few resemblances and similarities between the play and the film, the said resemblances are not material or substantial and the degree of similarities is not such as to lead one to think that the film taken as a whole constitutes an unfair appropriation of the plaintiff's copyrighted work. In fact, a large majority of material incidents, episodes and situations portrayed by defendants 1 and 2 in their aforesaid film are substantially different from the plaintiff's protected work and the two social evils viz. caste system and dowry system sought to be exposed and eradicated by defendants 1 and 2 by means of their aforesaid film do not figure at all in the plaintiff's play.

After going through the script of the play and the film the Court was inclined to agree with the opinion of the Courts below. It has already pointed out that mere similarities by themselves are not sufficient to raise inference of colourable imitation on the other hand there are quite a number of dissimilarities also. As such the Court was of complete agreement with the conclusions arrived at by learned Justice Murtaza Fazal Ali that there has been no breach on the part of the defendants of the plaintiff's copyright and concur with the judgment proposed to be delivered by him.

It appears from a comparison of the script of the stage play 'Hum Hindustani' and the script of the film 'New Delhi' that the authors of the film script have been inclined to some extend by the salient features of the plot set forth in the play script. There would be no doubt from the evidence that the authors of the film script had the knowledge of the scheme of the play. But on the other hand, the story depicted in the film was not the direct copy of the play as it travels beyond the plot outlined in the play, though, the theme of provincialism and relationship by inter-regional marriage was similar. The film is based on the theme aggressiveness and attitude of two families who are not from the same place, cast, province and community. Though, both the plots representing the same social evils like dowry system, provincialism and regionalism but apart from these facts other indifferent aspects are also clinched within the theme in the film.

Nonetheless, the question can arise whether there is an infringement of copyright even though the essential features of the play can be said to correspond to a part only of the plot of the film. This can arise even where changes are effected while planning the film so that certain immaterial features in the film differ from what is seen in the stage play. The relative position in which the principal actors stand may be exchanged or extended and embellishments may be introduced in the attempt to show that the plot in the film is entirely original and bear no resemblance whatever to the stage play. All such matters fell for consideration in relation to the question whether the relevant part of the plot in the film is merely a colourable imitation of the essential structure of the stage play. If the treatment of the theme in the stage play has been made the basic of one of the themes in the film story and the essential structure of that treatment is clearly and distinctly identifiable in the film story, the court might not necessarily examine all the several themes embraced within the plot of the film in order to decide whether infringement has been established. In the attempt to show that one is not guilty of infringement of copyright, it is always possible for a person intending to take advantage of the intellectual effort and labours of another to develop his own product that it covers a wider field than the area included within the scope of the earlier product, and in the common area covered by the two productions to introduce changes in order to disguise the attempt at plagiarism. If a reappraisal of the facts in the present case had been open, the Court surely would not have differed from the view taken on the facts by the High Court, but as the matter stands, the trial Court as well as the High Court have concurred in the finding that such similarities as exist between the stage play 'Hum Hindustani' and the film 'New Delhi' do not make out a case of infringement. The dissimilarities, in their opinion, are so material that it is not possible to say that the appellant's copyright has been infringed.

Thus, applying the principles enunciated above and the various tests laid down to determine whether in a particular case there has been a violation of the copyright the Supreme Court opined that the film produced by the defendants cannot be said to be a substantial or material copy of the play written by the plaintiff. The Supreme Court also found that the treatment of the film and the manner of its presentation on the screen is quite different from the one written by the plaintiff at the stage. The Court was also satisfied that after seeing the play and the film no prudent person can get an impression that the film appears to be a copy of the original play nor is there anything to show that the film is a substantial and material copy of the play. At the most the central idea of the play, namely, provincialism is undoubtedly the subject matter of the film along with other ideas also but it is well settled that a mere idea cannot be the subject matter of copyright. Thus, the present case does not fulfil the conditions laid down for holding that the defendants have made a colourable imitation of the play. On a close and careful comparison of the play and the picture for the central idea (provincialism which is not protected by copyright), from scene to scene, situation to situation, in climax to anti-climax, pathos, bathos, in texture and treatment and purport and presentation, it is clear that the picture is materially different from the play. As already indicated above, applying the various tests outlined above the Court was unable to hold that the defendants have committed an act of piracy in violating the copyright of the play.

Apart from this the two courts of fact, having considered the entire evidence, circumstances and materials before them have come to a finding of fact that the defendants committed no violation of the copyright. The Apex Court would also reluctant to disturb the findings of fact arrived at by the courts below particularly when after having gone through the entire evidence, it felt that the judgment of the courts below are absolutely correct. The result is that the appeal fails and is accordingly dismissed without any order as to costs.

Gramophone Company of India Limited Case[28]

Special features of this case are that it deals with the rights of the owner of copyrights to stop the infringing copies from being transmitted to another country.

Facts of the Case

The Gramophone Company of India Limited is a well known manufacture of musical records and cassettes. It receives information from the customs authorities at Calcutta that a consignment of re-recorded cassettes sent by the Universal Overseas Pvt. Ltd., Singapore to M/s. Sungawa Enterprise, Kathmandu, Nepal had arrived at Calcutta Port by ship and was awaiting dispatch to Nepal. The gramophone company was informed that these cassettes were pirated works and they claimed the rights over the consignment. They approached to the Registrar of Copyrights to take action under Section 53 of the Copyright Act, 1957. This provision enables the Registrar after making necessary enquiries as he deems fit to order that copies made out of India of a work which if made in India would infringe copyright, shall not be imported. The section also enable the Registrar to enter any ship, dock or premised where such copies may be found and to examine such copies.

All copies in respect of which an order is made prohibited or restricted under Section 11 of the Customs Act of 1962. The provisions of the Customs Act are to the effect in respect of those copies. All copies confiscated under the provisions of the said Act are not to vest in the Government but have to be delivered to the owner of the copyright in the work. As the Registrar was not taken expeditious action on the application of the Gramophone Company, the gramophone company apprehending that the pirated cassettes would then be transported to Nepal, filed a writ of mandamus to compel the Registrar to pass an appropriate order under Section 53 of the Copyright Act and to prevent release of the cassettes from the custody of the Customs Authorities. The learned Single Judge of the Calcutta High Court issued a rule nisi and made an interim order permitting the appellant to inspect the consignment of cassettes and if any of the cassettes were found to infringe the Gramophone's copyrights

28. *Gramophone Company of India Limited Vs. Birendra Bahadur Pandey and Other*, 1984 (2) SCC 534; (195-0-2000) 22 PTC Supp (1) 547 (SC); AIR 1984 SC 667.

they were to be kept apart until further orders of the Registrar. After causing the necessary inspection to be made the Registrar was directed to deal with the application under Section 53 of the Copyright Act in accordance with law after hearing the interested parties. The Registrar was directed to deal with the application within 8 weeks from the date of the High Court's order. In the event of any of the cassettes being held back by the Gramophone Company, which was not an infringement of any rights under the Copyright Act. The Gramophone Co. was to pay damages as assessed by the Courts. The consignee filed an appeal against this order made by the single judge.

Analysis of the Case

The division Bench of the Calcutta High Court examined this case under various provisions of the Copyright Act and on the established rules of international law viz. The Convention on Transit Trade of Landlocked States, 1965: Art. 11: Treaty of Trade with Nepal, Art. 10: Treaty of transit with Nepal; Art. 9: International Convention for the protection of literary and artistic works, 1971. Article 16 of the Universal Copyright Convention has already laid down the principle that the States shall endeavour to grant maximum facilities and undertake all necessary measures for the free an unhampered flow of goods from one country to the other.

However, the State also have a duty to co-operate effectively with each other to prevent infringement and circumvention of laws, rules and regulations of individuals' literary or artistic property and prevent any form of unfair competition. Special mention was made in relation to Article 16 of the Berne Convention which provides as follows:

> "Infringing copies of a work shall be liable to seizure in any country of the union where the work enjoys legal protection".

India is a party to the Berne Convention. Applying these international norms the Court then referred to the relevant sections of the Copyright Act. The first issue relates to whether the pirated cassettes that are in transit, amount to infringing copies and it was then examined whether the Registrar has power to deal with the importation of the infringing copies under Section 53 of the India Copyright Act. Section 52 of the Copyright

Act states that a copyright in a work shall be deemed to be infringed when any person: (i) makes for sale or hire or sells or lets for hire or by way of trade displays or offers for sale or hire or (ii) distributes either for the purpose of trade or to such an extent as to effect prejudicially the owner of the copyright, or (iii) by way of trade exhibits in public, or (iv) imports (except for the private and domestic use of the importer) into India any infringing copies of the work.

The Court then directed its attention to Section 53 as it deals with importation of infringing copies. Section 53 states: (i) The Registrar of copyrights on supplication by the owner of the copyrights in any work or by his duly authorised agent and on payment of the prescribed fees may agree making such inquiry as he deems fit, order that copies made out of India of the work which is made in India· would infringe copyright shall not be imported. (ii) Subject to any rules made under this Act, the Registrar of copyrights or any person authorised by him in his behalf may enter into any ship, dock or premises where any such copies as are referred to in sub-section (1) may be found and may examine such copies. (iii) All copies to which any order made under sub-section (1) applied shall be deemed to be goods of which the import has been prohibited or restricted under Section 11 of Customs Act, 1962 and all the provisions of that Act shall have effect accordingly:

Provided that all such copies confiscated under the provisions of this Act shall not vest in the Government but shall be delivered to the owner of the copyright in the work.

Section 53 of the Indian Copyright Act, thus empowers the Registrar of the Copyrights to make an order that the copies of the work which infringes the copyright shall not be imported and the effect of the order is that it attracts the provisions of the Customs Act including the liability to confiscate and the confiscated copies are then delivered to the owner of the copyrights. The subject of dispute relates to the word 'import' that is mentioned in Section 53 of the Copyright Act. In this case the goods were not brought into the country for commerce and trademark but for onward transmission to another country. The question then can they be said to be imported into the country for which an action arise under Indian Copyright Act.

The object of the Copyright Act is to prevent unauthorised reproduction of work or unathorised exploitation of the works and the object of this Act would be frustrated if infringing copies of the work are allowed to transit across the country. If goods are brought in only to go out they are in import in technical terms. The Court, however, did not accept any narrow interpretation to the word 'import' and rose to the occasion to stop that trafficking in industrial, literary and artistic property and it did not hesitate to conclude that the word 'import' means bringing into India from outside India and it cannot be limited to importation for commerce only. It includes importation for transit across the country. Such interpretation was held not to be inconsistent with any principle of international law and as such pass an order for an examination by the Registrar in accordance with Section 53 of the Indian Copyright Act. It directed the Registrar to examine the issues whether the copies infringed the Copyright of the complainant and conduct a quasi-judicial enquiry to determine the rights over the goods.

Gramophone Company of India Limited Case[29]

Facts of the Case

The Gramophone Company of India Limited which is the plaintiff in this case had produced audio records titled 'Hum Aapke Hain Kaun' under rights alleged to have been assigned to it by Rajashree Production Pvt. Ltd. who happen to be copyright owners of the Cinematographic work? The plaintiff claims that it has already sold 55 lakh audio cassettes and 40,000 compacts disc titled 'Hum Aapke Hain Kaun' and hope to sell an equal number of additional audio cassettes and compact discs with the result that the title 'Hum Aapke Hain Kaun', when used on a record, has come to be associated with the plaintiff alone. Its grievance is that the defendants too have launched an audio cassette by adopting 'Hum Aapke Hain Kaun' as its title with its design, colour scheme, get up and lay-out deceptively and confusingly similar to that of the plaintiff's and have even used a photograph of Salman Khan and Madhuri Dixit on the inlay cards. Both of them, it may be noticed, have acted in the film 'Hum Aapke Hain

29. *Gramophone Company of India Ltd. Vs. Super Cassette Industries Ltd.*, (1995) 1 Arb. LR 555: 1995 PTR 64: 1996 PTC (16) 252 DEL.

Kaun'. Hence, the suit of the plaintiff for permanent injunction restraining the defendants form manufacturing, selling, or passing of audio cassettes under the said title or from manufacturing, selling, or passing of audio cassettes under the said title or from using a carton or inlay card identical or deceptively or confusingly used by the plaintiff. Along with the suit, the plaintiff company also moved an application under Order 39, Rules 1 and 2 for grant of ad-interim injunction.

Analysis of the Case

Version Recording: A version recording is a sound recording made of already published songs by using another voice or voices and with different musicians and arrangers. Version recording in this regard neither copying nor reproduction of the original recording. A version recording is protected under clause (j) of sub-section (1) of Section 52 of the Act. It runs as under:

> "Certain acts not to be infringement of copyright, the following acts shall not constitute an infringement of copyright namely,
>
> (j) the making of records in respect of any literary, dramatic or musical work, if
>
> (i) records recording that work have previously been made by, or with the licence or consent of, the owner of the copyright in the work; and
>
> (ii) the person making the records has given the prescribed notice of his intention to make the records, and has paid in the prescribed manner to the owner of the copyright in the work royalties in respect of all such records to be made by him, at the rate fixed by the Copyright Board in this behalf:
>
> Provided that in making the records such person shall not make any alterations in, or omissions from, the work, unless records recording the work subject to similar alterations and omissions have been previously made by, or with the licence or consent of, the owner of the copyright or

unless such alterations and omissions are reasonably necessary for the adaptation of the work to the records in question.

On an examination of the facts of the case it was decided by the Courts that the injunction that was awarded in favour of the plaintiffs should be set aside as the Act permits version recording and the defendants were permitted to record the music subject to the condition that it should not use the cartoon or inlay card or any other packaging material similar to that of the plaintiffs and an alternate title must be given with a declaration in sufficiently bold letters that the record is not the original sound track but only a version record with voices of different artists, the word that it is not the original work should be clearly underlined.

Ambience Space Sellers Ltd. Case[30]

The significance of this case is that an action was claimed not only under the Copyright Act but also under the Law of Tort claiming an action under various other heads viz. *inducing* a breach of contract, passing off and for conversion.

Facts of the Case

The 2nd plaintiffs were owner of copyrights in various programmes that were produced in India. They had given the exclusive licences to the third plaintiff to broadcast these programmes on the TV channel known as 'Zee TV'. The first plaintiff was the sole agent who procured for the third plaintiff's advertisements in India. Thus the arrangement was that the 3rd plaintiff was receiving the programme from the owner (2nd plaintiff) and the advertisement from the 1st plaintiff would combine the two and broadcast the programme on Zee TV channel. The advertiser would choose the programme in which to advertise according to the timing of the programme and to the popularity of the programme. The defendants were the two companies' owner controlled and operated the Cable TV networks in several cities. Most of the viewers in cities like Bombay were connected to the Cable TV network. The cable TV networks had sophisticated equipments by which it was possible

30. *Ambience Space Sellers Ltd. Vs. Asia Industrial Technology Pvt. Ltd.*, 1998 (1) Raj. 319 (Bom.)

to blank out/switch off the signals sent by various broadcasters and interpose/substitute their own programme of materials.

The main allegation of the plaintiffs was that the defendants had blanked out the plaintiff's advertisement and substituted the defendant's advertisement during the period that the plaintiffs are broadcasting their advertisement. This was admitted by the defendants. The defendants claimed that they had a right to do so and they were entitled to do so.

The plaintiffs based their action on various ground. It alleged that the defendants had committed the torts of (a) inducing a breach of contract; (b) passing off; and (c) conversion. It also claimed an action for violation of copyright and broadcast reproduction rights.

Analysis of the Case and the principles evolved

Tort of inducing breach of contract and copyright: This tort has been recognised by the English Courts as well as the Indian Courts. Basically tortuous liability arises from a breach of duty primarily fixed by law. The Courts in general has developed this law and it is founded and structured on morality that is no one has a right to injure or harm others intentionally or ever innocently. The Supreme Court and various High Courts have assisted in the expansion of the rights under the Law of Torts so as to provide legal rights for social development and cultural refineness. The tort of inducing breach of contract has been well established. The first major decision in the English Court that has clearly laid down the elements of this tort is case of *Quinn Vs. Leathem.*[31] The case has clearly established that any wrongful interference with contractual relations without legal justification can give rise to an action under the Law of Torts. In this case the plaintiff used to regularly supply meat to a butcher. The plaintiff had employed certain persons who were not members of a particular union. The union asked the plaintiff not to employ non-members and to only employ their members. The plaintiffs refused to do so. Then the union convinced the employees of the butcher to boycott the work of the butcher, if plaintiff's meat was accepted by the butcher. As the butcher's employees threatened to boycott their work the butcher refused to take meat from the plaintiff. Thus, the plaintiff was not permitted to sell his meat

31. Reported in 1901 Appeal Cases, p. 495.

and thereby there was a clear interference in the contractual relationship between the plaintiff and the butcher due to the interference of the union. Such action is not acceptable under the Law of Torts and the third party who has induced a breach of a subsisting contract can be sued for inducing a breach of contract and when it cannot justify its action the third party can be sued under the Law of Torts.

Similarly, various other cases have accepted the principle laid down in *Quinn Vs. Leathem Case.*[32] For instance, in the case of *GWK Ltd. and Others Vs. Dunlop Rubber Co. Ltd.,*[33] the action was brought by two plaintiffs against the Dunlop Rubber Company. The first plaintiff was the manufacturer of motor cars who had a contract with the second plaintiff for the tyres to be installed for their cars. An agreement was made between the two plaintiffs that the tyres for the cars of first plaintiff should be fitted with tyres of the second plaintiff. When the cars were sent to an exhibition the defendants, who were the Dunlop Rubber Company, substituted their tyres on the night before the opening of the exhibition. They were aware of the agreement between the 1st and 2nd plaintiffs. Thus, the plaintiffs filed a suit against the defendant for knowingly interfering with the contractual rights and inducing a breach of a contract between the first and the second plaintiffs.

Various other cases have been cited by the plaintiff in this case to establish that the defendants have committed the tort of inducing of a breach of contract. The various elements of this torts are: (i) there must be a direct invasion of a subsisting contract; (ii) the unlawful act committed by a third party should prevent the performance of the subsisting contract; (iii) a third party should commit an unlawful act of inducing a breach of a subsisting contract.

The plaintiffs held that this case was similar to the facts of the case cited above in GKW's case wherein the tyres were changed without the knowledge and the consent of both the contracting parties and this was held to be a wrongful act. Similarly, in this case the defendants have switched-off the signals of the plaintiffs and did not permit the broadcast of the advertisement that was to be relayed in a particular programme. The defendants

32. *Supra.*
33. *Times Law Reports*, p. 376.

admitted that they had knowledge of the fact that the third plaintiff had a subsisting contract with the advertisers. The action of blanking out the signals in effect had prevented the contract between the plaintiffs whereby the third plaintiff was affected as he had to lose his contract of advertisements. This clearly is an actionable wrong as it was proved that the intention in switching-off/blanking out the plaintiff's advertisement and putting their own advertisement proceed that the defendants had deliberately interfered with a subsisting contract to capitalize the popularity of the plaintiff's programme.

Tort of Passing-off: The second cause of action was based on the tort of passing off. The plaintiffs relied upon the earlier cases to establish their claim under the tort of passing-off. In earlier cases *Illustrated Newspapers Ltd. Vs. The Illustrated London News and Sketch Ltd.* and *The Sporting and Dramatic Publishing Co. Ltd. Vs. Publicity Services (London) Ltd.,*[34] in these cases the plaintiffs were publishers of news papers. The defendants inserted supplements carrying their own advertisements and then bound the papers together and then deliver it to the readers. The chancery division held that such an action by the defendants amounts to a tort of passing-off for the defendants were trying to pass-off their supplements as if the supplements belong to the plaintiffs. People in general would mistake that the supplements are the parts of the paper belonging to the plaintiffs and the affect of it would be that the advertisers would go to the defendants for their advertisements and not to the plaintiffs, and passed order for restraining the defendants from inserting any supplement into the plaintiff's paper.

Citing the above said case the plaintiffs claimed in the instant case that the defendants should be restrained from showing their advertisements. The defendants in turn submitted that they were willing to display on the screen notice that the advertisements were not that of the plaintiffs so as to avoid the action of passing-off. Such disclaimer cannot be sufficient in this case as the defendant had displayed their advertisements for the sole purpose to capitalize on the popularity of the plaintiff's programme. If the defendants wished to display their own advertisements they were always at liberty to display their advertisements in various other programmes and therefore the advertisement

34. Reported in L.V. Reports of Patent Design and Trade Mark cases, p. 172.

with an improper motive to deliberately use the slot that was allotted for the plaintiffs clearly established the tort of passing-off.

An Action for Violation of Copyright and Broadcast Reproduction Rights: Under section 2(g) of the Cable Television Networks (Regulation) Act, 1995, a programme is defined as 'any television broadcast and includes any exhibition of films, features, dramas, advertisements and serials through video cassette recorders or video cassette players'. Under Section 6 no person shall transmit or re-transmit through a cable service any advertisement unless such advertisement is in conformity with the prescribed advertisement code. Proviso however, stated that this section would not apply to programmes of foreign satellite channels which can be received without the use of any specialized gadgets or decoder. The contention of the defendants was that the broadcast of the third plaintiff need not be in conformity with the advertisement code on the grounds that it was relayed from a foreign satellite channel. However, the plaintiffs submitted that the programme that was broadcast was a composite programme containing the original programme that was supplied by the second plaintiff along with the advertisements supplied by the plaintiffs and thus when it is broadcasted through a free to air programme the defendants were aware that the second plaintiffs have given an exclusive license to the third plaintiff and transmitted the signals to their subscribers. The claim made by the defendants is that the contractual agreement between the plaintiffs is not binding on them and that they are free to ignore the contract, was not accepted by the Court. When a person claims a copyright the right to broadcast and communicate to the public is granted under the Copyright Act.

Section 2(dd) of the Copyright Act defines a broadcast. A broadcast also means communication to the public *inter alia* by means of wireless diffusion and includes a re-broadcast. Section 2(f) of the Copyright Act, 1957 provides that a cinematograph film includes any work of visual recording on any medium produced through a process form which a moving image may be produced by any means and includes a sound recording accompanying such visual recording.

Section 2(ff) defines communication to the public. It means making any work available for being seen or heard or otherwise enjoyed by the public directly by means of display or diffusion other than by issuing copies of such work. Ultimately what was broadcast was one composite programme which includes the entertainment portion and the advertisement portion and the defendants had no right to infringe the copyright over this programme.

Moreover, Section 37 of the Copyright Act also confers the right known as broadcast reproduction rights. That was introduced in 1994. With the advent of many foreign broadcasting stations being available in India, Section 37 has incorporated new rights known as 'broadcast reproduction rights' whereby no one can re-broadcast the broadcast or cause of broadcast to be seen or heard by the public on payment of any charges without a licence from the owner. Thus, the defendant had no right to broadcast the programme without the licence from the plaintiffs. By inserting their own advertisements the defendants had violated the provisions of the Section 37 of the Copyright Act, 1957.

The next cause of action was based on the tort of conversion. The tort of conversion is said to have been committed when a person deals with goods in a manner inconsistent with the right of the owner. The elements of this tort are based on two conditions: (i) it is necessary to establish the right over the goods; and (ii) it should be established that the defendants have committed an act which is inconsistent with the owner's rights. Several cases have been cited by the plaintiffs to establish their rights. The first question relates to ownership over the signals and to claim the signals constitute as ownership of chattels and goods. The defendants in their counter submitted that the plaintiffs were only transmitting signals and that signals do not constitute as goods. They further stated that they had not distorted or affected the plaintiff's signals. The question therefore arose whether signals can be considered as goods or chattels under the Sale of Goods Act, 1930. Goods means any moveable property other that an actionable claim and money. In an earlier Supreme Court case of *The Commissioner of Sale Tax, Madhya Pradesh, Indore Vs. M.P. Electricity Board, Jabalpur,*[35] the Supreme

35. AIR 1970 SC 732.

Court held that the term 'movable property' cannot be construed in a narrow sense. The Supreme Court held that merely because electric energy is not tangible and cannot be removed or touched, for instance, like a book or piece of wood does not mean that it ceases to be movable property. The Supreme Court held that electric energy has all the attributes of movable property in as much as it can be transmitted, transferred, delivered, stored and possessed in the same way as in case of other movable property. Signals that are transmitted by the third plaintiff can also be transmitted, transferred, delivered, stored and possessed and they were in fact communicated by the defendants. As such signals can be considered as movable property within the meaning of the Sale of Goods Act, 1930.

The next issue is therefore, whether the plaintiffs can claim that the defendants had committed the tort of conversion. The programme in it's entirely included the entertainment and the advertisement. The defendants had shut out a portion of the programme by deleting the advertisement and substituting their own advertisement. This action amounted to a tort of conversion as they had denied the right of the plaintiffs who were entitled to advertise during the particular time and this right was denied by the defendants who had asserted their right contrary to the right of the plaintiffs. Thus, the plaintiffs have made out a *prima facie* case establishing a cause of action under the tort of conversion. The wilful and intentional act of defendants which has affected the plaintiffs right amounted to a tort of inducing a breach of contract and unlawful interference with the contract, a tort of passing-off, a tort of conversion as well as violation of copyrights and right of broadcast for which an injunction was accorded against the defendants restraining them from showing their own advertisements during the time slot that was given to the plaintiffs to advertise during a particular programme and this action was claimed under various heading under Law of Torts, as well as the statutory remedy he is granted under the Copyright Act, 1957.

The defendants filed a petition in appeal and the Division bench dismissed the petition and the defendants' application for leave to appeal to the Supreme Court was also denied. The defendants' special leave petition was denied by the Supreme Court. Special provisions have been inserted by Copyright

(Amendment) 1999, i.e. 15.01.2000, wherein the Central Government is given the power to apply Chapter-VIII to broadcasting organisations and performers in certain other countries. Section 40-A stated that if the Central Government is satisfied that a foreign country has made or has undertaken to make such provisions for the protection of broadcasting organisations and performers in that foreign country, these rights will be available under this Act and as such directs that the provisions of Chapter-VIII shall apply to broadcasting organisations whose headquarters is situated in a country to which the order related of the broadcast has been transmitted from a transmitter situated in a country to which the order relates as if the headquarters of such organisation were situated in India or such broadcast were made from India. This section provides protection to performance and sound recording that was made in another country as per Section 40-A(1)(b), (c), (d) of the Copyright Act, 1957. Similarly, the Central Government is empowered under Section 42-A of the Act to restrict the rights of foreign broadcasting organisations and performers.

The Gramophone Company of India Limited Case[36]

Facts of the Case

The plaintiff was the owner of a copyright in the sound recording of an audio cassette. He was also the owner of the copyright in lyrics embodied in the sound recording and had also designed a unique inlay card with distinctive design, colour combination, layout and get up for the said audio cassette which constituted as an artistic work under the provisions of the Copyright Act. The inlay card contained the photo of Lord Ganesh with photos of two singers Lata Mangeshkar and Usha Mangeshkar. This audio cassette was well received by the public. Later, the defendants launched an audio cassette in the market with the title 'Ganapati Aarti Ashtavinayak Geete' which was identical to plaintiff's audio cassette. The design, the colour scheme, the get up, and layout of the defendant's audio cassette was deceptively similar to that of the plaintiff. Further the songs also were in an identical sequence as that of the plaintiffs. However, the singer in the defendant's audio cassette was

36. *Gramophone Company of India Ltd. Vs. Super Cassette Industries Ltd.*, decided on 04.12.1998, Delhi High Court, reported in 1999 PTC (19) 2 (Del.).

Anuradha Podwal. The plaintiffs filed a suit against the defendants on the grounds that the defendants was passing-off its goods as that of the goods of the plaintiff and sought an action for restraining the defendants from issuing its sound recordings and from using the inlay card that was deceptively and confusingly similar to the inlay cards used by the plaintiff and from packaging or using labels which would infringe the copyright of the plaintiff.

Analysis of the Case

Primarily, the Copyright Act provides protection to the three broad categories of Section 2 of the Act which defines copyright work as (i) a literary, dramatic, musical or artistic work; (ii) a cinematographic film; and (iii) a sound recording. Musical work is defined in sub-section (p) of Section 2 which means a work consisting of music and includes any graphical notation of such work but does not include any words or any action intended to be sung, spoken or performed with the music. Clause (xx) of sub-section of Section 2 defines sound recording as recording of sounds from which such sounds may be produced regardless of the medium, on which such recording is the method, by which the sounds are produced and clause (m) defines an infringing copy as: (i) in relation to a literary, dramatic, musical or artistic work or reproduction thereof otherwise than in the form of a cinematograph film; (ii) in relation to a cinematograph film, a copy of the film made on any medium by any means, (iii) in relation to a sound recording or any other recording embodying the same recording made by any means; and (iv) in relation to a programme or performance in which such a broadcast, reproduction right or a performer's right subsists under the provisions of this Act, the sound recording or a cinematographic film of such programme or performance, if such a reproduction, copy or sound recording is made or imported in contravention of the provisions of this Act.

The scheme of the Act includes the rights that are conferred to the copyright holder[37] and also deals with the method of transfer of copyrights made by the copyright owners with their consent. However, there are certain acts permitted under the statute which cannot be considered as infringement of copyrights

37. Section 13 of the Indian Copyright Act, 1957.

and the act authorises the use of the copyrighted works in special circumstances. Special provisions are made with regard to version recording. Following acts shall not constitute an infringement of copyright, namely[38]:

(j) The making of records in respect of any literary, dramatic or musical work, if

(a) records recording that work have previously been made by, or with the licence or consent of, the owner of the copyright in the work; and

(b) the person making the records has given the prescribed notice of his intention to make the records, and has paid in the prescribed manner to the owner of the copyright in the work royalties in respect of all such records to be made by him, at the rate fixed by the Copyright Board in this behalf.

The special feature of this case was that the defendants have not denied the title claimed by the plaintiff for the original works. However, their submission was that they had sent necessary information to the plaintiff that they were using the original works for recording the songs to be rendered by another singer and had also enclosed a cheque for Rs. 2230 by way of royalty to make 5000 cassettes. They claimed that they were entitled to indulge in version recording under Section 52(1)(j) after payment of the necessary fees to the plaintiff. The fact was that they returned the cheque and they had informed the defendants not to make version recording. However, this section has to be read in harmony with other sections which confers exclusive rights over the original works to the copyright owners. The version recording cannot be considered as an infringement of the copyright within the meaning of Section 51 as the singers are different.

The Court however, consider that the fact that the plaintiff had returned the cheque and given clear instruction that it does not permit the version recording, gave the plaintiff the right to seek an injunction restraining the defendants from any further sound recording which would infringe the copyrights of the plaintiff. On the various factors placed before it, the Court was in favour of the plaintiff as all the three elements necessary for the

38. Section 52(1)(j) of the Copyright Act, 1957.

grant of injunction were present and as it was seen that the plaintiff would suffer irreparable injury if the injunction is not granted, the Court gave necessary direction to restrain the defendant form issuing any sound recording of the audio cassettes which would infringe the rights of the plaintiff.

Pepsi Co. Inc. Case[39]

In this case the issue of copyright protection for advertising slogans was considered. The Delhi High Court held in this case that the slogans are not *prima facie* protectable under the Copyright Act. They may be protected under the Law of Passing-Off. Here the plaintiff makes out such a case.

Facts of the Case

The plaintiffs alleged to have infringed upon their registered trade mark by using the words that are deceptively similar to the mark of the plaintiffs and also sought to restrain the defendants from infringing upon their slogan 'Yeh Dil Mange More'. The plaintiffs claimed to be the registered owners of the mark Pepsi, Pepsi Cola and Globe Device. They were also the registered owners of the copyright in the words 'Yeh Dil Mange More' and also registered the slogan under the Trade Mark Act. Huge publicity was based on this slogan and the plaintiffs alleged that the defendants had infringed upon the trade mark and copyright in relation to the phrase 'Yeh Dil Mange More'. In turn the defendants counter-claimed that the advertisement of the defendants was nothing more than a parody and was aimed at poking fun at the advertisement of the plaintiffs. This case has for the first time taken up the issue of comparative advertisement *per se* amounts to infringement of their rights. The defendants have used the word 'Pappi' which the defendants claim was neither visually nor phonetically similar to the word 'Pepsi'. The plaintiffs had registered the words 'Yeh Dil Mange More'. It claimed this phrase is an original literary work that has become distinct with the plaintiffs and that it had the rights of exploitation of the distinctive element. The word original does not mean that the work must be the expression of an inventive thought. The originality which is required under the Copyright

39. *Pepsi Co. Inc. and Another Vs. Hindustan Coca Cola and Other,* 2001 PTC 699 (DEL): 2001(3) RAJ 458 DEL: (2001)94 DLT 1172.

Act relates to the thought but the Act does not require that the expression must be in an original or novel form. But the work must not be copied from another work. It should originate from the author. The plaintiffs also relied upon the passage from Mac Carthy on Trade Marks and unfair competition to the effect that however, the theme of an advertisement is copyrightable if it embodies some definite concrete elements beyond the mere idea or concept.[40] Similarly, the plaintiffs also relied on Nimmer to this effect. Thus, it is arguable that the exclusively of the copyright in the words as a literary work is not lost by merging the words with music into a collective work compilation known as a musical work.[41]

Thus, the plaintiffs contented that it had the copyright over the phrase 'Yeh Dil Mange More'. In turn, the defendant submitted that there was no presumption on the ownership of the Globe Device in favour of the plaintiffs merely because the work is neither registered mark nor can the plaintiffs claim any copyright over the device to the effect that on the grounds of triviality there can be no copyright in the advertisement slogans, youthful appearances are social necessities, neither luxuries nor in the stringing together for advertisement purposes of a number of common law sentences.

The Court then referred to Section 2(o) of the Copyright Act which defines literary work. Section 2(o) stated literary work includes copyright programmes, table and compilations including copyright data bases.

Analysis of the Case

In this regard P. Narayanan[42] stated that advertisement slogans are not literary works whose statement was supported by Iyengar who also voted favouraly by saying that[43] in common place or trivial works there is no literary merit even as understood in this fact and mere advertising slogans are not literary works.

Considering the recent trends it was held that on a mere reading on the definition it is doubtful whether slogans are

40. Mac Carthy on Trade Marks and unfair competition, third edition.
41. Nimmer on Copyright Vol. I, 1996.
42. P. Narayanan on Copyrights, p. 42 on para 3.80.
43. Iyengar on Copyrights, p. 94.

subject of works and can be covered under the said definition or not. *Copinger and Skine James*[44] consider this and stated that no copyright on titles. It further contended that a mere advertising slogan is not a literary work within the meaning of the Copyright Act and therefore cannot claim any protection and the reliance was placed on remarkable case.[45] The titles of books, newspapers, periodicals and other copyright works are not generally in themselves the subject of copyrights. The reason is that there is usually no original literary work in the formation of several ordinary words into a title. The words or phrases chosen may be original in their application to produce the subject matter of the work which required much skilled and judgment. However, that skill and judgment is generally employed in choosing and selecting from common words and phrases and not in putting together words in an original for or in affording to others information instruction or pleasure. Whereas, it will usually be the case, the title forms part of a larger work or compilation, the copying of the title will rarely amount to the taking of a substantial part.

Although the task of devising, advertising slogans often requires a high level of skill and judgment as with titles, they will usually not qualify for copyright protection as original literary works. However, the value of an advertising slogan lies in its role in generating additional good will for a product or service and in acting as a badge for vehicle for the good will and in appropriate circumstances; a slogan may be protected as part of that good will. Thus, passing-off is not limited to names, but is wide enough to encompass other descriptive materials such as slogans, or visual images. The radio, television or newspaper advertising campaigns can lead the market to associate with the plaintiff's product, provided always that such descriptive material has become part of the good will of the product. The test is whether the product has derived from advertising a distinctive character which the market recognises. In most of the cases plaintiffs have failed to establish that their slogan is distinctive. It may be of course that the defendant's advertisement as a whole is deceptive. The mere fact that the words were registered does not

44. Copinger and Skine James on Copyright, 14th Edn., Vol. I, Para 21.20 and 21.35.
45. *Sinanide Vs. La. Maison Kosmeo*, 1939, the Law Times 365, 367, it also referred to para 2-10 of Copinger on Copyrights, 13th Edn, p. 23.

create any statutory right and therefore to claim that the copyright of this kind falls under a literary work, it must be established independent of any registration.

In *Camelin Pvt. Ltd. Vs. National Pencil Industries,*[46] the certificate of registration under the Copyright Act is only *prima facie* evidence of entries in the copyright register. It does not however establish that what was registered is in fact and in law copyrightable subject matter. On the basis of the above decisions the Delhi High Court in this instant case held that the advertising slogans are *prima facie* not protectable under the Copyright Act. They may be protective under the law of passing off in case the plaintiffs makes out such a case. However, it is admitted that the defendants had used the slogan in a mocking way only in the course of comparative advertising. This itself would not *prima facie* amount to infringement of copyrights.

In the television commercial of the defendants the advertisement was aimed at showing that the kids preferred Pepsi and described it as 'Cuchomvali Drink' and that 'Thums Up' is for grown up. These were shown in advertisement-I and in advertisement-II, the Pepsi and the phrase 'Yeh Dil Mange More' was used in a mocking manner, a covered drink was described as a sweet drink and it revealed the Glove Device with the mark Pappy. In advertisement-III and IV, the drink which resembled Pepsi was referred to as Pappy and termed as buchomvali while 'Thums Ups' was referred to as 'Bado Ke Liye' and 'Damdar Hai'. The commercials were evident that the defendant was comparing with the plaintiff's cola. The question was whether the act was disparagement of the plaintiff's products and thus, the case was viewed from the angle of false advertisement rather than the case of infringement of copyrights.

Vicco Laboratories and Another Case[47]

Facts of the Case

The petitioners carried on business as manufacturers of Ayurvedic Pharmaceutical products which was sold under the brand name of 'Vicco' and had acquired substantial reputation in the market. The first defendant was an advertising agency and

46. ILR 1985(II) Delhi 813, 829.
47. *Vicco Laboratories and Another Vs. Art Commercial Advertising Pvt. Ltd. and Others,* 2001 (2) CTMR 180: Supreme Court decision given on 13.08.2001.

has been the advertising agents in respect of the products manufactured by the petitioners. The second respondent is the Director and partner of the first respondent and was dealing with the petitioners on behalf of the first respondent. The other respondents are the proprietary concern and the concerned authority in charge of television in India in the name and style of 'Doordarshan' which is a television media. The petitioners had agreed to pay the entire costs of the production of a TV serial entitled 'Yehan Jo Hai Zindagi'. They claimed that the defendants were under their employment and that they were the owners of the said serial. Under the arrangement made between the plaintiffs and the defendants sixty episodes were produced and the petitioners had spent a crore of rupees for the products and the telecast of the said episodes and had also spent large sum of money on advertising to popularize the TV serial and it had become one of the most exclusive and popular serial. The petitioners claimed the exclusive right to use the title and claimed that the serial cannot be telecasted without the name of the petitioners as sponsors of the serial. They claimed to be the real producers and owners of the serial. The defendants however, denied the rights claimed by the plaintiffs. In their counter they have contested the suit on the grounds that it was agreed between the petitioners and the defendants that the copyright in the serial would rest exclusively with the defendants and not with the petitioners. The defendant's name was shown in the title of the said serial as the producer right from the beginning of the first serial and the petitioners had not protested against the same. The advertisement issued by the petitioners themselves in various newspapers to give wide publicity to the serial also indicates that the copyright over the serial lies with the defendants. They further contented that even assuming that the petitioners are the owners of the copyrights they had ceased to be such owners as they have acquiesced in the exercise of the rights by the defendants by their conduct. On an examination of the facts the question that arose was whether the two capacities of a sponsor and a producer can co-exist in one person. It was found that for the first twenty-six episodes the amount per episode paid by the petitioners was Rs. 1,20,000 and it also contained the expression 'service charges'. However, the trial Court rejected the contention of the plaintiffs that having borne the cost of production of the serial they should be considered as producers of the serial. There was no element of liability to render the account and nor was it established that the defendants were the agents of the petitioners within the meaning of Section 182 of the India Contract Act, 1872 and the trial Court summed up the position of the plaintiffs by stating that they were mere sponsors and not the producers of the serial. On appeal the High Court also notice the fact that the defendant's name appeared as producer in the titles of the serial and this was not protested nor objected to by the petitioners. This case was examined in the light of Section 17 of the Copyright Act.

Analysis of the Case

Section 17 of the Indian Copyright Act deals with the first owner of copyrights and subject to the provisions of this Act, the author of a work shall be the first owner of the copyrights therein provided that:

(a) In case if a literary, dramatic or artistic work made by the author in the course of his employment by the proprietor of a newspaper, magazine or similar periodical under a contract of service or apprenticeship, for the purpose of publication in a newspaper, magazine or similar periodical the said proprietor shall, in the absence of any agreement to the contrary, be the first owner of the copyright in a work in so far as the copyright relates to the publication of a work in any newspaper, magazine or similar periodical or to the reproduction of the work for the purpose of its being so published bit in all other respects the author shall be the first owner of a copyright.

(b) Subject to the provisions of clause (a) in the case of a photograph taken, or a painting or portrait drawn or an engraving or a cinematographic film made for valuable consideration at the instance of any person, such person shall in the absence of any agreement to the contrary, be the first owner of the copyright therein.

(c) In case of a work made in the course of the author's employment under a contract of service or apprenticeship to which clause (a) or clause (b) does not apply, the employer shall in the absence of any agreement to the contrary, be the first owner of the copyright therein.

(cc) In case of any address or speech delivered in public, the person who has delivered such speech on behalf of any other person, such other person shall be the first owner of the copyright therein notwithstanding that the person who delivers such address or speech or as the case may be, the person on whose behalf such address or speech is delivered is employed by any other person who arranges such address or speech or on whose behalf or premises such address or speech is delivered.

(d) In the case of a Government work, the Government shall in the absence of any agreement to the contrary be the first owner of the copyright therein.

(dd) In the case of a work made or first published by or under the direction or control of any public undertaking, such public undertaking shall, in the absence of any agreement, to the contrary be the first owner of the copyright therein.

The facts also clearly showed that an aggregate amount of money was paid to the defendants which was in fact a fixed price for sponsoring the said serial in order to link up their advertisement with the said serial and the defendants were not liable to render accounts to the petitioners for the expenditure that was incurred by them to produce the serial. Section 17 clearly states that unless and until the petitioners are able to establish that the defendants had produced the serial either: (a) as agents or the petitioners; or (b) in the course of their employment with the petitioners; and (c) for valuable consideration paid by the petitioners to them; (d) at the instance of the petitioner they cannot claim the right ownership the order made by the High Court and the petition was dismissed by establishing the rights to the defendants as owners of the serial.

Gee Pee Films Private Limited Case[48]

Facts of the Case

Plaintiff is a music company engaged in the business of music recording and deal with recordings of audio-video and film and non-film songs, having head office at Ballygunj, Circular Road, Kolkata. The defendant No. 1 is a singer of Bengali songs and defendant No. 2 is engaged in the business of manufacture and sale of cassettes, compact disk and other song recoding systems. The defendant No. 3 is the song lyricist and music composer, and defendant No. 4 is a relative of defendant No. 3 and claimed to be a lyricist, defendant No. 5 is also a lyricists and music composer. In 1999 the plaintiff commissioned defendant No. 3 and 5 to compose Bengali non-film lyrics and music proposed to be sung by defendant No. 1 and proposed to release those by way of cassettes and other sound recording systems. On payment by the plaintiff defendant No. 3 wrote the lyrics and composed the song titled 'Tanche Jakhan' and defendant No. 5 wrote the lyrics for another song 'Tomar Chhoante' which also sung by defendant No. 1. The tapes containing two songs were prepared and retained by the plaintiff and he claimed ownership for having paid adequate consideration to defendant No. 2 and 5. Subsequently the plaintiff came to know that defendant No.1 and 2 had released a music cassette containing the similar songs with few marginal cosmetic changes to the lyrics and made of fraudulent attempts to pass off the said two songs as different numbers by purporting to alter the titles of the said 2 numbers. The plaintiffs claim to be the owner of the two songs and in addition owner of the sound recording thereof. The Court granted an ex-party injunction in favour of the plaintiff. The defendants filed an appeal. The main contention of the defendants was that the copyright act provided ownership to the composer of the music.

Analysis of the Case

According to section 2(d) author means (ii) in relation to a musical work, the composer according to defendants even if it is accepted that the songs were written on the basis of commission

48. Gee *Pee Films Private Limited Vs. Pratik Choudhury and Others* (2002) 24 PTC 392 CAL.

given by the plaintiff or that these were composed on the bases of such payment, copyright remains with the lyricist and the composer. As per defendants unless it is alleged and established that those songs were written and composed in the course of plaintiff's employment under a contract of service or apprenticeship as provided in Section 17(c) of the Act, the plaintiff cannot have any copyright over the said songs. In terms of Section 17 of the Copyright Act, the first owner of the copyright subject to the provisions of this Act, the author of a work shall be the first owner of the copyright therein provided that (c) in the case of a work made in the course of the author's employment under a contract of service or apprenticeship, to which clause (a or b) does not apply, the employer shall, in the absence of any agreement to contrary, be the first owner of the copyright therein. The defendants further contended that the plaintiff couldn't claim any copyright even over the sound recording based on Section 2 (uu) states producer in relation to a cinematograph film or sound recording, means a person who takes the initiative and responsibility for making the work.

The plaintiff opposed the above contentions of the defendant and stated that the songs having been written and composed on the basis of payment of the commission, it should be presumed that the defendants wrote and composed those songs in the course of employment, under a contract of service and as such the plaintiff should be held to be the owner of the copyright on the lyrics and music as provided in Section 17(c) of the Act. The plaintiffs had taken the initiative of the recordings and borne all expenses by making payment of hire charges of the studios and remuneration to the musicians. The relevant passage from *Copinger and Skone James* on copyrights, referred earlier, was taken to prove that when a person makes necessary arrangements for recording a work he should be presumed to be the producer of the work. It is a fact that defendant No. 3 and 5 being the lyricist and composer of the disputed songs was the owner of the copyright over the songs. It is for the plaintiff to prove that these works were made in the course of employment under a contract of service and that there was no agreement to the contrary relating to the owner of the copyrights. The plaintiffs stated that it had commissioned the defendants to compose the songs. The word commissioned means according to Oxford advanced learners dictionary means 'give somebody the job of making something', for example: He commissioned an artist to paint a statute of his wife, on payment. It also means to give an order. The case cited in this connection was the decision of the Supreme Court of Bangladesh.

Suraiya Rahman Vs. Skill Development for under-privileged women,[49] in this case the plaintiff was under a contract of service to produce artistic works and designs that she had produced before entering into the service of the defendants, as their works were clearly set out that unless and until it is proved that the work has been conducted during the curse of employment the master cannot claim ownership over the work. Base on the above cases and on examining the facts of the case of the High Court of Calcutta held that the plaintiff cannot misinterpret the definition of producer as given in Section 2(uu) of the Act. In order to be a producer a person must take initiative as well as the responsibility of the recording. In addition to paying the expenses of recording including hire charges of the studio and remuneration of the musician, a person must also take the consequential legal liability for such recording. The court therefore came to the conclusion that the plaintiff did not prove a *prima facie* case of copyrights in his favour and the plea for injunction was not granted and the earlier decision was vacated.

Anil Gupta and Another Case[50]

Facts of the Case

The Delhi High Court has recently decided this case on the issue of copyright for an idea that was conceived for producing a TV serial based on match-making. In this case the plaintiffs conceived an idea to produce a TV programme and decided to name the concept 'Swayamvaram'. The plaintiffs claimed that they had devised a unique and novel concept of a woman selecting a groom in the public forum. The copyright was claimed for some essential elements of the programme which was based on the following concepts:

(a) It was a real life entertainment programme taking a real life situation;

49. (1997) PTC (17) 295.

50. *Anil Gupta and Another Vs. Kunal Das Gupta and Others,* (2002) 25 PTC 1: 2002 Del, I.T. 257.

(b) It was half an hour long TV show that was even shot outdoors;
(c) It provided the thrill of match-making;
(d) It provided a platform for unmarried girls to select a spouse from a long list of suitor;
(e) The parents of the girls and the boys were also associated in the process of match-making;
(f) The participants for the show were selected and short listed by the producers prior to the show;
(g) The producers ensured that there should not be any foul play or duplicity; and
(h) The mediation between the parties is made by a mature, articulate, vibrant woman anchor.

Thus, it seeks to promote secular and progressive method of selection of the spouse and in way help in the empowerment of women. This was actually the basic concept for which the plaintiff claimed copyright protection. The defendant had asked for the details of the programme that was made by the plaintiffs. The highlights of this concept were explained to the defendants. This was a novel idea and the plaintiffs had approached to the Doordarshan. Late, the plaintiffs saw an article in the *Financial Express* that the Sony TV was launching a serial with the title 'Subh Vivah'. In response to the plaintiff's letter to clarify the contents of the defendant TV show, the defendants replied that they were not making a copy of the 'Swayamvaram'. The main contention of the plaintiffs was as follows:

(a) They contended that there was misappropriation of the concept of the plaintiff's programme;
(b) When the defendants announced their plans to make a similar programme it had inflicted huge loss and damage to the commercial potential of the plaintiff's programme by luring away their advertising sponsors;
(c) The plaintiffs contended that there was *prima facie* evidence for claiming a grant of injunction as it was a clear case of breach of confidence on the part of the defendants;
(d) It was claimed that the action of the defendant is a clear case of a breach of trust or confidence which gives a broader right to the plaintiff, far wider that of a breach of copyright. As the idea and information have been

acquired by the defendant under confidentiality the plaintiff sought the remedy of injunctions to restrain the defendants from making a similar serial on the basis of the concept and format supplied by the plaintiff;

(e) They further contended that the law of confidential communication includes written and oral communications;

(f) Another contention is that there are no requirements that the idea should always be developed to its fullest extent. In certain cases, as seen in the present case, the mere fact that the concept was disclosed to the defendants does not permit the defendants to use it nor claim that the information has now fallen into public domain; and

(g) Next it was alleged that, it is not proper to claim that there were other people who knew of the concept or the format besides the defendants. The issue was that the doctrine of 'Spring Board' is applied in such situations and as the concept of 'Swayamvaram' was first initiated by the plaintiffs, they claimed ownership over the concept seeking a restrain order to stop the defendants from misappropriating their theme and claim unjust enrichment by using the same to the detriment to the plaintiff who had first conceived, evolved, presented and made the format and the concept for the first time as TV show. Thus, the plaintiff filed the suit to restrain the defendants from showing the TV serial 'Subh Vivah' based on the concept and format of the plaintiffs.

In their counter the defendants claim that the concept of 'Swayamvaram' was already in the public domain. (i) It was further contended that the narration of the plaintiffs that was given to the defendants was very vague with a very rough preliminary note and no presentation was given to the defendants. (ii) It was further stated that the onus was on the plaintiffs to identify the information that was supplied to the defendants and prove that it was confidential information and that the defendants were guilty of breach of confidentiality. (iii) The plaintiffs cannot be allowed to monopolies a concept which was in the public domain. It claimed that there cannot be a copyright on a subject matter or theme that is based on historical mythological believe. The defendants pointed at the difference between their show and the plaintiff's programme. It stated that the following points were missing in the plaintiff's programmes: (i) providing platform to young women to chose a spouse from a short list of potential suitors; (ii) involvement of the parents of the girl and the suitors; (iii) enabling selection of the spouses through various devises; (iv) rewarding the couple after the 'Swayamvaram' is concluded; (v) selection process through matrimonial bureau, etc.; (vi) empowerment of women by giving her power of selection; and (vii) giving gifts to the engaged couple as stridhan.

Thus, the defendants concluded that their show was different from the plaintiff's concept, and that this idea was already in the public domain even prior to 1996 as there were several similar shows in existence in various countries outside India, for example, 'Mr and Mrs' was shown on ATV between 1964 and 1988, and broadcast on UK during the 1990's 'Love at first sight' was broadcast on Sky since 1990. 'Blind Date' was broadcasted on ITV since 1995. This striking feature of the defendant's serial was as follows:

(a) the applicants for the show sent their photos, CVs, and personal information like their preferences, likes, dislikes, etc.;
(b) the applicants are then shortlisted by producers;
(c) each segment has one girl who has to choose from five boys;
(d) she ask a few questions to the five boys';
(e) their answers are shown to the girl and she shortlist three of them;
(f) she and her family then meet the three boys and their families; and
(g) there is an interaction and the girl shortlist one boy. Lastly, the boy and girl meet and take the final decision to marry or not to marry and if they marry within a year, their honeymoon is sponsored by the producers of the serial and are given the prizes.

Analysis of the Case

The main thirst of this case was on the legal rights for a concept or an idea and the protection and enforcement of these rights. It is a fact that this concept was shown on the small screen which has become an effective media of mass communication like radio and has a wide potentiality of gaining revenue, therefore, needs to be thoroughly examined. When a person creates an idea or a concept or a theme which is original, law must ensure that the people who created these ideas should be rewarded for their labour. The creators provide the raw materials which are vital for the entertainment industry. When these ideas are developed into concepts in more detailed manner and registered, it gives a greater right to the copyright holder. 'Swayamvaram' is a concept based on Indian mythology which was seen in the 'Mahabharat' and 'Ramayana'. However, the concept in these Indian mythologies was not a choice left on the bride but was based on the act of chivalry that was performed by any prince to seek the hands of the princes. The concept that was visualized by the plaintiff was totally different. A concept like the present one was given legal protection in various cases as seen in the case of *Talbott Vs. Television Corporation*[51], where the court given the concept a special right and held that:

> "I am satisfied that what was called the 'commercial twist' or the particular slant of the plaintiff's concept or idea does give it a quality which takes it out of the public knowledge. In my opinion the situation then was that the plaintiff had 'a saleable proposition' which had as its kernel the valuable concept of a programme which had the intent of exposing the lives of successful people. In my opinion not only was the text of the submission made available in confidence but the kernel of the concept whether it was conveyed in writing or orally was also made available in confidence."

And such confidential information has to be protected. The fact that a bare outline also can be protected is seen in the case of *Fraser Vs. Thames Television*,[52] wherein it was held that:

> "I do not think this requirement necessitates in every case a full synopsis. In some cases the nature of the idea may require extensive development of this kind in order to make the criterion. But in other the criterion may be made by a short unelaborated statement of an idea".

51. 1981, RPC, 1.
52. 1983, ALL E.R. 101.

And further in *Franchie and Others Vs. Franchie and Others,*[53] it was stated:

> "clearly a claim that the disclosure of some information would be a breach of confidence is not to be defeated simply by proving that there are other people in the world who know the fact in question beside the man as to whom it is said that his disclosure would be a breach of confidence and to those to whom he has disclosed them."

The court after considering all the abovesaid facts and on the legal mind given on this issue came to the conclusion that it is not proper to except the views of the defendant that once a concept is registered; under the Copyright Act the same comes under the public domain. In fact, when the concept is registered it can claim protection from the public as the very purpose of the Copyright Act is to grant monopoly interest and a right to restrain others from using the copyrighted work and the right of exploitation and communication to the public is given solely to the copyright owner. The concept of the proposed TV programme of the defendants with the title 'Subh Vivah' contain the basic salient features of the plaintiff's programme and it is based on the thrill of the match making as real life situation. The defendants therefore, cannot reap the fruits of the labour put in by the plaintiff in this regard. The plaintiffs had proved all the elements required for claiming an injunction as it *prima facie* proved that if the order of injunction is not granted to restrain the defendants it would give a premium to the defendants to rob and misappropriate the right of the plaintiff over his work. The injury that would be sustained by the plaintiffs was difficult to be measured in term of money and therefore an order was passed to restrain the defendants from transmitting or enabling the transmission by the television its programme entitle 'Subh Vivah'. However, it also stated that if the plaintiffs do not transmit their programme entitles 'Swayamvaram' within a period of four months; the defendants will be at liberty to transmit its programme 'Subh Vivah' after expiry of four months.

53. 1967, RPC 149.

Star India Private Ltd. Case[54]

Facts of the Case

The Plaintiffs were carrying on business acquiring copyright in films, TV serials, and programmes. They also produced and commissioned the production of these programmes. They had entered into an agreement with the defendants to create, compose and produce 262 episodes of the TV serial entitled 'Kyon Ki Saas Bhi Kabhi Bahu Thi'. This serial gained tremendous popularity and goodwill. A television commercial advertisement for a consumer product 'Tide Detergent' produced by the defendants use the words 'Kyon Ki Bahu Bhi Kabhi Saas Banegi' with identical characters of the original serial of the plaintiffs. The contention of the plaintiffs was that the defendants had not obtained proper consent or permission from the plaintiffs and that the defendants attracted patronage of the viewers of the plaintiffs' serial. It was alleged that the defendants made a false and deliberate misrepresentation of a connection with the plaintiffs' business and with the plaintiffs' TV serial thereby committing/attempt to commit a tort of passing-off and mis-representating that they were authorised by plaintiffs' popular serial.

The contention of the defendants was that they had depicted the age-old custom of the Saas handing over the keys and the responsibility of the house to the Bahu cannot be considered as an original artistic work. It was also averred that even assuming that there are some features in the defendants commercial that were similar to the serial of the plaintiffs, it did not amount to a reproduction or substantial reproduction of the serial and hence does not amount to infringement. The defendants in their counter pleaded that the plaintiffs cannot claim personal rights over the serials, more so in the law of trademark. The rights claimed were in relation to certain scenes in a serial, they cannot be identified and be equated to goods nor is it possible to establish the goodwill that is associated with movable item. The issue was then shifted to the regime of copyrights.

54. *Star India Private Ltd. Vs. Leo Burnett (India) Private Ltd.*, 2003(27) PTC 81 (BOM) 86-87:2003 (2) BOM. CR 655.

Analysis of the Case

The first question that was considered is whether the defendant's commercial is a copy of the plaintiffs' TV serial. Section 14(d)(1) of the Indian Copyright Act gives the owner of the copyright, the exclusive right to make a copy of the film including a photograph of an image forming a part thereof. Unlike the UK and Australian Copyright Acts the word copy is too defined in the Indian Copyright Act and therefore, the word copy has to be referred from the dictionaries of the English language. Imitating or making a film which bears likeness or striking resemblance to a copyrighted films would amount to making a cop of the film and therefore, infringement of the copyright in the film. The test of 'substantiality' has to comply with the guidelines set out by the Courts. The judgment of the apex court in *R.G. Anand vs. M/S Deluxe Films and others*[55] provided the guidelines to test the infringement of copyrights. The word 'copy' has been discussed in *Copinger and Skone James copyrights* as follows:

> "It has been stated that skill labour and judgment merely in the process of copying cannot confer originality and the mere copyist cannot have protection of his copy. Particularly therefore, where the reproduction is in the same medium as the original, there must be more than an exact reproduction to secure copyrights, there must be some element of material alteration or embellishment which suffices to make the totality of the work an original work. If the original, in the case of a painting is use merely as a model to give the idea of the new work or, in the case of a photograph merely as a basis to be network may be entitled to protection, but if the result is simply a slavish copy it will not be protected."[56]

Narrow copyright protection is accorded to a film/sound recording when compared to the literary, dramatic or artistic works. The reason perhaps could be that in case of literary, dramatic, or artistic works a copyright protection is granted only

55. AIR 1978 SC 1613 : PTC (Supp.) (1) 802 (SC).
56. In *R.G. Anand Vs. M/s Delux Films and Others*, AIR 1978 SC 16B, Supreme Court referred the definition of term 'copy' as given by Copinger and Skone James in their book 'Copinger and Skone James on Copyright', 1st South Asia Edition, 2008, Vol. I, p. 38.

on the proof of originality, while in the case of films and sound recordings a copy of the theme does not amount to infringement and if it is proved that there are some dissimilar features, the producer can escape liability.

In the instant case, the defendants were merely promoting their own product that is the 'Tide Detergent'. There was no material or real likelihood of any damage being cause to the plaintiffs by the acts of the defendants. The mere act of a TV advertisement by the defendants cannot prejudice respect of the characters in the serial because while the TV serial of plaintiffs were carried over for 262 episodes of over 87 hours with each episode of 30 minutes, the defendant's TV commercial advertisement was for 30 seconds only. Moreover, the fields of activity of the plaintiffs and of the defendants are totally different. When the fields of activity are different, it bears strong evidence that the act does not establish misrepresentation and the real likelihood of damage. The case does not fall within the realm of character merchandising, as the plaintiffs could not establish character merchandising in respect to the characters in the serial. On the contrary, the general public on viewing the TV commercial advertisements would infer that the defendants were promoting their own products and not to cause any misrepresentation relating to the plaintiffs. In the absence of likelihood to damage the interests of the plaintiffs, the court was of the opinion that the remedy of injunctions is not available to the plaintiffs, as the actions of the defendants do not amount to passing-off or of character merchandising. The plaintiffs were however, allowed to a separate action to claim damages on proof of any injury caused to them.

Zee Telefilms Ltd. Case[57]

Facts of the Case

This case is of special relevance as it seeks to provide copyrights on concepts which carry a special value especially when they form a basis for TV serial and short plays. The facts of the case were that the plaintiff was engaged in the business of television programming, video programmes, multi-media programmes, feature films, TV serials, etc. The concepts that

57. *Zee Telefilms Ltd. & Anr. Vs. Sundial Communications Pvt. Ltd. & Ors.*, 2003 (27) PTC 457 (Bom.) 472: 2003(5) BOM CR 404: 2003(3) MAH LJ 695.

were generated by the group of entrepreneurs who worked in different televisions network would create these concepts and register them with the film writers' association along with the titles which in turn were registered with the Indian motion picture producers' association. The concepts including notes, character sketches, detailed plots, episodes, etc., main story lines were included in these concepts which were registered. These concepts were also translated into pilot projects which contained the audio visual representation produces on video tapes and were ready for telecasting. The concept in issue was based on a family where 'Kanhaiyya' who was an avatar of Lord Krishna appears as a child and is a succor to them and helps them. He plays with the family members performs skill miracles and adds joy and happiness to the entire family. Based on this concept the details of the serial were worked out and ten episodes were sent to the defendant's office. In fact, the plaintiffs had asked whether to draw a non-disclosure agreement as the contents were confidential and not to be used or exploited in any manner without the consent of the plaintiff. The plaintiffs categorically stated that the ideas, concepts, thoughts and expressions expressed in these episodes were original and they claimed a right based on Section 13 of the Indian Copyright Act, 1957. When the director of the defendant company, Ms. Vinitha Nanda accepted the concepts and showed a positive response, the plaintiffs produced the pilot programmes and sent to the defendants.

The pilot programme was structured in the following ways:

> "A rich dysfunctional family; Internal feuds (within the family); Affected family member crisis and asks God for help. Lord Krishna appears in a human (child) form (of 'Kanhaiyya') in front of the family member who prays for help; 'Kanhaiyya' enters the house, posing as 'Krish' relative of the family member; 'Kanhaiyya' then proceeds to weave his magic and miracles around the family that is on the verge of breaking apart; 'Kanhaiyya' brings happiness to all."

Later, when there was no response from the defendants the plaintiffs approached the Sony Entertainment Television to telecast their serial and it agreed to produce this concepts. However, the plaintiffs later learned that the defendants were producing a similar serial based on their concepts. Later on, the Sony Television of the defendants was also producing a similar serial. The serial of the defendants was based on the same theme wherein there is a large family with internal quarrels and 'Kanhaiyya' coming down to help them in handling their problems. The defendants in answer to the suit filed by the plaintiffs restraining the defendants from infringing their copyright counterclaimed that their serial was conceived on the basis of the theory of 'Karma' which is the essence of Bhagwat Gita. It was emphatically stated that the theme of the defendants' serial is different and distinct from that of the plaintiffs. In the defendants' serial there was an orphan child who is blessed with sagacity and wisdom beyond his age. He is not God not was he supernatural or divine. He never appeared as Lord Krishna and the advice that the child offers is very casual and in the course of normal conversation. The defendants therefore state that the emphasis of his serial is on the natural rather than supernatural. In a way that it seeks to convey the message that one should do one's deeds act by him and not to look for divine help. In fact the plaintiff's pilot and concept was exactly the reverse. The three main claims in this case were as follows:

(a) It claimed an infringement of their copyright for their works titled 'Krishna Kanhaiyya';
(b) The issue also relates to breach of confidentiality that was reposed on the defendant; and
(c) The plaintiffs claim that the defendants had committed a wrongful act in the form of reverse passing-off of the plaintiff's work.

Analysis of the Case

The primary premise of the law of copyright is that there can be no copyright over an idea or a mere concept. This has been clearly stated by various Courts in India. In the case of *Indian Express Newspaper (Bom.) Pvt. Ltd. Vs Jagmohan,*[58] where **Justice Jamdar** observed that:

> "No doubt the contras theme of the articles published by the second plaintiff and that of the drama and movie is the same, though the emphasis in the drama and the movie is more on human bondage, particularly of Indian

58. AIR 1958 Bom. 229.

women. The articles published by Ashwini Sarin also contain an autobiographical account of the part actually played by him in the affair. He has presented the whole affair in his own style, but that at the most would give the plaintiffs copyright in respect of these articles. There cannot, however, be a copyright in an event which has actually taken place. There is a distinction between the materials upon which one claiming copyright has worked and the product of the application of his skill, judgment, labours and literary talent of these materials. Ideas, information, natural phenomena and events on which an author expends his skill, labour, capital, judgment and literary talent are common property and are not the subject of copyright."

Supreme Court also has laid down certain guidelines to determine whether the defendants had copied the special features of the copyrighted work of the defendants. The following rules were enunciated by the Supreme Court in the case of *R.G. Anand Vs. M/S. Deluxe Films and Ors.*,[59]

1. There can be no copyright in an idea, subject-matter, themes, plots or historical or legendary facts and violation of the copyright in such cases is confined to the form, manner and arrangement and expression of the idea by the author or the copyrighted work.
2. Where the same idea is being developed in a different manner, it is manifest that the source being common, similarities are bound to occur. In such a case the courts should determine whether or not the similarities are on fundamental or substantial aspects of the mode of expression adopted in the copyrighted work. If the defendant's work is nothing but a literal imitation of the copyrighted work with some variations here and there it would amount to violation of the copyright. In other words, in order to be actionable the copy must be substantial and material one for which the defendant is guilty of an act of piracy.
3. One of the surest and the safest test to determine whether or not there has been a violation of copyright is

59. *R.G. Anand Vs. M.S. Deluxe Films and Ors.*, AIR 1978 SC 1613: (1978) 4 SCC 118: PTC Suppl. (1) 802 (SC).

to see if the reader, spectator or the viewer after having read or seen both the words is clearly of the opinion and gets an unmistakable impression that the subsequent work appear to be a copy of the original.

4. Where the theme is the same but is presented and treated differently so that the subsequent work becomes a completely new work, no question of violation of copyright arises.
5. Where, however, apart from the similarities appearing in the two words there are also material and broad dissimilarities which negative the intention to copy the original and the coincidence appearing in two words are clearly identical no infringement of the copyright comes into existence.
6. As a violation of copyright amounts to an act of piracy it must be proved by clear and cogent evidence after applying the various tests laid down by the decided case laws.
7. Where, however, the question is of the violation of the copyright of stage-play by a film producer or a Director the task of the plaintiff becomes more difficult to prove privy. It is manifest that unlike a stage play film has a much broader perspective, wider field and a bigger background where the defendants can by introducing a variety of incidents give a colour, a complexion distinct from the manner in which the copyrighted work has expressed the idea. Even so, if the viewer after seeing the film gets a totality of impression that the film is by and large a copy of the original play, violation of the copyright may be said to be proved.

An earlier decision given in the case of *Harman Pictures NV Vs. Osborne,*[60] was also referred in this case wherein the observations given by Justice Golf, were also considered. He stated that the whole of the script must be read carefully and compared with the book to find out the similarity between the works. Thus, the question is whether the substantial portion of the work has been taken or not. Slight modifications are not sufficient. Concept as such was also accepted as a legally protected interest under the copyright laws in the case of

60. 1967 (1) WLR 723.

Anil Gupta and Another Vs. Kunal Das Gupta and Others,[61] as the concept and the theme of the serial belonging to the plaintiffs was original the Delhi High Court accepted it as a form of work that can claim copyright protection and restrain others who seek to use it. The second issue in this case relates to confidential information in confidence. This is a broad equitable doctrine wherein no person who receives information in confidence should take unfair advantage of it or profit from the wrongful use of publication of it. It is different from the law of copyrights and even if a person is not permitted to claim copyright over ideas or information is given only to material that has been reduced to permanent form the law of confidence protects all forms of confidential communication whether oral or written. While copyright is available against the whole world confidential information is a right that can be claimed against persons who receives this information with the note that it would not further be disclosed. The case in issue clearly shows that the concept and the theme of their serials were disclosed under great confidentiality. This information should not be used by the recipient in contradiction to the trust that was reposed when the concerned information was related to the other party. An action for a breach of confidence involves the following four elements:

(a) the plaintiff must identify clearly the information which he considers as confidential;
(b) he should prove that this information was handed over not to be revealed;
(c) this information should be treated as confidential; and
(d) the information has been used without seeking prior permission of the plaintiff.

On examination of the facts the Court held that the communication of the idea for the serial had been made in confidence and the idea was distinct having sufficient originality, commercial attractiveness and likelihood of realisation so as to fix the defendants with the obligation of utmost confidence which the defendants has clearly violated when they used the idea as a basis for their own television serials. The Court observed that the concept can be protected by restraining the defendants from using it.

---

61. (2002) DEL. LT 257.

The third issue relates to the claim of reverse passing-off. In this case the claim of the plaintiffs was that the defendants had indulged in an action of reverse passing-off. That is the defendants has attempted to misrepresent that the concept of the plaintiffs was actually belonging to them, that is, when an original idea or a concept that belongs to one person is used by another as if it belongs to him it gives rise to an action of reversing passing-off. This was clearly seen in recent case of *Bristal Conservatories Ltd. Vs. Conservatories Custom Built India,*[62] wherein the plaintiffs filed a complaint that the defendants were showing the photographs and designs belonged to the defendants. The customers were thereby misled into believing that the defendants were actually producing the said conservatories. The Apex Court held that the action of the defendants amounted to an act of reverse passing-off also. This claim was not dealt in detail in this case as there was proof that the defendants had committed a breach of confidence and had violated the copyright that was subsisting on the concept and as such no opinion was expressed on the issue of reverse passing-off resulting the dismissal of the present appeal.

Eastern Book Company and Others Case[63]

Facts of the Case

The appellants are involved in the printing and publishing of various books relating to the field of law. One of the well known publications of Appellant No. 1, Eastern Book Company, is the law report 'Supreme Court Cases' (SCC). The appellant publishes all reportable judgments along with non-reportable judgments of the Supreme Court of India in SCC. Yet another category included in SCC is short judgments, orders, practice directions and records of proceedings. The law report SCC was commenced in the year 1969 and had been in continuous publication ever since. The name 'Supreme Court Cases' had been coined by the appellants and they had been using the same continuously,

---

62. 1989 RPC 455.
63. *Eastern Book Company and Others Vs. D.B. Modak and Another,* (2008)1 SCC 1, Contempt Petition (C) arose out of Civil Appeal No. 6472 of 2004 and Civil Appeal No. 6905 of 2004 and CA No. 158 of 2006 in CA No. 6472 of 2004, decided on December 12, 2007.

exclusively and extensively in relation to the law reports published by them.

For the purpose of publishing the judgments, orders and proceedings of the Supreme Court, the copies of judgments, orders and proceedings are procured directly from the office of the Registrar of the Supreme Court of India. After the initial procurement of the judgments, orders and proceedings for publication, the appellants make copy-editing inputs wherein the judgments, orders and records of proceedings procured, which is the raw source, are copy-edited by a team of editorial staff and various inputs are put in the judgments and orders to make them user-friendly by making an addition of cross-references, standardisation or formatting of the text, paragraph numbering, verification and by putting other inputs. The appellants also prepare headnotes comprising two portions, the short note consisting of catch/lead words written in bold; and the long note, comprised of a brief discussion of the facts and the relevant extracts from the judgments and orders of the Court. Headnotes are prepared by Appellant No. 3, Surendra Malik. As per the Appellant No. 3 (Plaintiff No. 3 in the suits filed in the High Court), the preparation of the headnotes and putting of the various inputs in the raw text of the judgments and orders received from the Supreme Court Registry requires considerable amounts of skill, labour and expertise and for the said work a substantial amount of capital expenditure on the infrastructure, such as offices, equipments, computers and for maintaining extensive library, besides recurring expenditure on both the management of human resources and infrastructural maintenance, are incurred by the appellants-plaintiffs. As per the appellants, SCC is a law report which carries case reports comprising of the appellants' version or presentation of those judgments and orders of the Supreme Court after putting various inputs in the raw text and it constitutes an 'original literary work' of the appellants in which copyright subsists under Section 13 of the Copyright Act, 1957 and thus, the appellants alone have the exclusive right to make printed as well as electronic copies of the same under Section 14 of the Act. Any scanning or copying or reproduction done of or from the reports or pages or paragraphs or portions of any volume of SCC by any other person, is an infringement of the copyright in SCC within the meaning of Section 51 of the Act.

Respondent No. 2, i.e. Defendant, Spectrum Business Support Ltd. in Civil Appeal No. 6472 of 2004, had brought out a software called 'Grand Jurix' published on CD-ROMs and Defendant, Regent Data Tech Pvt. Ltd. in Civil Appeal No. 6905 of 2004, had brought out a software package called 'The Laws' published on CD-ROMs. As per the appellants, all the modules in the respondent-defendants' softwares packages had been lifted from the appellants' work. The respondents had copied the appellants' sequencing, selection and arrangement of the cases coupled with the text of the copy-edited judgments as published in the appellant-plaintiffs' law report SCC including the copy-editing, paragraph numbers, footnote numbers, cross-references, etc. and that such acts of the respondent-defendants constituted infringement of the appellant-plaintiffs' exclusive right to the same.

The appellant-plaintiffs moved to the High Court for temporary injunction against both the parties filing applications in Suit No. 758 of 2000 against Spectrum Business Support Ltd. and in Suit No. 624 of 2000 against Regent Data Tech Pvt. Ltd. before a Single Judge. The interim orders of injunction were passed in the suits from time to time. However, the respondent-defendants filed application for vacation of the stay order. By a common judgment dated 17-1-2001, the Single Judge of the High Court dismissed the appellants' applications for interim injunction and allowed the respondents' application for vacation of stay. However, before the Single Judge, the respondents conceded that the appellants have copyright in the headnotes and as such they undertook not to copy these headnotes in their CD-ROMs.

Aggrieved by the said order dated 17-1-2001 refusing to grant interim injunction, the appellants preferred appeals before a Division Bench of the Delhi High Court and the applications praying for interim relief were also filed in both the appeals. The applications praying for the interim relief were disposed of by a Division Bench on 9-3-2001 directing that during the pendency of the appeals the respondents will be entitled to sell their CD-ROMs with the text of the judgment of the Supreme Court along with their own headnotes which should not in any way be a copy of the headnotes and the text of the appellant-plaintiffs. On filing of contempt petitions for non-compliance with the above said order of the Division Bench dated 9-3-2001, another Division Bench of the High Court heard the interim appeals and by the impugned order dated 27-9-2002 held that the appellants could not claim copyright in the text of the judgment by merely putting certain inputs to make it user-friendly. The Division Bench of the High Court, however, held that there is originality and creativity in preparation of the headnotes, and, therefore, there would be copyright in the headnotes to the judgments prepared by the appellants. The Division Bench also held that so far as footnotes and editorial notes are concerned, it could not be denied that these are the publisher's own creations and based on the publisher's own research and thus, the appellants had copyright over them. By the impugned order, the Division Bench modified the judgment of the Single Judge in favour of the appellants by directing that the respondents would be entitled to sell their CD-ROMs with the text of the judgments of the Supreme Court along with their own headnotes, editorial notes, if any, which should not in any way be the copy of the headnotes of the appellants. It also directed that the respondents shall also not copy the footnotes and editorial notes appearing in the journal of the appellants. However, the Division Bench did not grant injunction protecting the copy-edited text of the appellants. Hence, they filed these appeals by special leave.

Before the Supreme Court the appellants claimed that the copyright subsists in SCC as a law report, as a whole based cumulatively and compendiously on all the substantial contributions of skill, labour and capital in the creation of various parts of SCC, i.e. headnotes, editorial notes, footnotes, the version of the copy-edited text of judgments as published in the appellants' law report, the selection of cases as published, the sequence and arrangement of cases as published and the index, table of cases, etc. which are published in each volume of SCC, that give the SCC volumes and thereby the complete SCC set, its character as a work as a whole. The appellants also claimed that the copyright subsists in the copy-edited version. The appellants did not claim copyright in the raw text of the judgments, certified copies of which are obtained from the Registry of the Supreme Court. The appellants did not claim a monopoly in publishing judgments of the Supreme Court; they were being published by other publishers also without copying from each other's publications. The appellants claimed copyright in the copy-edited version of the text of judgments as published in SCC which is a creation of the appellants' skill, labour and capital and there are contributions/inputs/additions of the appellants in creating their version of the text of judgments as published in SCC.

The appellants placed before the Court their contributions/ inputs to the text of the judgments received by them from the Registry of the Supreme Court. The appellants asserted that originality inheres in such aspects of its editorial process which are selected, coordinated and arranged in such a way that the resulting work as a whole constitutes an original work of the appellants. Thus, the questions that arose before the Supreme Court were:

(1) What shall be the standard of originality in the copy-edited judgments of the Supreme Court which is a derivative work and what would be required in a derivative work to treat it the original work of an author and thereby giving a protected right under the Copyright Act, 1957 to the author of the derivative work?

(2) Whether the entire version of the copy-edited text of the judgments published in the appellants' law report SCC would be entitled for a copyright as an original literary work, the copy-edited judgments having been claimed as a result of inextricable and inseparable admixture of the copy-editing inputs and the raw text, taken together, as a result of insertion of all SCC copy-editing inputs into the raw text, or whether the appellants would be entitled to the copyright in some of the inputs which have been put in the raw text?

(3) That is, whether by introducing certain inputs in a judgment delivered by a court it becomes 'original copy-edited judgment' and the person or authority or company who did so could claim to have embodied the originality in the said judgment and the judgment takes the colour of original judgment having a copyright therein of its publisher?

Analysis of the Case

It is clear that the decision of the Supreme Court would be confined to the judgments of the courts which are in the public domain as by virtue of Section 52 of the Copyright Act, 1957; there is no copyright in the original text of the judgments. To claim copyright in a compilation, the author must produce the material with exercise of his skill and judgment which may not be creativity in the sense that it is novel or non-obvious, but at the same time it is not a product of merely labour and capital. The derivative work produced by the author must have some distinguishable features and flavours to raw text of the judgments delivered by the court. The trivial variation or inputs put in the judgment would not satisfy the test of copyright of an author.

On this touchstone, the Court take into consideration the inputs put by the appellants in their journal 'SCC'. The appellants have added in the copy-edited version the cross-citations to the citation(s) already given in the original text; added names of cases and cross-citations where only the citation of the case is given; added citation and cross-citations where only name of the case is given; inserted citation in case history where only the title and year of the impugned/earlier order is given; presented in their own style of the cases when they are cited/ repeated in the judgment; provided precise references to the quoted matter in the judgment by giving exact page and paragraph number as in the original case source/treatise/ reference material; added margin headings to quoted extracts from statutes/rules, etc., when they are missing from the original text of the judgment; added the number of the Section/Rule/ Article/paragraph to the extract quoted in the original text; added the names of Judges on whose behalf opinion given by giving expressions, viz. for himself and Pathak, C.J., etc.; done verification of first word of the quoted extract and supplied emphasis on such verification; added ellipsis to indicate breaks in quoted extract; provided and supplied the matter inadvertently missed in quoted extracts in the original text of the judgment; completed/corrected the incomplete/incorrect case names or citations; renumbered correctly the clauses/sub-clauses in terms of the questions framed which were numbered in terms of answers to questions framed by learned Judge; changed the text as per corrigenda issued, which has been issued upon SCC editors request and suggestions; done compressing/simplification of information relating to the case history; followed certain norms at 'SCC' for giving case names; omitted the words like Section, Rule, etc. and given only the number of the Section/rule at the beginning of the quoted extract; made margin heading and the first clause/sub-section or initial matter of section/rule, etc. to run-on instead of being let to start from a fresh line; done compressing of unquoted reference and use of substantive parts; replaced the series of dots in the raw text with ellipsis; removed abbreviations such as sec., R., cl. and substituted them with full word, i.e. Section, Rule, clause; added hyphenation after the section/rule numbers which have alphabets suffixed to them; applied indentation of quoted extracts; removed full stops or word number and given full forms of abbreviations to enhance readability and clarity. In addition to the above, capitalisation and italicisation is also made wherever necessary in the raw text; and punctuation, articles, spellings and compound words are also checked and corrected, if required, in the original text.

The aforesaid inputs put by the appellants in the judgments would have had a copyright, had the Court accepted the principle that anyone who by his or her own skill and labour creates an original work of whatever character, shall enjoy an exclusive right to copy that work and no one else would be permitted to reap the crop which the copyright owner had sown. No doubt, the appellants have collected the material and improved the readability of the judgment by putting inputs in the original text of the judgments by considerable labour and arranged it in their own style, but that does not give the flavour of minimum requirement of creativity. The exercise of the skill and judgment required to produce the work is trivial and is on account of the labour and the capital invested and could be characterized as purely a work which has been brought about by putting some amount of labour by the appellants.

Although for establishing a copyright, the creativity standard applicable is not that something must be novel or non-obvious, but some amount of creativity in the work to claim a copyright is required. It does require a minimal degree of creativity. Arrangement of the facts or data or the case law is already included in the judgments of the court. Therefore, creativity of

'SCC' would only be addition of certain facts or material already published, case laws published in another law report and its own arrangement and presentation of the judgments of the court in its own style to make it more user-friendly. The selection and arrangement can be viewed as typical and at best result of the labour, skill and investment of capital lacking even minimal creativity. It does not as a whole display sufficient originality so as to amount to an original work of the author. To support copyright, there must be some substantive variation and not merely a trivial variation, not the variation of the type where limited ways of expression is available and an author selects one of them which can be said to be a garden variety. Novelty or invention or innovative idea is not the requirement for protection of copyright but it does require minimal degree of creativity. The Court opined that the aforesaid inputs put by the appellants in the copy-edited judgments do not touch the standard of creativity required for the copyright.

However, the inputs put in the original text by the appellants in (i) segregating the existing paragraphs in the original text by breaking them into separate paragraphs; (ii) adding internal paragraph numbering within a judgment after providing uniform paragraph numbering to the multiple judgments; and (iii) indicating in the judgment the Judges who have dissented or concurred by introducing the phrases like 'concurring', 'partly concurring', 'partly dissenting', 'dissenting', 'supplementing', 'majority', 'expressing no opinion', etc., have to be viewed in a different light. The task of paragraph numbering and internal referencing requires skill and judgment in great measure. The editor who inserts para numbering must know how legal argumentation and legal discourse is conducted and how a judgment of a court of law must read. Often legal arguments or conclusions are either clubbed into one paragraph in the original judgment or parts of the same argument are given in separate paragraphs. It requires judgment and the capacity for discernment for determining whether to carve out a separate paragraph from an existing paragraph in the original judgment or to club together separate paragraphs in the original judgment of the court. Setting of paragraphs by the appellants of their own in the judgment entailed the exercise of the brain work, reading and understanding of subject of disputes, different issues involved, statutory provisions applicable and interpretation of the same and then dividing them in different paragraphs so that chain of thoughts and process of statement of facts and the application of law relevant to the topic discussed is not disturbed, would require full understanding of the entire subject of the judgment. Making paragraphs in a judgment could not be called a mechanical process. It requires careful consideration, discernment and choice and thus, it can be called as a work of an author. Creation of paragraphs would obviously require extensive reading, careful study of subject and the exercise of judgment to make paragraph which has dealt with particular aspect of the case, and separating intermixing of a different subject. Creation of paragraphs by separating them from the passage would require knowledge, sound judgment and legal skill. In our opinion, this exercise and creation thereof has a flavour of minimum amount of creativity. The said principle would also apply when the editor has put an input whereby different Judge's opinion has been shown to have been dissenting or partly dissenting or concurring, etc. It also requires reading of the whole judgment and understanding the questions involved and thereafter, finding out whether the Judges have disagreed or have the dissenting opinion or they are partially disagreeing and partially agreeing to the view on a particular law point or even on facts. In these inputs put in by the appellants in the judgments reported in 'SCC', the appellants have a copyright and nobody is permitted to utilize the same.

For the reasons stated in the aforesaid discussion, the appeals are partly allowed. The High Court has already granted interim relief to the plaintiff-appellants by directing that though the respondent-defendants shall be entitled to sell their CD-ROMs with the text of the judgments of the Supreme Court along with their own headnotes, editorial notes, if any, they should not in any way copy the headnotes of the plaintiff-appellants; and that the defendant-respondents shall also not copy the footnotes and editorial notes appearing in the journal of the plaintiff-appellants. It is further directed by the Court that the defendant-respondents shall not use the paragraphs made by the appellants in their copy-edited version for internal references and their editors' judgment regarding the opinions expressed by the Judges by using phrases like 'concurring', 'partly dissenting', etc. on the basis of reported judgments in SCC. The judgment of the High Court is modified to the extent that in addition to the interim relief already granted by the High Court, the Court have also granted the above-mentioned additional relief to the appellants and in view of the decision rendered by the Court in the civil appeals, the Supreme Court meaningfully passed an order on the contempt petition and thus, the contempt petition was disposed of accordingly.

Principles Evolved in this Case

From the decision of the Supreme Court in the instant case it can be said that partly allowing the appeals, the Supreme Court held that copyright protection finds its justification in fair play. When a person produces something with his skill and labour, it normally belongs to him and the other person would not be permitted to make a profit out of the skill and labour of the original author and it is for this reason that the Copyright Act, 1957 gives to the authors certain exclusive rights in relation to the certain works referred in the Act. The object of the Act is to protect the author of the copyright work from an unlawful reproduction or exploitation of his work by others. Copyright is a right to stop others from exploiting the work without the consent or assent of the owner of the copyright. A copyright law presents a balance between the interests and rights of the author and that of the public in protecting the public domain, or to claim the copyright and protect it under the copyright statute. One of the key requirements is that of originality which contributes, and has a direct nexus, in maintaining the interests of the author as well as that of public in protecting the matters in public domain. It is a well accepted principle of copyright law that there is no copyright in the facts *per se*, as the facts are not created nor have they originated with the author of any work which embodies these facts. The issue of copyright is closely connected to that of commercial viability, and commercial consequences and implications. Copyright is purely a creation of the statute under the 1957 Act. What rights the author has in his work by virtue of his creation, are defined in Sections 14 and 17 of the Act. These are exclusive rights, but subject to the other provisions of the Act. In the first place, the work should qualify under the provisions of Section 13, for the subsistence of copyright. Although the rights have been referred to as exclusive rights, there are various exceptions to them which are listed in Section 52 of the Act.

For copyright protection, all literary works have to be original as per Section 13 of the Act. Broadly speaking, there would be two classes of literary works:

(a) **Primary or Prior Works:** These are the literary works not based on existing subject-matter and, therefore, would be called primary or prior works; and

(b) **Secondary or Derivative Works:** These are literary works based on existing subject-matter. Since such works are based on existing subject-matter, they are called derivative works or secondary works. The Copyright Act is not concerned with the original idea but with the expression of thought. Copyright has nothing to do with originality or literary merit. Copyrighted material is that what is created by the author by his own skill, labour and investment of capital, may be it is a derivative work which gives a flavour of creativity. The copyright work which comes into being should be original in the sense that by virtue of selection, coordination or arrangement of pre-existing data contained in the work, a work somewhat different in character is produced by the author. To claim copyright in a compilation, the author must produce the material with exercise of his skill and judgment which may not be creativity in the sense that it is novel or non-obvious, but at the same time it is not a product of merely labour and capital.

The Canadian Supreme Court in *CCH Canadian case,*[64] held that:

> "to be original under the Copyright Act the work must originate from an author, not be copied from another work, and must be the product of an author's exercise of skill and judgment. The exercise of skill and judgment required to produce the work must not be so trivial that it could be characterised as a purely mechanical exercise. Creative works by definition are original and are protected by copyright, but creativity is not required in order to render a work original. The original work

64. (2004) 1 SCR 339; 2004 SCC 13.

should be the product of an exercise of skill and judgment and it is a workable yet fair standard".

The 'sweat of the brow' approach to originality is too low a standard which shifts the balance of copyright protection too far in favour of the owner's right, and fails to allow copyright to protect the public's interest in maximising the production and dissemination of intellectual works. On the other hand, the creativity standard of originality is too high. A creative standard implies that something must be novel or non-obvious concepts more properly associated with patent law than copyright law. By way of contrast, a standard requiring the exercise of skill and judgment in the production of a work avoids these difficulties and provides a workable and appropriate standard for copyright protection that is consistent with the policy of the objectives of the Copyright Act. Thus, the Canadian Supreme Court is of the view that to claim copyright in a compilation, the author must produce a material with exercise of his skill and judgment which may not be creativity in the sense that it is not novel or non-obvious, but at the same time it is not the product of merely labour and capital.

On the face of the provisions of the Copyright Act, 1957 the principle laid down by the Canadian Supreme Court in CCH Canadian case would be applicable to copyright in the judgments of the Supreme Court. As provided for under Section 52(1)(q)(iv) the judicial pronouncements of the Supreme Court would be in the public domain and their reproduction or publication by any number of persons would not be infringement of the copyright of the first owner thereof, namely, the Government, unless it is prohibited. This being the position, the copy-edited judgments would not satisfy the copyright merely by establishing amount of skill, labour and capital put in the inputs of the copy-edited judgments and the original or innovative thoughts for the creativity are completely excluded. Accordingly, original or innovative thoughts are necessary to establish copyright in the author's work. To secure a copyright for the judgments delivered by the court, it is necessary that the labour, skill and capital invested should be sufficient to communicate or impart to the judgment some quality or character which the original judgment does not possess and which differentiates the original judgment from the printed one. The derivative work produced by the author must have some distinguishable features and flavours to raw text of the judgments delivered by the court. The trivial variation or inputs put in the judgments would not satisfy the test of copyright of an author. On this touchstone, the inputs put by the appellants in their journal 'SCC' shall be considered. The principle where there is common source the person relying on it must prove that he actually went to the common source from where he borrowed the material, employing his own skill, labour and brain and he did not copy, would not apply to the judgments of the courts because there is no copyright in the judgments of the courts, unless so made by the court itself.

It is made clear that this decision would be confined to the judgments of the courts which are in the public domain as by virtue of Section 52 of the Act there is no copyright in the original text of the judgments but on the other hand any inputs put in the judgments of the SC and reported in any journal has a copyright because it require special skills, labour, investment, etc. and using this matter without consent of the creators is the infringement of the copyright of the creator.

Academy of General Education, Manipal & Another Case[65]

Facts of the Case

'Yakshagana' is a form of ballet dance. It has its own heritage. Indisputably, Dr. Kota Shivarama Karanth ('Dr. Karanth'), a Jnanapeeth awardee, who was a Novelist, Play Writer, Essayist, Encyclopediationist, Cultural Anthropologist, Artist, Writer of Science, Environmentalist. He was a director of the appellant institute. He developed a new form of 'Yakshagana' named as 'Yaksharanga. On or about 18.6.1994, he executed a Will in favour of the respondent. He expired on 9.12.1997.

'Yaksharanga' ballet dance as developed by Dr. Karanth was performed in New Delhi on or about 18.9.2001. Respondent filed a suit for declaration, injunction and damages alleging violation of the copyright in respect of the said dance vested in her in terms of the said Will stating that Dr. Karanth developed a new distinctive dance, drama troop or theatrical system which was

65. *Academy of General Education, Manipal & Another Vs. B. Malini Mallya*, (2009) 4 SCC 256.

named by him as 'Yaksharanga' which in his own words mean 'creative extension of traditional Yakshagana' and thus, the appellants infringed the copyright thereof by performing the same at New Delhi without obtaining her prior permission. It was stated that Dr. Karanth had composed seven verses or prasangas for staging 'Yaksharanga' ballet apart from bringing in changes in the traditional form thereof on its relevant aspects, namely, Raga, Tala, Scenic arrangement, Costumes, etc. These prasangas are: (i) Bhishma Vijaya; (ii) Nala Damayanthi; (iii) Kanakangi or Kanakangi Kalyana; (iv) Abhimanyu or Abhimanyu Vadha; (v) Chitrangadha or Babruvahana Kalaga; (vi) Panchavati; and (vii) Ganga Charitha. Plaintiff-Respondent admittedly claimed copyright in respect of 'literary and artistic works' in her favour in terms of clauses 11 and 12 of the said Will dated 18.6.1994, which read as under:

> "Since I left the house 'Suhasa' I have been living in a specially built house 'Manasa' of Smt. Malini Mallya, who has built it with borrowed money at her cost. She had joined my service as Copyist and later, she secured an employment in Life Insurance Corporation of India. Ever since 1974 till now in my old age she has been serving me with exemplary devotion and sincerity. And in this occasion I must also acknowledge with gratitude that she diligently cared and nursed my wife Leela Karanth during her prolonged illness till her last day. And she has cared and looked after me also during my illness which at times had been quite serious, enfeebling me for long period. In recognition of her devotion and sincere affection towards me in 1986 I have dedicated one of my novels namely, 'Antida Aparanji' to her. I have also placed on record her invaluable services to me in my memoirs, 'Hunchu Mansina Hathu Mukhagalu', 1991 edition. In my opinion, very long enduring and a signal service she has done to me and to my literary works is, in writing a bibliography of all my books, a highly meritorious and scholarly work involving so much of pains taking research, that it has been acclaimed and rated as the first of its kind in Kannada and highly appreciated by Critics and Scholars. Apart from this, she has collected and edited all my stray writings from 1924

onwards, upto date in eight sumptuous volumes which are being published by Mangalore University. This work also has brought her deserving fame and appreciation of scholars. Such painstaking service in this direction has brought to light several of my hitherto untraced, forgotten and unknown writings and thereby giving them extended or renewed lease of life. For all these services, I hereby declare that after my death copyrights in respect of all my literary works shall vest with Smt. Malini Mallya and she alone shall be entitled to receive royalties of all my books and she shall be entitled to print, publish and republish and market the same. Whatever she may earn thereby shall be her exclusive income and property. No one else shall have any right or claims for the same. From time to time I have distributed among my children all gold and silver jewels and ornaments and other valuables, which were gifted to me by my friends and admirers. And I have distributed all copper and bronze vessels and utensils among my children while leaving my former home 'Suhasa' keeping only bare essential and necessary things and articles. Whatever movable properties, books, fittings, furniture, utensils, etc. belonging to me into this house 'Manasa' and my car and cash money in hand after my death shall go to Smt. Malini Mallya only. No one else shall have any claim or right over the same. Any outstanding due to me and Bank Deposits and whatever assets or properties not mentioned above, that is, residuary after my death shall belong to Smt. Malini Mallya alone."

Plaintiff-Respondent, *inter alia,* prayed for passing a judgment and decree against the defendants-appellants granting the following reliefs:

1. A declaration that the plaintiff is the exclusive copyright holder in respect of 'Yaksharanga' Ballets, namely, Bhishma Vijaya, Kanakangi, Nala Damayanthi, Panchavati, Gaya Charitha, Chitrangadha, Abhimanyu Vadha, and for consequential permanent injunction restraining the Defendants, their agents, employees, etc. From staging or performing any of the above said 7 Ballets or Prasangas or any parts thereof;

2. Directing the Defendants to pay to the plaintiff damages of Rs. 15000 towards infringement of her copyright on account of staging or performing Abhimanyu Vadha on 18-9-2001 at New Delhi;
3. Directing the Defendants to pay to the plaintiff interest on Rs. 15000 at 15% p.a. from 18-9-2001 till now which is Rs. 9500; and
4. Directing the Defendants to pay future interest on Rs. 15000 at 15% p.a. till payment of the entire amount.

Appellants in their written statement, however, denied and disputed any copyright of the said dance in Dr. Karanth alleging that whatever work he had done was in the capacity of a Director of the Yaksharanga Kendra with the assistance, finance and staff provided by the Organisation of Mahatma Gandhi Memorial College Trust in respect whereof a Committee was formed under him by the Board of Trustees. It was furthermore contended that Dr. Karanth was appointed as the President of the Executive Committee of Yaksharanga Kendra for a period of three years by the appellant and while holding the said post only he expired.

By reason of a judgment and decree dated 14.11.2003, the District Judge, Udupi decreed the said suit declaring the plaintiff-respondent as a person having the exclusive copyright in respect of seven Prasangas and that she had acquired the same by reason of a Will as a residuary legatee and the defendants-appellants or their employees or agents were restrained from performing the said seven Ballets or Prasangas or any parts thereof in any manner as evolved distinctively by Dr. Karanth.

Appellants aggrieved thereby and dissatisfied therewith preferred an appeal before the Karnataka High Court which was marked as R.F.A. No. 271 of 2004. By reason of the impugned judgment and order dated 5.12.2007, the said appeal has been dismissed. The appellant then moved before the Supreme Court.

Analysis of the Case

The Copyright Act, 1957 was enacted to amend and consolidate the law relating to copyright. Section 2 is the interpretation section. Section 2(c) defines 'artistic work' to mean,

(i) a painting, a sculpture, a drawing (including a diagram, map, chart or plan), an engraving or a photograph, whether or not any such work possesses artistic quality;

(ii) a work of architecture; and

(iii) any other work of artistic craftsmanship.

The word 'author' is defined in Section 2(d) to mean,

(i) in relation to a literary or dramatic work, the author of the work;

(ii) in relation to a musical work, the composer;

(iii) in relation to an artistic work other than a photograph, the artist;

(iv) in relation to a photograph, the person taking the photograph;

(v) in relation to a cinematograph film or sound recording, the producer; and

(vi) in relation to any literary, dramatic, musical or artistic work which is computer-generated, the person who causes the work to be created.

The term 'communication to the public' as defined in Section 2(ff) reads as under:

> 'communication to the public' means making any work available for being seen or heard or otherwise enjoyed by the public directly or by any means of display or diffusion other than by issuing copies of such work regardless of whether any member of the pubic actually sees, hears or otherwise enjoys the work so made available.
>
> *Explanation:* For the purposes of this clause, communication through satellite or cable or any other means of simultaneous communication to more than one household or place of residence including residential rooms of any hotel or hostel shall be deemed to be communication to the public.

Section 2(ffa) defines the word 'composer', in relation to a musical work, to mean the person who composes the music regardless of whether he records it in any form of graphical notation. Section 2(h) defines "dramatic work" to include any piece of recitation, choreographic work or entertainment in dumb show, the scenic arrangement or acting, form of which is fixed in writing or otherwise but does not include a cinematograph film.

Section 2(o) defines 'literary work' to include computer programmes, tables and compilations including computer databases.

Section 2(qq) defines 'performer' to include an actor, singer, musician, dancer, acrobat, juggler, conjurer, snake charmer, a person delivering a lecture or any other person who makes a performance.

Section 2(y) defines 'work' to mean any of the following works, namely:

(i) a literary, dramatic, musical or artistic work;
(ii) a cinematograph film; and
(iii) a sound recording.

Section 13 which occurs in Chapter III of the Act provides that subject to the provisions thereof and the other provisions of the said Act, copyright shall subsists throughout India in the following classes of works, that is to say:

(a) original literary, dramatic, musical and artistic works;
(b) cinematograph films; and
(c) sound recording.

Section 17 of the Act deals with 'First owner of copyright', in terms whereof, subject to the provisions of the Act, the author of a work shall be the owner of the copyright therein. Proviso (d) appended thereto states that in the case of a Government work, Government shall, in the absence of any agreement to the contrary, be the first owner of the copyright therein. Sections 22, 23 and 52(1)(a), (i) and (l) of the Act, which are relevant for our purpose read as under:

Section 22: Term of copyright in published literary, dramatic, musical and artistic works, except as otherwise hereinafter provided, copyright shall subsist in any literary, dramatic, musical or artistic work (other than a photograph) published within the life time of the author until fifty years from the beginning of the calendar year following the year in which the author dies.

Explanation: In this section, the reference to the author shall in the case of a work of joint authorship, be construed as a reference to the author who dies last.

Section 23(1): In the case of a literary, dramatic, musical or artistic work (other than a photograph), which is published anonymously or pseudonymously, copyright shall subsist until sixty years from the beginning of the calendar year next following the year in which the work is first published:

Provided that where the identity of the author is disclosed before the expiry of the copyrighted period, copyright shall subsist until sixty years from the beginning of the calendar year following the year in which the author dies.

Section 23(2): In sub-section (1), references to the author shall, in the case of an anonymous work of joint authorship, be construed, (a) where the identity of the authors is disclosed, as references to that author; (b) where the identity of more authors than one is disclosed, as references to the author who dies last from amongst such authors.

Section 23(3): In sub-section (1), references to the author shall, in the case of a pseudonymous work of joint authorship, be construed, (a) where the names of one or more (but not all) of the authors are pseudonymous and his or their identity is not disclosed, as references to the author whose name is not a pseudonym, or, if the names of two or more of the authors are not pseudonyms, as references to such of those authors who dies last; (b) where the names of one or more (but not all) of the authors are pseudonyms and the identity of one or more of them is disclosed, as references to the author who dies last from amongst the authors whose names are not pseudonyms and the authors whose names are pseudonyms and are disclosed; and (c) where the names of all the authors are pseudonyms and the identity of one of them is disclosed, as references to the author whose identity is disclosed or if the identity of two or more of such authors is disclosed, as references to such of those authors who dies last.

Explanation: For the purposes of this section, the identity of an author shall be deemed to have been disclosed, if either the identity of the author is disclosed publicly by both the author and the publisher or is otherwise established to the satisfaction of the Copyright Board by that author.

Certain acts not to be infringement of copyright—As per section 52(1): The following acts shall not constitute an infringement of copyright, namely:

(1) a fair dealing with a literary, dramatic, musical or artistic work not being a computer programme for the purpose of: (a) Private use including research; (b) criticism or review, whether of that work or of any other work; (i) The performance, in the course of the activities of an educational institution, of a literary, dramatic or musical work by the staff and student of the institution, or of a cinematograph film or a sound recording, if the audience is limited to such staff and students, the parents and guardians of the students and persons directly connected with the activities of the institution or the communication to such an audience of a cinematograph film or sound recording. (ii) The performance of a literary, dramatic or musical work by an amateur club or society, if the performance is given to a non-paying audience, or for the benefit of a religious institution.

Before entering to the submissions made by the learned counsel for the parties, the Court noticed the issues framed in the suit by the lower courts, which are:

1. Does plaintiff prove that late Dr. Shivaramaji Karanth had acquired copyright in respect of seven 'Yakshagana' Prasangas and also in respect of 'Yakshagana' dramatic or theatrical form i.e., Bhishma Vijaya, Nala Damayanthi, Kanakaangti or Kanakangi Kalyana, Abhimanyu or Abhimanyu Vadha, Chitrangadha or Babruvahana Kalaga, Panchavati Chritha followed in the plaint?
2. Has the plaintiff became entitled to the said right under the Registered Will dated 18.06.1994?
3. Does the plaintiff prove that her right under the said Will was infringed by the defendants?
4. Does the plaintiff liable for the actual loss or damage suffered, if any, by the defendants?

The Court opined that indisputably, in view of the submissions made at the bar, respondent had acquired copyright in respect of seven 'Yakshagana' Prasangas as also in respect of 'Yakshagana' dramatic or theatrical form as a residuary legatee in terms of clause 12 of the Will dated 18.6.1994. However, the Court noticed that whereas the trial court has proceeded on the basis that clause 12 of the Will shall apply in the instant case, the High Court opined that clause 11 thereof is attracted, stating:

> "No doubt, by reading para-2 of the 'Will' in isolation, one can certainly arrive at the conclusion that the bequest made in favour of the plaintiff is in the nature of residuary bequest. But, that is not at all, in the 'Will' Ex. P-1, I have already referred to para No. 11 of the 'Will' while dealing with the topic dramatic works *vis-a-vis* literary work and therefore if the 'Will' is read in its entirety and if we take into account, the benefits that flow from the bequest made by Dr. Karanth in favour of the plaintiff, it is not as if the plaintiff received the bequest only in respect of the things which form the residuary as mentioned in para-12 of the 'Will' but the plaintiff also was given the copyrights in respect of literary works and all books as well as the right to print, republished and mark the literary works as well as the books."

Referring to the new Encyclopaedia Britannica and Halsbury's Laws of England, that a literary work with dramatic elements in it would also be literary work, the High Court observed:

> "Dramatic works also could contain in its, passages of great literary taste, as in the case of great plays of William Shakespear. Therefore, the main classification as literary work and dramatic work cannot be construed to mean that dramatic work has nothing to do with literary work. The only difference I see in them is that the dramatic work (Plays) forms the text upon which the performance of the plays rests whereas a 'literary work' enables one to read the printed words. Neither of the two can be produced without the imaginative skill of the author."[66]

It was furthermore held by the court that:

> "all the above changes brought about by Dr. Karanth in

66. Karnataka High Court which was marked as R.F.A. No. 271 of 2004.

> respect of Yakshagana Ballet leads to the inference that the imaginative faculties of Dr. Karanth permeated the entire Yakshagana Prasangas and thus a new look was given to the Yakshagana Ballets. I, therefore, hold that the bequest of copyright in literary works and books in favour of the plaintiff by Dr. Karanth will have to be treated as the bequest covering the dramatic works also since I have also drawn the conclusion that the dramatic works is also a form of literature. Therefore, necessity of mentioning copyright separately in respect of dramatic works does not arise. The plaintiff, therefore, is entitled to copyright even in respect of the dramatic works namely the seven prasangas, by virtue of bequest made in her favour in respect of copyrights and books."

Broadly speaking, a dramatic work may also come within the purview of literary work being a part of dramatic literature. The new Encyclopaedia Britannica (Vol. IV), 15th Edition provides the following information about 'Dramatic Literature'. 'Dramatic Literature means the texts of plays that can be read, as distinct from being seen and heard in performance.'

The Supreme Court, however, noticed that the provisions of the Act make a distinction between the 'literary work' and 'dramatic work'. Keeping in view the statutory provisions, there cannot be any doubt whatsoever that copyright in respect of performance of 'dance' would not come within the purview of the literary work but would come within the purview of the definition of 'dramatic work'. The Court, however, do not mean to suggest that any act of literary work will be outside the purview of the Will dated 18.6.1994. The Court, thus, performed its duty only for the purpose of clarifying the provisions of the Act with reference to the findings arrived at by the High Court.

For the aforementioned reasons, the Court agreed with Dr. Dhavan, learned counsel for respondent, that paragraph 12 of the Will, namely, residuary clause shall apply in the instant case apart from the areas which are otherwise covered by paragraph 11 of the Will. The residuary clause will apply because it is well settled that no part of the stay lies in limbo. It was also not a case where respondent in any manner whatsoever waived her right.

The learned trial judge on issue No. 4 opined that plaintiff had not been able to prove actual loss or damage particularly having regard to the fact that Dr. Karanth had associated himself with the appellants for a long time. The learned trial judge recognized the equitable interest vested in the plaintiff-respondent. A declaratory decree, therefore, was passed.

The Supreme Court noticed at this stage that the form of injunction granted both by the learned trial judge as also by the High Court in favour of the plaintiff-respondent. The operative part of the judgment of the trial court reads as under:

> "Defendants or their employees or agents are restrained from performing the above said Ballets or Prasangas or in parts thereof in any manner as evolved distinctively by Dr. Karanth by way of permanent injunction."

The High Court, however, directed:

> "As far as the restraint order passed by the Trial Court by granting permanent injunction to the plaintiff is concerned, the same is modified by ordering that if the appellants desire to stage any of the seven Yaksharanga Prasangas in the manner and form as conceived in all respects viz., costumes, choreography and direction by Dr. Karanth, the appellants can do so only in accordance with the provisions of the Copyrights Act, 1957 in view of copyright in seven prasangas vesting with the plaintiff."

Decree for injunction is an equitable relief. The courts while passing a decree for permanent injunction would avoid multiplicity of proceedings. The court while passing such a decree is obligated to consider the statutory provisions governing the same. For the said purpose, it must be noticed as to what is a copyright and in respect of the matters the same cannot be claimed or otherwise the same is lodged by conditions and subject to statutory limitation. In this regard renowned of the case *R.G. Anand vs. M/s Delux Films & Ors.*,[67] may be referred where the Supreme Court after a careful consideration and elucidation of the various authorities and the case laws on the subject emerged the following propositions:

1. There can be no copyright in an idea, subject-matter, themes, plots or historical or legendary facts and

67. (1978) 4 SCC 118.

violation of the copyright in such cases is confined to the form, manner and arrangement and expression of the idea by the author of the copyrighted work.

2. Where the same idea is being developed in a different manner, it is manifest that the source being common, similarities are bound to occur. In such a case the courts should determine whether or not the similarities are on fundamental or substantial aspects of the mode of expression adopted in the copyrighted work. If the defendant's work is nothing but a literal imitation of the copyrighted work with some variations here and there it would amount to violation of the copyright. In other words, in order to be actionable the copy must be a substantial and material one which at once leads to the conclusion that the defendant is guilty of an act of piracy.
3. One of the surest and the safest test to determine whether or not there has been a violation of copyright is to see if the reader, spectator or the viewer after having read or seen both the works is clearly of the opinion and gets an unmistakable impression that the subsequent work appears to be a copy of the original.
4. Where the theme is the same but is presented and treated differently so that the subsequent work becomes a completely new work, no question of violation of copyright arises.
5. Where, however, apart from the similarities appearing in the two works there are also material and broad dissimilarities which negative the intention to copy the original and the coincidences appearing in the two works are clearly incidental no infringement of the copyright comes into existence.
6. As a violation of copyright amounts to an act of piracy it must be proved by clear and cogent evidence after applying the various tests laid down by the decided case-laws.
7. Where, however, the question is of the violation of the copyright of stage play by a film producer or a director the task of the plaintiff becomes more difficult to prove piracy. It is manifest that unlike a stage play a film has a much broader prospective, wider field and a bigger

> background where the defendants can by introducing a variety of incidents give a colour and complexion different from the manner in which the copyrighted work has expressed the idea. Even so, if the viewer after seeing the film gets a totality of impression that the film is by and large a copy of the original play, violation of the copyright may be said to be proved.

Yet again in *Eastern Book Company & Ors. Vs. D.B. Modak & Anr.,*[68] Apex Court held that:

> "**Section 57:** The Copyright Act is not concerned with the original idea but with the expression of thought. Copyright has nothing to do with originality or literary merit. Copyrighted material is that what is created by the author by his own skill, labour and investment of capital, may be it is a derivative work which gives a flavour of creativity. The copyright work which comes into being should be original in the sense that by virtue of selection, coordination or arrangement of pre-existing data contained in the work, a work somewhat different in character is produced by the author. On the face of the provisions of the Copyright Act, 1957, we think that the principle laid down by the Canadian Court would be applicable in copyright of the judgments of the Apex Court. We make it clear that the decision of ours would be confined to the judgments of the courts which are in the public domain as by virtue of Section 52 of the Act there is no copyright in the original text of the judgments. To claim copyright in a compilation, the author must produce the material with exercise of his skill and judgment which may not be creativity in the sense that it is novel or non-obvious, but at the same time it is not a product of merely labour and capital. The derivative work produced by the author must have some distinguishable features and flavour to raw text of the judgments delivered by the court. The trivial variation or inputs put in the judgment would not satisfy the test of copyright of an author."

The High Court, in the opinion of Supreme Court, should have clarified that the appellants can also take the statutory

68. (2008) 1 SCC 1.

benefit of the provisions contained in clauses (a), (i) and (l) of sub-section (1) of Section 52 of the Act. Section 52 of the Act provides for certain acts which would not constitute an infringement of copyright. When a fair dealing is made, *inter alia,* of a literary or dramatic work for the purpose of private use including research and criticism or review, whether of that work or of any other work, the right in terms of the provisions of the said Act cannot be claimed. Thus, if some performance or dance is carried out within the purview of the said clause, the order of injunction shall not be applicable.

Similarly, appellant being an educational institution, if the dance is performed within the meaning of provisions of clause (i) of sub-section (1) of Section 52 of the Act strictly, the order of injunction shall not apply thereto also. Yet again, if such performance is conducted before a non-paying audience by the appellant, which is an institution if it comes within the purview of amateur club or society, the same would not constitute any violation of the said order of injunction. Thus, the appeal was thus dismissed with aforementioned modification in the order of injunction.

The discussion made in the abovementioned cases and the opinion of different Courts show that the copyright protection from the traditional modes of infringement in India has some roots to take care of the copyright of the person concerned, though not strong and effective enough, but electronic or digital modes of the infringement in this electronic age is real problem for the copyright creations in India. The protection extends only to the copyright as understood in the traditional or manual aspects not in modern aspects. Thus, on-line copyright issues also need to be adequately protected. To meet the ever increasing challenges, as posed by the changed circumstances and latest technology, the existing laws are required to be so interpreted that all facets of copyright are adequately covered or new law should be enacted, as required. This can be achieved by applying the 'purposive interpretation' technique, which requires the existing laws to be interpreted in such a manner as justice is done in the fact and circumstances of the case. Alternatively, existing laws should be amended as per the requirement of the situation. The existing laws can also be supplemented with newer ones, specifically for dealing with the contemporary issues and problems. The Information Technology Act, 2000 necessitates a new outlook and orientation, which can be effectively used to meet the challenges posed by the copyright regime in this age of information technology. Till day, the country has no sound and strong legal base for the protection of copyrights in economic perspective, the judiciary should play an active role in the protection of this right. The situation is, however, really alarming one and the existing legal system should be made more equipped so that it can effectively take care of any problem associated with copyright infringements.

The Courts while considering the question of grant of reliefs (where parameters are not laid down), supplanted the statutory provisions by the norms accepted by the international community and would be justified in seeking guidance from the treaties and conventions on the subject so long they are not inconsistent with the municipal laws. The courts undoubtedly will be bound by the constitutional mandates and the laws. It will have to strike a delicate balance between public welfare and private interests so that an atmosphere conducive, to respect, for the copyright of the nationals and the member-states are created which would help to increase international trade and encourage the citizens to strive for excellence to produce intellectual property which will be recognized and enforced by all courts of the member-States.

In India, there is a highly matured and developed legal system firmly embedded in the rule of law. The approach of judiciary in safeguarding the basic human rights and the majesty of law is amply reflected in the various decisions of the Apex Court and the High Courts. The courts have frowned upon arbitrary actions of the administrative authorities or unfair and arbitrary approach of the authorities in their decision-making process. There is judicial insistence on the application of the principles of natural justice and fair play by the authorities who make orders that may have an adverse impact on the rights of a person. As a safeguard against arbitrariness, the authorities are required to make reasoned orders and their decisions are required to be communicated to the concerned parties. The proceedings of courts are normally held in the open. With its independence secured against any arm twisting by outside forces, the role that the Indian Judiciary can play in safeguarding the legally recognized rights like the copyright can put to envy any enlightened judicial system of any developed country. The fairness of the procedures reflected in our laws and recognition of equal rights of even aliens by virtue of Article 14 as fundamental rights should generate sufficient confidence in our legal system to encourage the entrepreneurs to be sure of the protection of their copyright which is recognised by the municipal laws. How far the judiciary can be instrumental in protection of private and other rights like copyright will ultimately depend upon the perceptions of those who have to pay for use. It is therefore, important that they thoroughly understand the nature of the rights recognized by law, the need of their protection, the steps required to be taken as also the urgency of the matter. The establishment of Judicial Academy for providing periodic training and refreshers can keep the decision-makers abreast of the needs of time and situations and make them responsive of the important role that they have to play.

Thus, Indian Judiciary has to play a very significant role in protecting the infringement of copyright in India. The main problem in this regard is to find out the modes of infringement and ways for its protection because in this electronic age the modes of infringing the copyright are so easy that it is quite difficult to find out the cases of the infringement of copyright. More and more careful consideration on the part of judiciary is required to take the cognizance of the modern infringement. The prime task for which the researcher has undertaken this job is to find out the cases which are infringing the copyrights in one hand and the areas injuring the national economy of the country on the other.

6

CONCLUSION

> "Justice is the first virtue of social institutions, as truth is of systems of thought. A theory however elegant and economical must be rejected or revised if it is untrue; likewise laws and institutions no matter how efficient and well-arranged must be reformed or abolished if they are unjust. The only thing that permits us to acquiesce in an erroneous theory is the lack of a better one; analogously, an injustice is tolerable only when it is necessary to avoid an even greater injustice. Being first virtues of human activities, truth and justice are uncompromising."[1]
>
> —*John Rawls*

The supreme task of copyright law has been to motivate the creation of intellectual works for the public welfare subsequently enriching the public domain and next important object has been to secure economic recognition to those who are engaged in the thought creation process and also those who are engaged in the dissemination process. However, due to global recognition and marketable value addition it is becoming competitive with industries who earn by exploiting the intellectual works of the creators. Today, copyright is moving from being an author's concern to the concept of 'industrial property' resulting in the

1. A Theory of Justice, 2005 reissue (Harvard University Press, 1971), Chapter 1: Justice as Fairness, The Role of Justice, pp. 3-4

change of the role of copyright which is now playing the supreme task even upto the extent of overshadowing the limitations imposed upon the limited monopoly in public interest. It has now-a-days converted into a considerable contributor to the state revenues.

From the discussion made in the foregoing chapters it may be concluded that originally, copyright is based on the economic philosophy that no person is allowed to profit from the weirs of the others. Profit in this sense bears its ordinary meaning of earning income, the share of which shall go to the author of the work (as he has expended his intellect) or his assigns, licensees, etc. (who have invested their income to market or sell that 'intellectual product'.) In the field of law it is often quoted 'Ignorantia juris non execusat' that ignorance of law is no excuse. One cannot take this defence in the court of law. Most of the people who know the law pretend not to, and go full steam ahead in photocopying copyrighted materials in substantial parts or sometime in totality. They consider it legitimate since they are paying the photocopier for his labour and service which is far much more rewarding than to pay the author for his intellect or publisher for expenditure. But people often practice the same in Schools, Colleges and Universities without even a bit of guilt, moreover not even consider it immoral so long as they are paying for the pages and many of them are not even aware that it is an illegal act.

The different areas of infringement of copyrights have been identified in this work. Some of the areas are oldest traditional areas or modes of infringement like copying manually but after the arrival of the technological and the digital technology, areas of infringement has really increased remarkably. Infringement by way of burning of CDs/DVDs, exploitation of creations through internet mail server, telecasting movies through cable communication, leaving copy or creation in the server, downloading the creation of authors without consent and uploading the cinematographic and musical works on the internet without obtaining authority, are some areas of rampant infringement of copyright with which the creators/owners as well as investors are poorly suffering, not only in India but throughout the globe. The researcher has also gone through one area of the infringement of copyright which is latest and caused due to arrival of the digital environment and that is home tape recording of audio and video programme for future days without paying anything to the owner/creator.

From the abovesaid discussion it is also sufficiently clear that the copyright development started in European countries mainly in UK and its neighbouring countries like France, Denmark, Germany, Rome but later on the development of copyright law in England was not as quicker as the development of the US Copyright law. The Copyright law of USA, which got its origin from the Constitution of the USA,[2] initially started developing slowly but got the real momentum after its globalisation specially after the establishment of the WTO and implementation of TRIPs guidelines, the US law-makers started treating copyright law *at par* with the changes of technological improvement by making different changes and passing new laws like the remarkable Audio Home Recording Rights Act, 1992, No Electronic Theft (NET) Act, 1997 and Digital Millennium Copyright Act, 1998, etc. The study of historical development also shows that the modern copyright law has developed in USA, which is also called the father of modern copyright law. The US law-makers always ready to knock the door of the laws whenever any challenges arrive. The US Copyright laws are only laws which, for the first time, tried to prevent the infringement of copyright from the challenges posed by the technological and digital advancement. The US government also conducted many conferences on different issues related to Copyright like CONFU (Conference on Fair Use), CONTU Process, etc. to meet the challenges forwarded by the technological and digital progress. Thus, it can be said that the development of Copyright law, till date has been made in two phase primarily, in the UK where the ancient or traditional copyright laws have developed and secondly, in the USA where the modern copyright laws have been developing. But still neither English Copyright law nor US Copyright laws are able to protect the copyrights of its citizen particularly from the non-traditional, electronic and digital mode of infringement. In spite of regular changes in copyright laws of both countries, they are suffering from the pain of electronic and digital fever in particular and incomplete satisfaction in general.

---

2. Article 1, Section 8, Clause 8 of U.S. Constitution, 1787.

Indian Copyright law is though primarily considered to be overshadowed by the English copyright law but the globalisation and economic value addition to IPR in general and copyright in particular, India has really changed its dimension and in the passage of time our legislature provided us own colour and taste in the field of Copyright law. Now-a-days, in the process of copyright creation works India is one of the largest in the world but the protective mechanism is weakest one which is very discouraging. The present law, i.e. Copyright Act, 1957 is amended many times only to keep balance with the development, i.e. to keep pace with time and following the changes observed in the international principles like TRIPs etc., but still, the copyright and related laws of India are suffering from the policy sickness and not able to protect many areas of the copyright violations. The Indian laws of copyright have certainly failed to cope with the technological advancement in order to protect the copyright from the infringement as the nature of the copyright becomes international one. One can copy the creation of any person only by a click of mouse. Indian copyright law is not *at par* with the technological, digital and electronic advancement of the age.

From the deep study of the legislations, cases and laws relating to infringement of copyright in India and its impact on the copyright of the creators, it can be concluded that India by the amendment of its copyright law in 1999 in the opinion of the researcher, has weakened the computer software protective provisions which were more effective in 1995 and considered as most progressive among the developing world. Even though Information Technology Act, 2000 includes huge penalties for the unauthorised copying of softwares, the immunities available in other laws prevent successful prosecutions of the cases by the Indian judicial system. This should be seriously looked into in India. India is still not a signatory of the most effective treaties to meet the technological challenges of WIPO, i.e. WIPO Copyright Treaty (WCT) and WIPO Performance and Phonograms Treaty (WPPT).

Another important area which has not perfectly covered by the current Indian copyright legislation is the liability of service providers for copyright infringement. On the other hand, the Information Technology Act, 2000 exempts ISPs from liability if they can prove that they had no knowledge of the occurrence of the alleged act and that they had taken sufficient steps to prevent a violation. However, the existing provisions of both Copyright Act and Information Technology Act do not clearly prescribe liability limits of service providers. For example, if a person makes a representation to a service provider claiming copyright infringement on the material available on the network, the service provider will be liable only if he fails to take steps within a 'reasonable time' to remove the infringing material from the network. If the service provider fails to prevent infringement of copyright in the above circumstances, the plea of not having knowledge of infringement is still available to him. If the service provider removes the material from the network in pursuance to the representation made by a person, which later on proves false, the service provider will not be liable to the person whose material has been removed. The Indian position in respect to the liability of service providers for copyright infringement must be made more explicit so that ISP can properly discharge its responsibilities.

Most of the infringement of copyright has been made in the name of 'fare use'. Recognising a 'fair use' defense gives a user free access to whatever copyrighted works happen to be created by the creator. Thus, in presence of transactional barriers in bargaining, the fair use doctrine serves the important function of facilitating diffusion without significantly chilling creativity. It has been now settled that fair use rule has evolved as an equitable response to market failure as a way to ensure that socially desirable uses will not be blocked. But in reality one of the sole causes of failure of the measures for the protection of copyright infringement is the defense of 'fair use' because there is no guideline to determine the term 'fair use' in Indian copyright laws. Sometimes socially responsible citizens are also not convinced as whether an act is the fair use or not? Actually the purpose of incorporation of 'fair use' was very clear but its application is not proper and most of the time it has been misused by the user. Once Justice Govdon, Professor of law, Boston University, School of Law, argued that if a market does not develop for a creative work or use because high transaction costs impede bargaining, then prohibiting copying makes little sense from economic uses, without providing any monetary return to creators.[3]

Another important aspect of the Copyright law which is not properly dealt with in the present law relating to copyright in India is the steps to encourage and motivate the people by providing awareness regarding copyright infringement and its consequences. Even police personals who can play major role in combating piracy, are not copiously aware of various provisions of the law relating to copyright. There is lack of adequate number of personnel who can fully devote to copyright-related crimes alone. The police are more concerned with usual law and order problems and copyright-related crimes are attached least priority. The awareness level among end-users is also very low. While buying a copyrighted product, majority of consumers do not look at copyright notification (e.g. C or P). As long as price is low (as generally is the case with pirated products) users do not mind even buying pirated products.

Present Indian copyright legislation and related laws certainly provides the mechanism for the protection but the another serious aspects not properly anticipated by the Indian law-makers is challenge of the enforcement of the prescribed laws. The enforcement is lacking at different levels. First, users (consumers) themselves are not aware about the fundamentals for copyright. According to statistics, given earlier, the domestic software industry has been bleeding losses of over half a billion dollars due to the piracy nexus. When we will have a fundamental base of copyright protection that allows us to unleash more innovations from the Indian technical community and provides more protection to them, only then there will be more investment in innovations from the venture capitalists. Moreover, copyright protection can also mean more jobs in the IT industry such as software experts, programmers, etc.

Another aspect which has been revealed throughout the study is that law related to copyright in India has failed to compete with the advancement in the field of technology. Almost nine years have elapsed since last amendment of Copyright Act has gone through to make the law more effective and meaningful. Lots of technological changes have been made in the field of science and technology but no changes have been seen in

3. Wendy J. Gordon & Robert G. Bone, Copyright, 1999, p. 202.

copyright law though in most cases it is infringed by the use of those technological devices. In fact, in modern times copyright law and related laws are generally violated by the use of electronic or technological or digital instruments, etc., technology is developing day-by-day but in this relation copyright laws are not revised and it becomes frozen in time which is not desirable. Only by incorporating the remarkable changes required due to technological advancement, the copyright laws shall be able to serve its purpose.

Since the beginning of this decade a 'core group' of Governmental officials, local industrialists, academicians and lawyers have been favouring new amendments to the Copyright Act leading to the implementation of WCT and WPPT principles but all discussions are going fruitless due to coldhearted attitude on the part of the governmental department concerned.

Thus, if this will be the position the original creator will never be awarded and moreover, the nation will continue losing its revenue from the area of copyright industry. This practice is to be curbed by any means by taking appropriate action.

SUGGESTIONS

Dr. Sundarárajan has aptly writes that Copyright reform in India suggests a fundamental rethinking of India's approach to the public interest in particular, the right of the public to use works that are protected by copyright. India has long recognised that excessive restrictive copyright laws may impede public education, particularly where knowledge from advanced countries is needed for modernisation.[4]

The researcher does not suppose to step into the shoes of the legislature and precisely propose the draft enabling laws which are the bounden duty and the sacred domain of the legislature. However, that do not make us bashful as responsible citizens from the suggestion as to what should the law-makers keep in mind while drafting the enabling provisions which shall diminish the free and unauthorised accessibility to the copy-righted works. The copyright law is a form of societal

4. Dr. Mira T. Sundararajan, Digital Learning in India: Problems and Prospects; http;//cyber.law.harvard.edu/home/dl_india

governance. The Copyright law must be examined in the context of social development.[5]

From the discussion made throughout the research project, the author prefers the following suggestions which shall not only make the present copyright laws of India *at par* with the international instruments but also help the country to have a proper and complete law of copyright.

Imposition of Liability of Internet Service Provider

Internet Service Provider is very important body to the process of Internet Service of this electronic age. ISP is taking sufficient considerations for providing its services but in India, still, the liability of service provider is not expressly covered under present Copyright Act, 1957. The Information Technology Act, 2000 exempts ISPs from liability if they can prove that they had no knowledge of the occurrence of the alleged act, and that they had taken sufficient steps to prevent an infringement. In order to be exempt from liability, the Indian Act requires the service provider to exercise due diligence to prevent the commission of copyright infringement whereas, the Act does not provide the meaning of the term due diligence. There is a need for a consensus on the meaning of the term due diligence because the primary function of ISPs is to build and provide the Internet service. The I.T. Act must include sections that address the financial aspect of the transaction, and the relationship between an ISP and a third party because this is vital in determining the identity of the violator. The American concept of contributory infringement can also be incorporated into the Indian copyright legislation so that if any person with knowledge of the infringing activity, induces, causes, or materially contributes to the infringing conduct of another, the person can be made liable.

Introduction of Digital/Audio Books for Visually Challenged Users

The author consider that persons with disabilities are still not active partners with government in the development and implement of legislations and polices that most significantly affect their lives and, towards the end, also propose that persons

5. Succinctly highlighted by Prof. (Dr.) Prabuddha Ganguli in a seminar of Intellectual Property Right in Strategic Management in July 2007.

suffering from aural or print disabilities must be made an active participant in working out exceptions to the existing copyright law as to secure an enabling environment for them in terms of accessibility to copyrighted material in their 'language', i.e. the Braille code or audio formats. The organisations of disabled persons may be usefully consulted in all matters regarding the rights of disabled persons in furtherance of the principles enshrined in the U.N. Declaration on the Rights of Disabled persons.[6] Supply of the accessible copies free of cost is not advocated but only that the conversion of literary work into accessible format by an authorised entity must be permitted without the consent of the right holder. This need of access must be in the nature of right not as an obligation from the right holders, however, it is equally important to safeguard their rights under the statute. In fact, efforts have been made to provide accessible books for the blind for example Ramakrishna Mission School agreed to convert the books of NIOS (National Institute of Open Schooling) after Prof. N.K. Ambasht, Former Chairman, NIOS contacted them. Books were then ordered in appreciable quantities for the use of the blind students. Copyright restrictions were also waived-off so that reproduction of the text into accessible braille format could be made without fear of copyright infringement but it is not final, it is only the beginning. The Government must take initiatives, by some provision of law, to constitute an authority which shall convert copyrighted printed books into accessible file for aurally and visually challenged. The access of the converted file may be controlled by technological measures including access codes, encryption technologies, so that the contents of the work cannot be copied and can be operated by licensed persons only. Thus, only one license per copy should be allowed. This way, only the user shall have to fill in the access codes in the same computer where the licensed file is installed and shall not be operable in absence of the compact disk which contains the copyrighted work. This shall prevent lending of the work to multiple users who have not paid the cost of acquiring the accessible copy and are free riding on the author's labours.

6. Point 12 of the U.N. Declaration on the Rights of Disabled Persons.

Prevention of Unauthorised Burning of the Computer Software

Similar is the condition in duplicating compact disks (CD's) and DVD's. It is a click of a button without a pinch of guilt for us. One considers it as a legitimate act. The computer users is ready to pay for the hardware and is least bothered to check whether the software installed in it by the vendor is original or not. This unfortunately is the present state of affairs. Proper immediate action is required for the protection of the original CD's and DVD's. Although the growth story for the software market in India continues to show promise, the market is losing millions of rupees as softwares like Adobe, McAfee, Microsoft and Symantec continue to be sold for mere pennies on the roadsides. Last estimated, the Business Software Alliance seized about $2.1 million worth of pirated software in 2006. The worst is yet to come as internet penetration rises to newer heights, says Joseph Fitz Gerald, Symantec, vice-president, in an interview to ET[7].

Establishment of Special Trained Police Personnel

The government (both union and state) shall also think about the special class of police who shall be specially trained and expertise as required. They should be appointed especially to take care of copyright and related matters and fully devoted to copyright and related crimes, the percentage of which is very high in this age. Chief Justice of Delhi High Court Mr. S.B. Sinha, in a seminar also emphasised the need for the training of judicial and police officers in all aspects for the implementation of IPR laws so that there shall be adequate protection to the manufacture of genuine products and the consumer shall be exposed to the danger of purchasing/consuming fake products.

Introduction of Awareness and Education Programme

In the field of copyright there can be two ways of infringement of copyright. Firstly, the persons who are copying the original works of the authors without knowing whether this is the case of copyright infringement or not. Secondly, the persons who are intentionally infringing the copyright of the authors by copying it without permission from the authors. In India, in case of literary and artistic work the infringement by way of first

7. *Economic Times*, 12.02.2007.

category are higher than the case of second category though in other part of the globe the ratio is reverse. The above category of infringement can be minimised simply by conducting awareness and education programme regarding copyright. The governmental departments and non-governmental organisations should come together to fight with this menace in order to protect the IPR in general and copyright in particular. Counterfeit products were flourishing because there was a ready market in the country for such cheap, look-alike products. The acceptance of counterfeit products by consumers comes in the way of the implementation of laws which is the result of lack of awareness, education and information. The below mentioned category of persons should specially be given awareness and education to make them understand the basic of copyright and to provide them the knowledge about the infringement of copyrights, copyrighted products and its economic and social importance. They should also be made conscious to understand the distinction between the copyright notifications of 'C' not 'P', etc. They should be aware and educated for combating the copyright infringement in India:

- **General:** A public awareness programme should be developed to educate the general public, of the risks of using the Internet and other means to obtain infringing copies of the copyrighted works. The awareness of the copyright regime is lacking much and in consequence lessening the fear of the law. The photocopier, who may not know a, b, c, of language, is likely to know the a, b, c, of law. Copyright law in India has, though, traversed a great deal of legislative path but has not covered the same journey on the awareness front. The law may easily hold a person liable for infringement even it was done innocently in ignorance of law. Only the quantum of damages may be mitigated. However, as a member of a civil society, it is our duty to spread the message and make people aware on the do's and don'ts of copyright law. More the people become aware less the cases of infringement of copyright will be there.
- **Police:** A police personnel, who can play a major role in combating piracy, should be made fully aware of various provisions of the law. Lack of adequate number of

personnel who can fully dedicate to copyright crimes alone also affecting the protective measures in this field. The police should be made more concerned with copyright-related crimes by inducting more training programme and educational workshops on the copyright laws and its infringement, etc.

- **End-Users:** The awareness level among end-users is to be increased so that at the time of buying a copyrighted product the consumers shall be able to differentiate between copyright notification (e.g. C or P). The users/ consumers do not mind buying pirated products as because they don't have the idea about the impact of such purchase. Governmental and non-governmental steps should be encouraged to impart more awareness and educational programmes and workshops for the users of the copyrighted materials. The participation of the academicians and experts in the awareness and educational programme should be increased to make the end-users aware about the pros and cons of infringement of copyright.

Establishment of Self-Enforcement Body

For one, Indian law certainly provide for copyright protection from some manual modes of infringement. But the challenge here is the enforcement of the prescribed laws. The enforcement is lacking at different levels. In India, where neither users nor sellers are aware of the copyrighted products as they are running after margin of profits only, the self-enforcement body can only be helpful in preventing the copyright infringement. Thus, an active and strong self-enforcement body should be set-up who can be able to protect the copyrighted works of the authors or investors at the preliminary stage.

Introduction of Specialised Copyright or IPR Court

A dedicated specialised Fast Tract IP court like consumer court along with specially trained copyright law enforcement personnel to tackle infringement and piracy cases would be established. At present, Indian courts are already overburdened with serious civil and criminal cases with them and IP cases are also brought to the same court so copyright cases are not taken care of properly. Setting up of specialized fast track IP courts can also help to get around the massive backlog of civil and criminal cases pending in the Indian Court system. Failing that, chiefs of all the high courts should appoint special judges to try copyright infringement criminal and civil cases, imposing deadlines for resolving them finally. These courts or special judges should at least be responsible for completing a set number of 'model' cases with deterrent penalties to deliver a message to the Indian public about infringement which has never been delivered. Hence, the need is for having more resources to be allocated to aid courts and getting proper law enforcement to take serious note of copyrights infringement. The extent of damages could even have potential jail term like US along with string statutory pecuniary damages. In short, the Indian courts need to be given some guidance as how to deal with copyright infringement cases.

Introduction of Technological/Digital/Electronic Protective Measures

Charles Clark's renowned remark 'the answer to the machine is in the machine'[8] is perfectly suited in the modern situation. Indeed, the perfect reply to the technological abuses is the application of technological innovation. It is a fact that we have technological barriers in the prevention of copying intellectual property in terms of copyright. A strong technological protection system can be placed in e-books so that only those for whom it has been manufactured or created can have the access. 'Encryption technology' can also helps in reducing the traditional symptoms of market failure encountered in the analog world, by making it possible to license and enforce copyright, even in cases of mass distribution of copyrighted work. On the third place the password-based access can be applied either at the level of service and contents or at the level of user or receiver.

The technological handicaps in India have remained as a depressing factor in the spread of copyright piracy in electronic environment.[9] Anti-circumvention and other similar advance techniques empowered, the right holders of their right, to choose

---

8. Charles, Clark, 'The Answer to the Machine is in the Machine', in: P. Bernt Hugenholtz (ed.), The Future of Copyright in a Digital Environment, The Hague: Kluwer Law International, p. 139.
9. Committee Report, Copyright Piracy in India available at manpatra.

their audience and have absolute control over the consumption of their works. The access provisions and anti-circumvent laws have to be perceived and enacted as an important set of laws. Law to permit access has to be guarded with technology as both are intrinsically interlinked. Though, some laws are in pipeline still the Government has to look at the enforcement of technical measures like user-friendly digital rights management systems which will certainly supportive in curbing the activities of infringement of copyrights in India.

Power of Licensing Body should be Increased

A licensing body has a major and effective role in policing the Copyright or Performer's rights. It also cuts down unnecessary litigation, extreme expenses and difficulty for the individual owner of copyright or performers rights to enforce his rights both in the country of origin and outside. The right to sue for infringement of Copyright or Performer's rights of licensing bodies is recognised in most of the countries (i.e. Australia, USA, UK, Nigeria and Canada, etc.) if the owners of the copyright are so desired but in India it is not available. Normally, in no country the statute provide prosecuting powers on these bodies for any infringement of rights they licensed. But when these entities are empowered by their members, whether in the capacity of an assignee, licensee or merely as an agent, the Courts have endorsed such rights and allowed the licensing bodies to bring legal actions for the infringement of the copyrights or performer's rights. So the appropriate directions on the part of the judiciary in the form of judicial guidelines or changes in the existing laws on the part of legislature, are highly desired to empowered the Copyright Societies in India to sue for the infringement of copyright or performer's rights, which shall obviously increased the quality of protection and decrease the quantity of infringement cases. The function of suing the infringer of copyright or performer's rights (if) carried out by a licensing body will help the government or regulating body effectively in the process of making collective administration, which should be welcomed for the effective regulation of the infringement cases of copyright in India. It will also prove more convenient for the owners of these rights as once they are the members of a licensing body, they can be satisfied that the latter will spot and further take care of any infringement of their rights (though the cost of litigation is borne by them).

Dynamism should be Brought in Copyright Act

The Copyright Act should not be given a meaning that is frozen in time, but should be interpreted in such a way that, it can take into account the technological advancements, provided that the interpretation is consistent with its purpose. The unauthorised circumvention of locking devices should be specifically made actionable at the instance of copyright owners and their exclusive licensees. The use of devices which enables the unauthorized use of computer programme should be banned. The Copyright Act, 1957 is, therefore, required to be amended to provide that copyright owners and their exclusive licensees may have the right to prevent the commercial manufacture, storage, distribution and possession for commercial purposes of devices which are designed to facilitate the unauthorized circumvention of locks or other devices applied to protect computer programmes from unauthorized copying.

Further to modernise the Copyright Act, particularly, in its enforcement procedures and penalty levels. Bringing the law fully into compliance with the WIPO treaties to prepare for new era of e-commerce, particularly WCT and WPPT of 1996, shall really be an addition to make this law updated and capable to deal with the challenges of technological progression.

Improvisation of Internet Use Education Programme

A provision for the establishment of Internet Use Education Programme should be made, with a view to educate the general public concerning the value of copyrighted works and the effects of the theft of such works on those who creates them and for whom it has been created, and also educate the general public concerning the privacy, security and other risks of using the Internet to obtain illegal copies of copyrighted works. The Internet Use Educational Programme shall develop materials appropriate to Internet users in different sectors of the general public where criminal copyright infringement was a concern. The unauthorized recording of motion pictures in a motion picture theater was to be made an offence punishable by imprisonment for not more than three years and fine or both, and for the second or subsequent offence, imprisonment upto six years could be imposed like section 8 of US Prevention of Surreptitious Recording in Motion Pictures Act, 2004. All these provisions of the PSRMP Act can provide useful guidelines for introducing similar changes in the Indian copyright law by making suitable adaptation in its context.

Formation of National Anti-Piracy Task Force

Central Government should create a National Anti-Piracy Task Force to take criminal and civil actions against infringement. If this is not achievable, provide resources to the states to equip and train state IP Task forces. The Home Ministry should take the lead in providing this training and resources, and the Home Minister should issue a strong and widely publicized condemnation of infringement and the damage caused by it to India and urges all police forces to take immediate action to root it out.

Term of Copyright should be Shortened

It is often said that shorter term of required safety is the better way of protection in the field of security and in some quarters, it has also been suggested that the copyright terms should be shortened, thereby increasing the size of the 'public domain' available for creative manipulation. Copyright owners' authority to control the preparation of 'derivative works' should be reduced for the same reason.[10] Thus if the work will be protected for the lesser time the case of the infringement shall be lesser like Patent.

Incentive-based Creation should be Encouraged

If the purpose of the copyright law is to provide incentive for creative intellectual efforts that will benefits the society at large, an unduly prolonged protection of copyright would obviously block the benefits of the creative genius to the public. The society greatly contributes to an individual's thinking at various levels of development of his personality and a creative genius therefore,

10. Neil Weinstock Netanel, **Copyright and a Democratic Civil Society,** 106, *Yale Law Journal*, 283 (1996), referred by William W. Fisher in his Article: Theory of Intellectual Property, New Essays in the Legal and Political Theory of Property, Cambridge University Press, 2001.

owes a duty to the society to release the fruits of his attainment for the general good. Thus, a social renaissance should be created so that the society will paid due admiration to the act or creation of the copyrighted materials in the country like India which is always remembered since the beginning of the civilisation for its creative culture.

Intensive Training for Judges etc.

To make out the complexities of the issues governing the ever expanding field of copyright, there should be an intensive training given to those who participate in legislative process and dispense justice so that the necessary legislative changes are duly identified and incorporated and the law correctly interpreted and enforced. The help of academicians who have specialized in the field can be sought in order to assist the legislative process that is required to be undertaken to fine-tune the copyright law to effectively cope up with infringement of copyright including computer software piracy, the alarming music piracy and other aspects discussed above. The Chief Coordinating Officer of the Indian Music Industry (IMI), an association of music companies recently lamented that though the number of seizures, raids and arrests is higher, the conviction rate is zero in one State.[11] The act of infringement can be stopped by swift action, collection of the relevant evidence by the investigating agencies specialized in the field and by entrusting the trials by the Judges well equipped with knowledge of relevant copyright and related laws.

Need to Redefine the Term 'Fair Use'

A fair dealing with a literary, dramatic, musical or artistic work [not being a computer programme] for the purposes indicated in Section 52(1)(a), does not constitute an infringement of copyright. Fair use defence allows the public to use not only facts and ideas contained in the copyrighted work but also expression itself in certain circumstances. The doctrine of 'fair use' has been called the worst troublesome in the law of copyright. It encourages the infringement in liberal sense of application because there are no guidelines for determining whether a particular act is fair or not and no fixed criterion has

11. News item in *Times of India* dated 05-06-2004.

emerged till date to measure the act of fair use such as judicial precedent or customary laws. Certain factors such as the purpose and character of the use, nature of copyrighted works, the amount and substantiality of the portion used and effect of the use, etc. upon which the term 'fare use' is determined. On the other hand, many users continue to be frustrated by lack of specific, quantitative guidelines to determine whether a use is fair. But, fair use was designed to be flexible, so that it could evolve with new circumstances and new types of uses. Uncertainty is the price we pay for that flexibility. Thus, the term 'fair use' must be re-defined specifically so that the cases of the infringement of copyright shall be lessen. People intentionally infringing the copyright but taking the shadow of the 'fair use' shall be prevented from doing so only if it shall be re-construed in a clear and specified words.

Frequency of Raid should be Increased

Significant increase of the number of *suo moto* raids against infringement at all levels is highly required. This also requires a significant increase in the resources and manpower in the IPR cells and the local police forces. The organisation like BSA and NASSCOM as helping in conduction of raids occasionally should be involved in the process regularly on the basis of terms etc. The NGOs should also be sensitised to get in concern about this serious problem of the nation.

Customs Departments should be Empowered

Proper steps should be taken to empower customs to initiate more raids to check the cases if infringements and also to seize and destroy pirated goods. Currently, many seized goods are resold to shops working with the Customs Service. This TRIPs-inconsistent practice must be stopped. Additionally, the customs process continues to be cumbersome.

Infringement should be made Strict Non-Bailable Crime

The acts of infringement of copyright though an offence but need to make it more dreadful crime. It should be made a serious non-bailable as it is undermining one of the strongest, fastest growing industries in India. Deterrent penalties should be imposed on infringers and a clear standards for damages in civil cases, including implementation of strong statutory damages which must include pecuniary damages and long-term jail resulted real deterrence, should be established.

Amendments in Existing Copyright Law, Suggested

Now it is considered appropriate to further amend the provisions of the Copyright Act, 1957 to incorporate the following observations:

- To extend effective copyright protection to the composers of Indian music, which is not available to them under the existing laws, which presupposes a system of notation used in western music aiming to protect the interest of the author's assignor in regard to the assignment of the copyright and the issue of license.
- To provide effective protection to the owner of copyright and related rights in the context of technological developments affecting the reproduction of works by, *inter-alia,* bringing them within the scope of copyright, the subsequent hire or sale of copies of cinematography films, computer programs and sound recordings.
- To further clarify the law in respect of cable, satellite and other means of simultaneous communication of works to more than one households or private place of residence, including the residential rooms of a hotel or hostel.
- To make adequate provision for the special nature of computer programs-related literary works and for the protections of computer generated works.
- To extend to authors, in respect of the original copies of their paintings, sculptures and drawings and original manuscripts of literary, dramatic or musical works, *a droit de suite* or resale share right.
- To include within the scope of copyright in artistic works the right (Subject to appropriate exceptions), to display the work in public.
- To re-define properly the term 'fair use' and provide the specific and clear guidelines about the fair use act under the copyright Act.
- To include the provision of digital/Audio books conversion specifically for the disabled to be enabled to get the copy of the work in their version.

- To make the copyright infringement crime a non-bailable one and also to increase the punishment and fine for the infringement acts. The minimum punishment should be five years which may be extended upto seven years and a fine should not be less than two lakh but upto five lakh.

New technological solutions need to be worked out to face the modern challenges along with the use of digital or electronic technology. Encryptions technology, digital identification numbers, digital rights management information system, anti-circumvention measures and conditional access are some of the concept to be achieved. It is only the advance modern technological tools through which we can prevent electronic copyright infringement.

At the end there would always be some group who circumvent the system which will certainly become a temporarily hurdle for which we shall have to create a socially motivated strong civil society. The strong civil society can help in the process of enforcement of copyright law in this civil society and hold back the cases of infringement of copyright to enrich the Indian revenues by contributing to the GDP of India like developed countries, i.e. United Kingdom, USA, etc. by alluring more and more investment in this knowledge creation-based industry.

BIBLIOGRAPHY

Books

Ahuja, Dr. V.K., *Law of Copyright and Neighbouring Rights: National and International Perspectives*, Lexis Nexis Butterworths, 2007.

Armstrong, Elizabeth, *Before Copyright: The French Book-Privilege System 1498-1526*, Cambridge University Press, Cambridge, 1990.

Bainbridge, David I., *Introduction to Computer Law*, Pitsman Publishing, London, 1993.

Band, Jonathan, *Digital Millennium Copyright Act Guide*, American Library Association, 2006.

Bansal, Ashwani Kumar, *Economic Rights of the Copyright Owner with Special Reference to the Right to Communication in Law of Copyright, From Gutenberg's Invention to Internet*, Prof. A.K. Kaul, V.K. Ahuja, eds., Faculty of Law, University if Delhi, 2001.

Beier, Friedrich-Karl, and Schricker, Gerhard, eds., *From GATT to TRIPS—The Agreement on Trade-Related Aspects of Intellectual Property Rights*, Weinheim: VCH, 1996.

Benko, Robert P., *Protecting Intellectual Property Rights: Issues and Controversies, American Enterprise Institute for Public Policy Research*, Washington, D.C., 1989.

Besen, Stanley M., *New Technologies and Intellectual Property: An Economic Analysis*, National Science Foundation, 1990.

Bhagwati and Hirsch, eds., *The Uruguay Round and Beyond: Essays in Honour of Arthur Dunkel*, Heidelberg: Springer, 1998.

Bhandari, Dr. M.K., *Law Relating to Intellectual Property Rights*, 38, Central Law Publications, 1st ed., 2006.

Birrell, Augustine, *Seven Lectures on the Law and History of Copyright in Books*, Rothman Reprints Inc., 1899 (1971 reprint).

Birrell, *The Law and History of Copyright in Books,* Cassell and Co., London, 1899.

Bowker, R.R., *Copyright: Its History and Its Law,* Houghton Mifflin, 1912.

Brian, Rowe, *History of Copyright in India,* Oxford, October 1, 2008.

Briggs and Burke, *The Print Revolution in Context, A Social History of The Media,* Oxford, 2002.

Bronscont, Anne W., *Who Owns Information? From Privacy to Public Access,* Basic Books, New York, 1990.

Bruch, Stephen and Stabinsky, Doreen (eds.), *Valuing Local Knowledge, Indigenous People and Intellectual Property Rights,* Island Press, 1995.

Burner, Hans Peter, *Closing the Technology Gap, Technological Changes in Indian Computer Industry,* Sage Publications, New Delhi, 1995.

Burrell, Robert & Coleman, Allison, *Copyright Exceptions: The Digital Impact,* Cambridge University Press, 2005.

Calestous, Juma and Jackton, Owjang B. (eds.), *Innovation and Sovereignty,* African Centre for technological studies, Nairobi, Kenya, 1989.

Chaktravarthy, Raghavan, *Recolonistion-GATT,* The Uruguay Round and the Third World, Malaysia, 1991.

Clapes, and Lawrence, Anthony, *Software: Legal Battle for Control of the Global Software Industry,* Quorum Books, 1989.

Colell, Mas, Whinston, Michael D. and Green, Jerry R., *Microeconomic Theory,* Oxford University Press, 1995.

Copinger and James, Skone, Copinger and Skone James on *Copyrights,* 13th ed., 2001, & K.M. Garnett, G. Davies and G. Harbottle (eds.), 15th ed., South Asian Edition, 2008.

Cornish, W. R., *Cases and Materials on Intellectual Property,* London, Sweet & Maxwell, 5rd ed., 2005.

Cornish, W.R., *Intellectual Property,* (London, Sweet & Maxwell), Universal Law Publishing, Delhi. India, 3rd ed., 1966, 1st Indian Reprint 2001.

Correa, Carlos M., *Intellectual Property Rights, the WTO and Developing Countries: The TRIPS Agreement and Policy Options,* Zed Books, Third World Network, 3rd Printing, 2002.

Curtis, George Ticknor, A treatise on the law of copyright in books, dramatic and musical compositions, letters and other manuscripts, engravings and sculpture: as enacted and administered by England and America: with some notices of the history of literary property, New Jersey, The Lawbook Exchange, 2005.

Davies, Gillian & Hung, Michele E., *Music and Video Private Copying: An International Survey of the Problem and the Law*, Sweet & Maxwell: London, 1993.

Davies, Gillian, *Copyright and the Public Interest*, 2nd ed., Sweet and Maxwell. 2002.

Davis, G., *Copyright and the Public Interest*, 2nd ed., London, Sweet & Maxwell, 2002.

Drahos, P. and Braithwaite, J., *Information Feudalism*, New Work, The New Press, 2003.

Drahos, Peter and Braithwaite, John, *Information Feudalism: Who Owns the Knowledge Economy?*, London: Earthscan, 2002.

Drone, Eaton S., *A Treatise on the Law of Property in Intellectual Productions*, Little, Brown, & Co., 1879.

Dubey, Muchkund, *An Unequal Treaty, World Trading Order After GATT*, New Age, 1996.

Elgar, Edward, *New Frontiers is the Economies of Innovation and New Technology: Essays in Honour of Paul A. David* (eds.), Cristiano Antonelli, Dominique Forany, Bronwyn H. Hall, W. Edward Stainmuller, Cheltenham, UK, 2006.

Fisher, William W., *Theories of Intellectual Property in New Essays in the Legal and Political Theory of Property*, Cambridge University Press, 2001.

Fishman, Stephen, *The Copyright Handbook: How to Protect and Use Written Work*, 2nd ed., Berkeley, Calif.: Nolo, 1994.

Gadbaw, R. Michael, and Richard, Timothy J. (eds.), *Intellectual Property Rights Global Consensus*, Global Conflict, Westview Press, London, 1988.

Gantz, John and Rochester, Jack B., *Pirates of the Digital Millennium, Upper Saddle River: Financial Times*, Prentice Hall, NJ, 2005.

Geller, Paul Edward, *International Copyright Law and Practice*, Matthew Bender, 2000.

Gervais, Daniel, *The TRIPS Agreement: Drafting History and Analysis*, 3rd ed., London: Sweet & Maxwell, 2008.

Goldstein, Paul, *Copyright's Highway: From Gutenberg to the Celestial Jukebox*, New York: Hill and Wang, 1995.

Goldstein, Paul, *International Copyright: Principles, Law, and*

Practice, Oxford University Press, 2001.

Gopalakrishnan, N.S., *Intellectual Property and Criminal Law*, NLSIU, 1994.

Gopalkrishnana, N.S. and Agitha, T.G, *Principles of Intellectual Property*, Eastern Book Company, Lucknow, 1st ed., 2009.

Gopinath, K. (eds.), *International Conference on IPR in Computer Software and Their Impact on Developing Countries*, IIS, Bangalore, 1992.

Gordon, Wendy J. & Bone, Robert G., *Copyright*, 1999.

Gorman, Robert A. and Ginsburg, Jane C., *Copyright: Cases and Materials*, New York: Foundation Press, 2002.

Hal, R. Varian, *Microeconomic Analysis*, W.W. Norton & Co Inc., 3rd ed. 1992.

Hesse, Carla, *Publishing and Cultural Politics in Revolutionary Paris*, 1789-1810. Berkeley: University of California Press, 1991.

Iyengar, T.R. Srinivasa, *The Copyright Act*, 1957, 5th ed., Law Book Company, 1985.

Iyer, V.R. Krishna, Reddy, Chinnappa O, Desai, D.A. and Sachs, Rajinder, *Peoples' Commission on GATT*, Centre for Study of Global Trade System and Development, New Delhi, 1995.

Jain, M.P., *Outlines of Indian Legal History*, 5th ed., Wadhwa & Co., Reprint 2001.

Jhawala, H.M., *Intellectually Property and Competition Law in India*, C. Jamnadas & Co, Mum., 1997.

Jose, Alvarez, *International Organizations as Law-Makers*, New York: Oxford University Press, 2005.

Kaul, A.K. and Ahuja, V.K., *Law of Copyright: From Gutenberg's invention to Internet, in Law of Copyright: From Gutenberg's invention to Internet*, Prof. A.K. Koul and Dr. V.K. Ahuja, eds., Faculty of law, University of Delhi, 1st ed. 2001, New Delhi.

Keayla, B.K., *TRIPs System Analysis and Implication Centre for Study of Global Trade System and Development*, New Delhi, 1997.

Kumari, Dr. T. Vidya, *Copyright Protection Current Indian & International Perspective*, Asia Law House, Hyderabad, New ed., 2004.

Lal, Nathuni, Lal's *Commentary on the Copyright Act, 1957* (Act 14 of 1957) with the Copyright Rules, and Neighbouring Rights, 4th ed., Delhi Law house, 2006.

Lange, David Mary, France, La and Mayers, Gary, *Intellectual*

Property: Cases and Materials, St. Paul: West Group, 1998.

Lessig, Lawrence, *The Future of Ideas*, New York: Vintage Books, 2001.

Locke, John, *Two Treatises of Government*, P Laslett (eds.), Cambridge University Press, 1988. (revised in 1690).

Lowenstein, Joseph, *The Author's Due : Printing and the Prehistory of Copyright*, University of Chicago Press, 2002.

Mackay, Mackay L., *A Dictionary of Scientific Quotations*, Paperback, Jan., 1991.

Maggs, P.B., *Internet and Computer Law: Cases, Comments and Questions*, St. Paul, Minn.: West Group, 2001.

Marihuana, P., *Law of Copyright and Industrial Design*, 3rd ed., 1980.

Martial, James Mitchie, *The Epigrams*, Penguin, 1978.

McCarthy, J. Thomas, *McCarthy on Trade Marks and Unfair Competition*, 3rd ed., Clark Boardman Callaghan, Vol. 111, 1996.

McCarthy, J. Thomas, *The Rights of Publicity and Privacy*, New York: C. Boardman, 1992.

Mittal, D.P., *Law Relating to Copyright, Patent and Trademark and GATT*, Taxman Allied Services (P.) Ltd., 2005.

Nair, K.R.G. and Kumar, Ashok (eds.), *Intellectual Property Rights*, Allied Publication, New Delhi, 1994.

Narayanan, P., *Intellectual Property Law*, 4th ed., Eastern Law House, 2004.

Narayanan, P., *Law of Copyright & Industrial Designs*, 2nd ed., Eastern Law House, 1995.

Nimmer, Melville & Nimmer, David Nimmer on *Copyright*, Matthew Bender, 1997.

Okediji, Ruth, *Welfare and Digital Copyright in International Perspective: From Market Failure to Compulsory Licensing*, in International Public Goods & Transfer of Technology Under a Globalized Intellectual Property Regime, Jerome Reichman & Keith Maskus, eds., Cambridge University Press, 2005.

Patterson, L. Ray and Lindberg, Stanley W., *The Nature of Copyright: A Law of Users' Rights*, Athens: University of Georgia Press, 1991.

Patterson, L., *Copyright in Historical Perspective*, Vanderbult University Press, Nashville, 1968.

Philip, Jermy, *Introduction to Intellectual Property Rights*, First Edition, Butter worth, London, 1986.

Polanski, Paul, Przemyslaw Chapter 10 of the *Internationalization of Internet Law*, IUS Gentium, Vol. 2, 2008.

Prasad, Akhin & Agarwala, Aditi, *Copyright Law Desk Book Knowledge, Access & Development*, Universal Law Publishing Co., New Delhi, 1st ed., 2009.

Pratap, Ravindra, *India at the WTO Dispute Settlement System*, New Delhi: Manak, 2004.

Putnam, G.H., *The question of Copyright*, 2nd ed., The Knicker Bocker Press, New York, 1896.

Raju, K.D., *Intellectual Property Law, WTO and India*, New Era Law Publication, 2005.

Rawls, John, *Theory of Justice*, Harvard University Press, 1971, reissue, 2005.

Robert, Nozick, Anarchy, *State and Utopia*, New York, Basic Books, 1974.

Ryder, Rodeny. D., *Intellectual Property and the Internet*, 1st ed. Lexis Nexis, 2002.

Samuels, Edward, *The Illustrated Story of Copyright*, New York: Thomas Dunne Books, 2000.

Senftleben, Martin, *Copyright, Limitations and Three-Step Test: An Analysis of the Three Step Test in International and EC Copyright Law*, Prof. P. Bernt Hugenholtz, eds., Kluwer Law International, 2004.

Shermen, B., and Strowel, A., *Of Authors and Origins*, Oxford, Clarendon, 1994.

Smith, Eric H., *Trade Losses Due to Piracy and Other Market Access Restrictions Affecting the US Copyright Industries: A Report to the US Trade Representative*, The Alliance, Washington, 1990.

Sterling, Bruce, *The Hacker Crackdown: Law and Disorder on the Electronic Frontier*, New York: Bantam Books, 1992.

Sterling, J.A.L., *World Copyright Law*, London Sweet and Maxwell, 3rd ed., 2008.

Stewart, S.M., *International Copyright and Neighbouring Rights*, 2nd ed., London, Butterworths, 1989.

Stewart, Terence P., *The GATT Uruguay Round: A Negotiating History* (1986-94), Hague, Kluwer Law International, 1999.

Stim, Richard, *Getting Permission: How to License and Clear Copyrighted Material Online and Off*, Berkeley, Calif.: Nolo, 2001.

Tapscott, Don, *The Digital Economy: Promise and Peril in the Age of*

Networked Intelligence, New York: McGraw-Hill, 1995.

Thairani, Kala, *How Copyright works in Practice—The Copyright Act, 1957 and Judicial Interpretation* (A case law study in perspective), Popular Prakashan, 1996.

Vaidhyanathan, Siva, *Copyrights and Copywrongs: The Rise of Intellectual Property and How it Threatens Creativity*, New York: New York University Press, 2001.

Wadhera, B.L., *Law Relating to Patent Trademarks, Copyrights, Designs and Geographical Indications*, Universal Law Publishing Co., 3rd ed., 2004.

Wadlow, C., *Enforcement of Intellectual Property in European and International Law*, London: Sweet & Maxwell, 1998.

Wallerstein, Mitchel. B. (eds.), *Global Dimensions of Intellectual Property Rights in Science and Technology*, National Academy Press, 1993.

Watal, *Intellectual Property Rights in the WTO and Developing Countries*, Kluwer Law International, 2001.

Articles

Abichandani, Justice R.K., *Role of Judiciary in the Effective Protection of Intellectual Property Right*, available at: http://www.gujarathighcourt.nic.in/Articles/roleofjudicary.htm

Abiomats, Philp, Copyright Misuse and Anti-Competitive Software Licenses Restrictions: Laser Comb. America Inc V Reynolds, *University of Pittsburgh Law Review*, Vol. 52. Spring 1991.

Adelman, Martin J. and Baldia, Sonia, Prospect and Limits of the Provision in the TRIPS Agreement: The Case of India, *Vanderbilt Journal of Transnational Law*, Vol. 29, 1996.

Alan, Story, Intellectual Property and Computer Software: a Battle of Competing Use and Access Visions for Countries of the South, Issue paper-10, International Centre for Trade and Sustainable Development/United Nations Conference on Trade and Sustainable Development, Geneva, May 2004.

Alikhan, S., The Role of the Berne Convention in the Promotion of Cultural Creativity and Development: Recent Copyright Legislation in Developing Countries, *Journal of Indian Law Institute*, Vol. 28, 1986.

Aull, Ashly, Fair Use and Educational Uses of Content, available at http://cyber.law.harbard.edu/home/dl_fairuse.

Bainbridge, David I., Computer Programs: More Exceptions to Infringement, *Modern Law Review*, 591, 1993.

Baxi, Upendra, Copyright Law and Justice in India, *Journal of Indian Law Institute*, 1986.

Bechtold, Stefan, Digital Rights Management in the United States and Europe, *American Journal for Compulsory Law*, 2004.

Bender, David, Protection of Computer Programs: The Copyright Trade Secret Interface, *University of Pittsburgh Law Review*, Vol. 47, Spring 1986.

Besek, June M., Copyright : What Makes A Use Fair?, *Educause Review*, Vol. 38, November/December, 2003.

Best, Michael, What's Mine is Mine and What is Yours is Yours: The Politics of Copyright on the Internet, 2003, available at http://web.uvic.ca/Shakespear /Annex/Articles/SAA1997.html.

Blanke, Jordan M., Vincent Van Gogh, Sweat of the Brow and Database Protection, *American Business Law Journal*, Summer 2002.

Bronkers, Marco C.E.J., The Impact of TRIPS: Intellectual Property Protection in Developing Countries, *Common Market Law Review*, Vol. 31, 1994.

Carleton, Dennis M., Lotus Development Vs Borland International: Determining Software Copyright Infringement is not as Easy 1-2-3, *University of Pittsburgh Law Review*, Vol. 56, Summer 1995.

Carlos, Braga and Prima, Alferto, The Economics of Intellectual Property Rights and the GATT: A view from the South, *Vanderbilt Journal of Transnational Law*, Vol. 22, No. 243, 1989.

Carren, Daughtrey, S., Reverse Engineering of Software for Interoperability and Analysis, *Vanderbilt Law Review*, Vol. 41, 1994.

Chafee, Zecharia, Reflections on the Law of Copyright, *Columbia Law Review*, 503, 1945.

Charles, Clark, The Future of Copyright in a Digital Environment, P. Bernt Hugenhotltz, eds., The Hague: Kluwer Law International, 1996.

Chin, Andrew, Antitrust Analysis in Software Product Markets: A First Principles Approach, *18 Harvard Journal of Law and Technology*, 2004.

Chothani, Poorva, Managing Copyright in the Digital Era,

available at http://www.managingip.com.

Cohen, Julie E., WIPO Treaty Implementation in the United States: Will Fair Use Survive?, *European Intellectual Property Review*, 1999.

Cullet, Philip, Human Rights, Knowledge and Intellectual Property Protection, *JIPR*, Vol. 11, January, 2006.

Dalal, Praveen and Gupta, Shruti, The Unexplored Dimensions of Right To Privacy, *IJCL*, Vol. III, No. 2, May 2004.

Dalal, Praveen, A work analysing the law pertaining to copyright in India, available at http://india.indymedia.org/en/2005/07/210809.shtml.

Damodaran, EMR for Glivec: A TRIPS dictated 'Cure'? *Financial Express*, Jan. 9, 2004.

Davidson, Duncan, Common Law Uncommon Software, *University of Pittsburgh Law Review*, Vol. 47, Summer 1986.

Days, Alai S., The Boundaries of Copyright: Its Proper Limitations and Exceptions, Sydney, Australian Copyright Council, 1999.

Dhar, Biswajit and Rao, Niranjan, Dunkel Draft on TRIPS, Complete denial of Developing Countries Interest, *EPW*, February, 1992.

Dinwoodie, Graeme B., A New Copyright Order: Why National Courts Should Create Global Norms, U. Pa. L. Rev. 2000.

Dinwoodie, Graeme B., The Development and Incorporation of International Norms in the Formation of Copyright Law, Oh. St. L. J., 2001.

Elsmore, Matt., Intellectual Property Rights within the International Community, Southampton Institute On Line Law Review, April, 1998, at http://www.solent.ac.uk/law/netsc.html.

Engle, Eric Allen, When is Fair Use Fair?: A Comparison of E.U. and U.S. Intellectual Property Law, 15 Transnational Law, 2002.

Falcon, Joseph Richard, Managing intellectual Property Rights: The Cost of Innovation, Vol. 6, *Duq. Bus LJ*, 2004.

Frischman, Brett & Moylan, Dan, The Evolving Common Law Doctrine of Copyright Misuse: A Unified Theory and Its Application to Software, Berkeley Tech. L.J., 2000.

Gadbaw, Michael R., Intellectual Property and International Trade: Merger of Marriage of Convenience, *Vanderbilt Journal of Transnational Law*, Vol. 22, 1989.

Gallini, Nancy T. & Trebilcock, Michael J., Intellectual Property Rights and Competition Policy: A Framework for the Analysis of Economic and Legal Issues, in Competition Policy and Intellectual Property Rights in the Knowledge-Based Economy, *Economics of Legal Relationships*, Vol. 3, 1998.

Gana, Ruth L., Has Creativity Died in the Third World? Some Implications of the Internationalization of Intellectual Property, *Denver J of Int. L. & Policy*, Vol. 24, 1995.

Ganguli, Prof. (Dr.) Prabuddha, Intellectual Property Right in Strategic Management, July, 2007.

Ganguli, Professor Prabuddha, Relevance of Copyright and Related Rights for SMEs at www.ircc.iitb.ac.in/IPCourse04/copyright_ PGWIPO.doc.

Ganley, Paul, The Internet, Creativity and Copyright Incentives, *Journal of Intellectual Property Rights*, Vol. 10, 2005.

Garret, W.H. Barid, Toward A perceptive View of Copyright Protection for non literal elements of Computer Programs: Recent Developments in the Courts, *Virginia Law Review*, Vol. 79, 1993.

Geiger et al., Christophe, Declaration on a Balanced Interpretation of the Three-Step-Test' in Copyright Law, *IIC*, 39, 2008.

Geiger, Andrea, A View From Europe: The high price of counterfeiting, and getting real about enforcement, 2008-04-30, available at http://thehill.com.

Geiger, Christophe, Right to Copy Vs Three-Step Test: The Future of the Private Copy Exception in the Digital Environment, CRI, 2005.

Gerald, Herman, Roundtable: Intellectual Property and the Historian in the New Millennium, Public Historian, Spring 2004.

Gervais, Daniel J., The Internationalization of Intellectual Property: New Challenges From the Very Old and Very New, 12 Fordham Intell. Prop. Media & Ent. L.J.,2002.

Gervais, Daniel J., Traditional Knowledge & Intellectual Property: A TRIPS—Compatible Approach, 2005 *Mich. St. L. Rev.* 2005.

Gifford, Daniel J., The Antitrust/Intellectual Property Interface: An Emerging Solution to an Intractable Problem, *Hofstra L. Rev.*, 2002.

Ginsburg, Jane, A Tale of Two Copyrights: Literary Property in Revolutionary France and America, *Tulane Law Review*, Vol. 64, 1990.

Givler, Peter, Copyright: It's for the Public Good, *Chronicle of Higher Education*, Vol. 45, May, 2003.

Goldstein, Paul, Infringement of Copyright in Computer Programs, *University of Pittsburgh Law Review*, Vol. 47, Summer 1986.

Greenhouse, Linda, The Supreme Court; Protected Works; 20-Year Extension of Existing Copyrights is Upheld, *New York Times*, January 2003.

Hal, R. Varian, Copying and Copyright, 19 J. Econ. Persp., 2005.

Hanna, Ramsay, Misusing Antitrust: The Search for Functional Copyright Standards, *Stanford Law Review*, Vol. 46, January1994.

Hans, Werner Moritz, Assignment of Computer Software for Use on a Data Processing System and the Applicability of Know how Licensing Rules, *IIC*, Vol. 21, 1990.

Harnad, S., For Whom the Gate Tolls? How and Why to Free the Refereed Research Literature Online Through Author/Institution Self-Archiving, 2001, at http://cogprints. soton.ac.uk/documents/disk0/00/00/ 16/39/index.html.

Hartzog, Neal, Gaining Momentum: A Review of Recent Developments Surrounding the Expansion of the Copyright Misuse Doctrine and Analysis of the Doctrine in its Current Form, *Mich. Telecomm. & Tech. L. Rev.*, 2004.

Helfer, Laurence R., Regime Shifting: The TRIPS Agreement and New Dynamics of International Intellectual Property Lawmaking, *Yale J. Int'l L.*, 1, 2004.

Hugh, Laddie, Copyright: Over-strength, Over-regulated, Over-rated?, *E.I.P.R.* ,1996.

Hughes, Justin, The Philosophy of Intellectual Property, 77 *George Town Law Journal*, 1980.

Ignatin, Gary R., Let the Hackers Hack: Allowing Reverse Engineering of Copyrighted Computer Programs to Achieve Compatibility, *University of Pennsylvania Law Review*, Vol. 140, May 1992.

James, T.C., Copyright Law of India and the Academic Community, Vol. IX, *JIPR* 207 (212), May, 2004.

Kaplan, Binyomin, Determining Ownership of Foreign

Copyright: A Three-Tier Proposal, 21 *Cardozo L. Rev.*, 2000.

Landes, William M., and Posner, Richard A., The Political Economy of Intellectual Property Law, AEI Press, Washington, 2004, available at http://www.aei.org./docLib/20040608_Landes.pdf.

Leaffer, Marshall, Protecting U.S. Intellectual Property Abroad: Toward a New Multilateralism, *Iowa L. Rev.*, 1991.

Lemley, Mark A., and Brien, David W.O., Encouraging Software Reuse, *Stanford Law Review*, Vol. 49, January 1997.

Lessig, Lawrence, The Future of Ideas, New York: Vintage Books, 2001.

Lewis, Gerald J., Lotus Development Corp., V Paperback Software International: Board Copyright Protection for user Interfaces Ignores the Trend Towards Standardization, *University of Pittsburgh Law Review*, Vol.52, Spring 1991.

Litman, Jessica, Copyright as Myth, *University of Pittsburgh Law Review*, Fall, 1991.

Loeber, Dietrich A., Socialist Features of Soviet Copyright Law, *Columbia Journal of Transnational Law*, Vol. 23, 1984.

Lucie, M.C.R. Guibault, Copyright Limitations and Contracts-Analysis of the Contractual Overiddabililty of Limitations on Copyright, Prof. P. Bernt Hugenholtz (eds.), *Kluwer Law International*, Vol. 55, 2002.

May, Christopher, A Global Political Economy of Intellectual Property Rights: The New Enclosures, The Routledge, 2000.

May, Christopher, The Venetian Moment: New Technologies, Legal Innovation and the Institutional Origins of Intellectual Property, Prometheus, 2002.

Mazzoleni, Roberto, and Nelson, Richard R., The Benefits and Costs of Strong Patent Protection: A Contribution to the Current Debate, *Research Policy*, 27, 1998.

McCarthy, Rory, Egypt to Copyright the Pyramids and Antiquities, *The Guardian*, 2007.

Mennell, Peter S., An Analysis of the Scope of Copyright Protection for Application Programs, *Stanford Law Review*, Vol. 41, May 1989.

Mennell, Peter S., Tailoring the Legal Protection for Computer Software, *Stanford Law Review*, Vol. 39, July 1987.

Meurer, Michael J., Vertical Restraints and Intellectual Property Law: Beyond Antitrust, 87 *Minn. L. Rev.*, 2003.

Mills, John G., Possible Defenses to Complaints for Copyright Infringement and Reverse Engineering of Computer Software: Implications for Antitrust and I.P. Law, 80 J. Pat. & Trademark Off. Soc'y, 1998.

Nachame, D.M., Intellectual Property Rights in the Uruguay Round: An Indian Perspective, *EPW*, February, 1995.

Netanel, Neil Weinstock, Asserting Copyright's Democratic Principles in the Global Arena, 51 *Vand. L. Rev.*, 1998.

Netanel, Neil Weinstock, Locating Copyright within the First Amendment Skein, 54 *Stan. L. Rev.* 2001.

Netanel, Neil, Copyright and a Democratic Civil Society, 106 *Yale Law Journal*, 1996.

Nimmer, David, A Tale of Two Treaties Dateline: Geneva, December 1996, 22 *Colum.-VLA J.L. & Arts*, 1997.

Nimmer, David, Time and Space, IDEA, 1998.

Nimmer, Melville, Does Copyright Abridge the First Amendment Guarantees of Free Speech and Press?, 17 *UCLA L. Rev.*, 1970.

Norm, Alsta, A Dry Period, Forbes, April, 1995.

O'Rourke, Maureen A., Fencing Cyberspace: Drawing Borders in a Virtual World, 82 *Minn. L. Rev.*, 1998.

Okediji, Ruth Gana, Copyright and Public Welfare in Global Perspective, 7 *Ind. J. Global Legal Stud.*, 1999.

Okediji, Ruth L., Public Welfare and the Role of the WTO: Reconsidering the TRIPs Agreement, 17 *Emory Int. L. Rev.*, 2003.

Okediji, Ruth, Development in the Information Age: Issues in the Regulation of Intellectual Property Rights, Computer Software and Electronic Commerce, UNCTAD/ICTSD, 2003.

Okediji, Ruth, Toward an International Fair Use Doctrine, 39 *Colum. J. Trasnat'l L.*, 2000.

Okediji, Ruth, TRIPs Dispute Settlement and the Sources of (International) Copyright Law, 49 *J. Copyright Soc'y U.S.A.*, 2001.

Osorio, Carlos, A contribution to the understanding of illegal copying of software, Working paper, June 2002, available at http://opensource.mit. edu/papers/osorio.pdf.

Palmer, Tom G., Are Patents and Copyrights Morally Justified?, The Philosophy of Property Rights and Ideal Objects, *Harvard* Journal of Law and Public Policy, Vol. 13, No. 3, 1990.

Patel, Surendra J., Intellectual Property Rights in the Uruguay Round: A Disaster for the South, *EPW*, May, 1989.

Patry, William, Choice of Law and International Copyright, 48 *Am. J. Comp. L.*, 2000.

Patterson, L. Ray, Folsom Vs Marsh and Its Legacy, *Journal of Intellectual Property Law*, Spring 1998.

Patterson, L. Ray, The DMCA: A Modern Version Of The Licensing Act Of 1662, 10 *J. Intell. Prop. L.*, 2002.

Petersmann, Ernst Ulrich, The GATT/WTO Dispute Settlement System: International Law, International Organizations and Dispute Settlement, 1996.

Petersmann, Ernst-Ulrich, Why Do Governments Need the Uruguay Round Agreements, NAFTA and the EEA?, *Swiss Rev. Int'l Econ. Rel.* (Aussenwirtschaft), 1994.

Pilieci, Vito, Copyright Deal could Toughen Rules Governing info on IPods, Computers, Canwest News Service, May, 2008, available at http://www. canada.com/vancouversun/ story.html.

Raskind, Leo J., The Uncertain Case for Special Legislation for Protecting Computer Software, *University of Pittsburgh Law Review*, Vol.47, Summer 1986.

Ravishankar A., and Archak, Sunil, Intellectual Property Rights and Agricultural Technology: Interplay and Implications for India, 35 *EPW*, 2000.

Ress, Manon, Compulsory Licensing under the Appendix to the Berne Convention, 2004, available at http://www.dtifueyo. cl/Simposio/papers% 20presentados/Ress-Berne-v9.pdf.

Ricketson, S., & Ginsberg J., International Copyright and Neighbouring Rights: The Berne Convention and Beyond, Oxford: Oxford University Press, 2nd ed., 2006.

Ricketson, Sam, The Berne Convention for the Protection of Literary and Artistic Works: 1886-1986, London, Centre for Commercial Law Studies, Queen Mary College & Kluwer Law International, 1987.

Ricketson, Sam, U.S. Accession to the Berne Convention: An Outsider's Appreciation, 8 *Intell. Prop. J.*, 1987.

Roffe, Pedro, Control of Anti-Competitive Practices in Contractual Licenses under the TRIPS Agreement, in Intellectual Property and International Trade: The TRIPS

Agreement 280, Carlos M. Correa and Abdulqawi A. Yusuf, eds., 1998.

Sahai, TRIPs Review: Basic Rights must be Restored, 36 *EPW*, 2001.

Salah, Basalamah, Compulsory Licensing for Translation: An Instrument of Development, Vol. 40, *IDEA*, 2000.

Salant, Jonathan D., Disney Locks in Copyrights to Mickey, Goofy and Gang, *San Francisco Chronicle*, 17 October 1998.

Scott, Brendan, Copyright in a Frictionless World, available at http://firstmonday.org/issues/issue6_9/scott/index.html.

Sinha, S. B., Article presented in the inauguration of a seminar on new IPR laws organised by the Associated Chambers of Commerce and Industry of India (ASSOCHAM), *The Hindu*, September 22, 2002.

Sun, Haochen, Overcoming the Achilles Heel of Copyright Law, *Northwestern Journal of Technology and Intellectual Property* 5, 2007.

Sundarajan, Dr. Mira T., Digital Learning in India: Problems and Prospects, available at http://cyber.law.harvard.edu/home/dl_india.

Teter, Timothy, Merger and Machines: An Analysis of the Pro-Compatibility Trend in Computer Software Copyright Cases, *Stanford Law Review*, Vol. 45, April 1993.

Tiwary, Anu and Rajan, Shruti S., Proprietary Rights on Common Property? The Dilemmas of Copyright Protection of Case Law Reporters, Vol. II, *JIPR*, January, 2006.

Tripathy, R.C., Grover, S.S. and Chakravarthy, A.K., Computer Software and Intellectual Property Rights Present Status in India and Future Direction, *Electronics and Planning*, Vol. 21, January, 1998.

Uchtenhagen, Ulrich, The GATT Negotiations Concerning Copyright and Intellectual Property Protection, *IIC*, Vol. 21, 1990.

Uritz, Daniel, The Myth of Intent in Equal Protection, *Stanford Law Review*, Vol. 41, July 1989.

Weinreb, Lloyd, Copyright for Functional Expression, *Harvard Law Review*, Vol. 111, 1998.

Wilkins, Jon S., Protecting Computer Programs as Compilations under Computer Associates V Altai, *Yale Law Journal*, Vol. 104, November 1994.

Woodmansee, M., The Construction of Authorship: Textual Appropriation in Law and Literature, University Press, 1994, also published as a law journal issue, *Cardozo Arts and Entertainment Law Journal*,1992.

Journals

All India Reporter
American Business Law Journal
American Journal for Compulsory Law
Berkeley Tech. Law Journal
Calcutta Law Times
Cardozo Arts and Entertainment Law Journal
Cardozo Law Review
Chronicle of Higher Education
Columbia Journal of Transnational Law
Copyright and Patent Cases
Criminal Law Journal
Criminal Weekly Notes
Denver Journal of International Law & Policy
Denver Journal of International Law and Policy
Duquesne Business Law Journal
Economic and Political Weekly
Educause Review
Electronics and Planning
Emory International Law Review
Entertainment Law Journal
European Intellectual Property Review (EIPR)
Fordham Intellectual Property Media & Entertainment Law Journal
George Town Law Journal
Harvard Journal of Law and Technology
Harvard Law Review
Hofstra Law Review
IDEA: The Intellectual Property Law Review
Indian Journal of Constitutional Law (IJCL)
Intellectual Property Review
International Review Of Intellectual Property And Competition Law (IIC)
Iowa Law Review
Journal of Copyright Society
Journal of Economic Perspectives

Journal of Indian Law Institute
Journal of Intellectual Property
Journal of Intellectual Property Law
Journal of Intellectual Property Rights
Journal of Patent & Trademark Off. Society
Journal of Transnational Law
Kluwer Law International
L.V. Reports of Patent Design and Trade Mark Cases
Manupatra Intellectual Property Reports
Michigan State Law Review
Michigan Telecommunications and Technology Law Review
Minnesota Law Review
Modern Law Review
New York Times
North Carolina Law Review
Patent Design and Trade Mark cases
Patent Trademark Copyright Cases
Patent, Trademark & Copyright Journal(PTC)
San Francisco Chronicle
Santa Clara Computer and High Technology Law Journal
Stanford Law Review
Supreme Court Cases
Swiss Review on International Economic Relation. The Routledge
The Weekly Law Reports (WLR)
Tulane Law Review
University of Pennsylvania Law Review,
University of Pittsburgh Law Review
Vanderbilt Journal of Transnational Law
Vanderbilt Law Review
Virginia Law Review
Yale Journal of International Law

Conventions, Declarations, Reports and Treaties

Agreed Statement to World Intellectual Property Organization Copyright Treaty Article 10, 1996.

Agreement between the World Intellectual Property Organisation and the World Trade Organisation, Geneva, 22 December, 1995.

Agreement Establishing the World Trade Organization,

Marrakesh, 15 April 1994, 33 *Inti Le. Mat.* 1144 (1994); Annex 1C: 1869 U.N.T.S. 299.

Agreement on Trade-Related Aspects of Intellectual Property Rights, April 15, 1994, Marrakesh, 15 April 1994, 33 *Inti. Leg. Mat.* 1197,1994.

Agreement on TRIPS, Including Trade in Counterfeit Goods, Geneva, 1993.

Committee Report (Chapter II), Copyright Piracy in India, available at www.manupatra.com.

Constituent Assembly Debate, Vol. IV. parliamentofindia. nic.in/ls/debates.

Convention Establishing the World Intellectual Property Organisation, Stockholm, 14 July 1967.

Convention for the Protection of Industrial Property, Paris, 20 March, 1983.

Convention for the Protection of Literary and Artistic Works, Berne, 9 September 1886.

General Agreement on Tariffs and Trade: Multinational Trade Negotiations, Final Act embodying the Results of the Uruguay Round of Trade Negotiations, Marrakesh, 15 April 1994.

Geneva Treaty of International Registration of Audio-Visual Works, 1989.

India, Economic Survey, 2006.

International Copyright Order. 1999.

International Covenant on Civil and Political Rights, New York, 16 December 1966, *Int'l Leg Mat* 368, 1967.

International Covenant on Economic, Social and Cultural Rights, New York, 16 December 1966, 6 *Int'l Leg Mat* 360, 1967.

International Intellectual Property Alliance Special Report India, 2007.

MHRD Report on Copyright Piracy, 2006.

Report of the Joint Select Committee on IP, the Gazette of India Extraordinary, 12.02.2007.

Study Conducted by *Software Publishers Association, a US-based body*, published in 2006.

Survey conducted jointly by Business Software Alliance (BSA) and NASSCOM in May 2006.

The Convention for the Protection of Producers of Phonograms against the Unauthorized Duplication of their Phonograms,

Geneva, 1971.
The Convention Relating to the Distribution of Program-Carrying Signals Transmitted by Satellite, 1974.
The Gazette of India, Extraordinary.
The International Convention for the Protection of Performers, Producers of Phonograms and Broadcasting Organizations, 1961.
The UCC (and PROTOCOLS), 1952.
Trade Act of 1974(US).
TRIPS agreement, 1994.
U.N. Declaration on the Rights of Disabled Persons.
Universal Declaration of Human Rights, 1948.
Vienna agreement for the protection of Typefaces and their International Deposit, 1973.
Vienna Convention on the Law of Treaties, May 23, 1969.
WIPO Convention.
WIPO Copyright Treaty, 1996.
WIPO Study on Limitations and Exceptions of Copyright and Related Rights in the Digital Environment.
World Intellectual Property Organisation, Rome Convention.
World Intellectual Property Organization Copyright Treaty, 1996.
World Intellectual Property Organization Performances and Phonograms Treaty, 1996.
World Intellectual Property Organization, Guide to the Berne Convention for the Protection of Literary and Artistic Works (Paris Act 1971) 23 (1978).

Statutes

Audio Home Recording Act of 1992 (US)
Broadcasting Services Act, 1992 as amended May, 2002 (US)
Civil Procedure Code 1908
Copyright (Amendment) Act, 1983(India)
Copyright Act, 1842
Copyright Act, 1847
Copyright Act of 1709
Copyright Act, 1911 (Imperial Copyright Act)
Copyright Law of Germany 1965, as amended on May 8, 1998.
Copyright, Designs and Patents Act of 1988, (UK).
Government of India Act 1935.
Imperial Copyright Act 1911(UK)

Indian Copyright Act, 1914
Indian Copyright Act, 1957
Indian Penal Code 1872
Information Technology Act, 2000
The Constitution of India.
The Copyright Rules, 1958
The Netherlands' Copyright Act of 1912
The Paris Act of July 24, 1971
The States Reconstructions Act 1956 (37 of 1956)
The Statute of Anne 1710
The Technology, Education, and Copyright Harmonization (TEACH) Act, 2000.
Trade Act of 1974 (US)
U.S. Constitution 1787
US Digital Millennium Copyright Act, 1998

Websites

http://www.copyright.gov.in
http:// www.cyber.law.harbard.edu
http://www.culturaleconomics.atfreeweb.com
http://www.iia.net.au
http://www.usinfo.state.gov
http://www.wipo.int
http://www.wipo.org
http://www.solent.ac.uk
http://www.loc.gov.
http://cogprints.soton.ac.uk
http:// www.papers.ssrn.com
http://www.bit.ly
http://www.wto.org
http://www.iprsonline.org
http://www.chaos.org.uk
http://w ww.thecornerhouse.org.uk
http://www.dklevine.com
http://www.news.bbc.co.uk
http://forum.grasscity.com
http://www.wired.com
http://www.china-laws-online.com
http://news.zdnet.co.uk
http://www.mbc.com

http://www.firstmonday.org
http://www.opensource.mit.edu
http://www.ustr.gov
http://www.thehill.com
http://www.europa.eu.int
http://www.web.uvic.ca
http://ww.canada.com
http://www.managingip.com
http://www.dtifueyo.cl
http:// www.aci.org.
http:// www.en.wikipedia.org
http://www.canada.com
http://www.forthehearts.net
http://www.law.cornell.edu
http://www.med.govt.nz
http://www.policy.meadholm.com
http://www.manupatra.com
http://www.parliamentofindia.nic.in/ls/debates

News Papers
The Hindu
The Telegraph
The Times of India
The Financial Express
The Economic Times

Magazines
Yojana
Forbes
Employment News (Kurukshetra)

Index